PENSION ASSET MANAGEMENT:
The Corporate Decisions

Sidney Cottle, Project Director

Leo C. Bailey

William R. Cottle

J. Michael Murphy

Roger F. Murray

A research study prepared for the
FINANCIAL EXECUTIVES RESEARCH FOUNDATION

Pension Asset Management:
The Corporate Decisions

Copyright 1980

Financial Executives Research Foundation
633 Third Avenue, New York, New York 10017

International Standard Book Number 0-910586-36-5
Library of Congress Catalog Card Number 80-69793
Printed in the United States of America
M 1318

First Printing

As the research arm of Financial Executives Institute, the basic objective of the Research Foundation is to sponsor fundamental research and publish authoritative material in the field of business management with particular emphasis on the principles and practices of financial management and its evolving role in the management of business.

Publication of a research study should not be interpreted as constituting endorsement by the Board as a whole, or by individual Trustees.

PROJECT ADVISORY COMMITTEE

James J. Kerley, Chairman
Executive Vice President
Monsanto Co.

Arnold F. Brookstone
Vice President-Finance & Treasurer
Stone Container Corporation

William Gray
Senior Vice President
Harris Trust and Savings Bank

Norvell G. Jones
Manager, Pension Asset Management
Monsanto Co.

Vincent J. Motto
Assistant Treasurer
Exxon Corporation

David Redo
Manager, Trust & Thrift
Bechtel Corp.

Robert C. Thompson
Vice President-Finance
Shell Oil Company

Eugene M. White, Jr.
Assistant Treasurer
Tenneco, Inc.

Benjamin R. Makela
Research Director
Financial Executives Research Foundation

FOREWORD

The management of America's private pension plans becomes more critical each year. Because:

o They involve the old age security of an increasing number of people in the American work force.

o They make up a large and increasingly significant share of the nation's marketable securities.

o Contributions to these funds have risen until they account for nearly one-quarter of corporate pre-tax profits.

o The federal government has become involved through the provisions of the Employee Retirement Income Security Act (ERISA).

This management responsibility falls heavily on the corporate financial executives of this country.

Help in meeting that responsibility is found in the study reported in the following pages. Sponsored by the Financial Executives Research Foundation, the study was conducted by FRS Associates, an organization well known for its meticulous work in financial research.

The study, prepared under the direction of Sidney Cottle, brings together in a single volume the significant criteria for the responsible and responsive management of pension fund assets.

The Foundation is most appreciative of the devoted work of the authors. We recommend the work to all members of the Financial Executives Institute. They will find here, in easy to read terms, a clear insight into the basic elements of modern pension asset management.

CHARLES R. ALLEN
President, FERF

ABOUT THE AUTHORS

SIDNEY COTTLE

Sidney Cottle is President of FRS Associates, a subsidiary of Zinder Companies, Inc., which provides specialized research and consulting on the investment decision-making process and investment management. Dr. Cottle was formerly Director of Finance and Financial Institutional Research at Stanford Research Institute and a member of the faculty at the Graduate School of Business, Stanford University. He is the author of articles in professional financial journals and coauthor with Benjamin Graham and David L. Dodd of *Security Analysis* (fourth edition). He is also coauthor of other books on investments.

LEO C. BAILEY

Leo C. Bailey is Executive Director of the Florida State Board of Administration, managing a $4 billion balanced retirement fund. From 1970 to 1978, he was Senior Vice President and Investment Manager at the College Retirement Equities Fund and introduced a number of successful combinations of traditional investment approaches, portfolio controls based on modern concepts and techniques, and international diversification. His investment career also includes executive positions in the insurance and brokerage fields.

WILLIAM R. COTTLE

William R. Cottle is Vice President of FRS Associates. His academic training and experience have been in corporate finance and investment research. He has undertaken research primarily on the analytical aspects of the investment process and pension fund management.

J. MICHAEL MURPHY

J. Michael Murphy, C.F.A., is a security analyst with Capital Research Company and also a consultant with emphasis on performance measurement and diagnosis. He is a registered principal with the National Association of Security Dealers and a registered investment advisor. Formerly, he was Vice President, Investment Planning & Control, American Express Investment Management Company. He is the author of articles in investment publications.

ROGER F. MURRAY

Roger F. Murray, Professor Emeritus of Finance, Columbia University Graduate School of Business, is a corporate director and independent financial consultant. He is a member of the Pension Research Council, the Investment Policy Panel of the Pension Benefit Guaranty Corporation, and the New York State Teachers' Retirement System Investment Advisory Committee. A past president of the American Finance Association, Dr. Murray is the originator of the Individual Retirement Account concept.

ACKNOWLEDGMENTS

The dimensions of this study required the combined efforts and capabilities of a number of people. In this connection, the project director wishes to express appreciation to the Project Advisory Committee. The members were particularly effective in defining the relevant issues, reviewing drafts, and providing constructive suggestions.

For their considerable assistance, the project director also thanks the following individuals who participated in the planning stage of the study or reviewed specific portions of it:

Gary L. Bergstrom
Martin L. Leibowitz
M. Rollin Pelton
William F. Sharpe

Harcourt Wood undertook a pension fund survey that provided important information from interviews with executives in 40 corporations located in a number of cities across the United States. The study greatly benefited from the responses of those corporate executives. Gary B. Barrett edited the full study and made numerous helpful suggestions in the course of the project.

Benjamin Makela, Director of Research of the Financial Executives Research Foundation, provided valuable assistance and guidance in formulating the project and in arranging meetings with the Project Advisory Committee as the study progressed.

The project director expresses deep appreciation to the other authors for their extraordinary effort and major contribution; however, he bears the responsibility for the total study and the specific conclusions.

PREFACE

The study reported here is designed for executives responsible for investment management of their corporations' pension funds.[1] It concentrates on aspects and principles of investing that are particularly important to corporate action. In this manner, the study seeks to provide maximum assistance to corporate executives in exercising informed judgment and reaching effective decisions.

Increasingly, corporate executives are finding it essential to possess informed opinions in four principal areas:

- Investment objectives established for a pension fund and, if there are multiple managers, for each manager

- The broad strategy to be employed by a manager in achieving prescribed objectives

- Criteria employed in selection of a manager or managers

- The manner in which portfolio performance is to be measured and appraised.

In concentrating its attention on these four areas, the study provides within a single volume a spectrum of investment principles and information that otherwise would need to be selected and drawn from a large number of books and articles and from corporate sources. The emphasis is on the practical and

---

[1]Overall responsibility for a corporation's pension fund may reside in a specific officer or a committee. In contrast, primary operating responsibility in terms of regular communication with managers, transmission of funds, monitoring performance, and related duties usually resides in a designated executive. In small enterprises, the individual will usually be the corporate finance officer who performs this duty along with his or her other responsibilities. In large enterprises, the individual may be designated as the corporate pension executive and not only devote full time to pension matters but may also have staff assistance. The terms "corporate executive," "corporate finance officer," and "corporate pension executive" are used interchangeably in the study to refer to the corporate official bearing particular responsibility for the corporation's pension fund.

usable and not on the theoretical. It is designed to assist the corporate executive in exercising specific judgments and making specific decisions. It is also designed so that those who wish to refer particularly to a specific major step in the decision process will find in the appropriate chapter or chapters a reasonably inclusive exposition.

The scope of the study needs to be made clear at the outset. First, although it is concerned with defined benefit pension plans, information contained in certain chapters, such as Chapters V, VI, and VII which examine strategic decisions and the investment process, should also be helpful to those corporate officers responsible for profit-sharing funds.

Second, with the exception of a single chapter on international diversification, the study pertains exclusively to domestic marketable securities (stocks, bonds, and money market instruments). These securities typically constitute 90% or more of total pension fund holdings.[2] In recent years there has been a growing interest in foreign securities and real estate. Considerable research has been undertaken on the diversification aspect and other attributes of foreign security holdings. Chapter VIII sets forth major findings from that body of research. In contrast, research that would provide comparable information on the results of investing in real estate is, for the most part, in its early stages.

Third, the study is not meant to be a comprehensive treatise on the investment process in its entirety. It provides an overview of such extensive functions as security analysis and portfolio management. In this manner, it seeks to identify and keep within manageable limits those aspects of particular importance to the corporate executive. Moreover, an in-depth treatment of these and other parts of the investment process would involve writing another book on investments (and one three times as long as this one).

[2]For the 1974–78 period, private noninsured pension funds placed 90.5% of their market-valued assets in these investment vehicles. See *Statistical Bulletin*, July 1979, Securities and Exchange Commission.

CONTENTS

EXECUTIVE SUMMARY

Decisions in regard to investment management of pension fund assets are among the major decisions to be reached by corporate management. Their importance will increase significantly over the next decade. This study is concerned with investment decisions critical to effective management of pension assets.

The study is designed for executives responsible for investment management of their corporations' pension funds. It concentrates on those aspects of investing that are most important to corporate decision and action. The purpose of the study is to provide maximum assistance to corporate executives in developing informed opinions and exercising effective judgment in regard to four dominant aspects of pension fund management:

- Setting investment objectives
- Formulating investment strategy
- Selecting external managers
- Measuring and diagnosing performance.

The study is structured in terms of basic investment concepts, essential information, critical judgments, and key decisions entailed in coping with these four aspects of pension fund management as they relate to U.S. securities and security markets. In addition, a chapter is devoted to major considerations in investing in foreign securities.

1

A CORPORATE OVERVIEW

The cost of pension plans and the size of pension assets have reached the point that, for an increasing number of corporations, the effectiveness with which assets are managed requires careful consideration. Giving due consideration to fiduciary responsibility, the important factors are the returns that can be expected from investments principally in stocks and bonds and the degree of risk entailed. To bring these factors into perspective, Chapter I provides a corporate overview of the increase in pension costs and assets, the risk-return characteristics of stock and bond markets, and the risk-return tradeoff in investing.

SETTING INVESTMENT OBJECTIVES

Setting investment objectives for a pension fund and, in the case of a multimanager fund, for individual managers has always been important, but the process is now at the center of a rapidly expanding research effort. This effort is devoted to developing both procedures and research inputs necessary to formulate explicit objectives. In view of the scope and significance of objective setting, it is considered from three standpoints: corporate and investment factors, risk-return forecasts, and asset allocation.

Giving due consideration to fiduciary requirements under ERISA, the plan sponsor must consider both corporate and investment factors in determining the appropriate investment objectives for a fund. (Chapter II)

- Corporate factors include actuarial and liability projections for the corporation's retirement plan, the impact of these requirements on the projected financial position of the corporation, the significance of different funding methods, cash flows into and out of the fund, and the degree of risk aversion of corporate management.

- Major investment factors encompass the time horizon (projection period for setting objectives, life cycle of the fund, and period over which performance is measured), priority given to liquidity needs, significance of real versus nominal returns, and risk and return. Risk and return are the key considerations in making investment decisions and thus the factors of overriding importance in setting objectives.

- The manner in which risk-return objectives are developed and stated is changing significantly. Rather than the traditional intuitive appraisal of risk and return and specification of objectives solely in words, the trend is toward appraising risk and return in a formal, systematic framework and specifying them in quantitative terms.

Establishment of specific risk-return objectives for a pension fund requires forecasts of the future. The plan sponsor therefore needs to be familiar with (1) the role of forecasting in objective setting, (2) the historic risk-return behavior of security markets, and (3) the general nature of the forecasting process. (Chapter III)

- Corporate executives responsible for setting pension fund objectives must base their decisions principally on the estimated *average* return for stocks, bonds, and money market instruments over the forecast period and on the probable extent to which the return realized in any year might depart from the average.

- It is highly desirable that appropriate corporate executives understand the general nature of economic forecasts and assumptions that support the risk-return projections used in setting portfolio objectives. This understanding is important in increasing the effectiveness of communication between plan sponsor and investment manager.

Allocation of the assets of a fund among stocks, bonds, and money market instruments relative to the structure of liabilities is the primary determinant of the amount of risk assumed and the rate of return sought. The asset allocation decision is therefore critically important. (Chapter IV)

- Asset allocation is determined primarily by the risk-return tradeoff decision. To a point, sponsors will assume additional risk if the estimated additional return is expected to more than compensate for the risk. In view of the importance of the asset-mix decision, various procedures have been developed to understand and quantify the risk-return tradeoff.

- Although different analytical methods may be used, simulation techniques are particularly applicable. In this manner, it is possible to estimate the effect of changes in the stock/bond/money market instrument ratios on the expected level and volatility of portfolio returns. A number of systems are available for analyzing and appraising asset-mix changes.

From the foregoing, it is to be seen that investment objectives constitute long term risk-return targets developed principally from careful consideration of the risk-return tradeoff provided by security markets. They are typically based on estimated *average* performance over a span of years of broad indexes for stock and bond markets and are thus representative of the results of passive management, because neither timing nor selection is involved. Using these expectations, *normal* risk-return targets are established. These targets can be set forth in such terms as the *normal* asset mix, level of equity diversification, quality of issues to be held, and bond maturity distribution. (They can also be stipulated in such statistical terminology as beta and standard deviation.)

FORMULATING INVESTMENT STRATEGY

Strategy also pertains to the risk-return tradeoff. From an investment standpoint, strategy essentially involves establishing the extent to which risk in its different forms can in the short term depart from long term quantified norms or averages stipulated in the objectives. These departures represent the quest of active management for additional return that more than compensates for the additional risk assumed. Thus strategy determines the extent and nature of these departures and thus the extent to which a fund can be actively managed.

The major portion of most pension funds will be actively managed. Under these circumstances, strategy plays a critically important role because it determines the extent to which active management can deviate from the norms established by investment objectives. Accordingly, strategy needs to be considered within an active management context. (Chapter V)

- Active management entails selection and market timing. Selection changes the composition of principally equity and fixed income holdings to take advantage of perceived mispricing of groups of issues and individual issues in the marketplace. Market timing entails changing the asset mix (stock/bond/money market instrument ratios) to take advantage of perceived overpricing or underpricing of *classes* of assets relative to one another.

- The major styles of active stock managers are: (1) diversified managers—hold all industries of investment consequence and have no strong and continuing bias toward any single industry or sector of the market; (2) undiversified managers— specialize in selected sectors of the market, such as high growth stocks; (3)

rotator managers—shift portfolio composition to hold those industries and sectors considered attractive; (4) module managers—hold stocks in modules each of which consists of issues in a specific sector of the market.

- The major components of active bond management are: yield pickup swaps, substitution swaps, sector spread swaps, and rate anticipation shifts. The first three types of action entail shifting issues or sectors to take advantage of short term perceived mispricing. The last is based on anticipated significant changes in the overall level and term structure of interest rates.

An understanding of the basic principles on which the investment process rests is essential in judging the capabilities of a manager in the selection process, deciding on appropriate objectives and strategy for an individual manager, and appraising performance. The investment process may be divided into two large parts: (1) analysis, timing, and selection and (2) portfolio construction and management. (Chapters VI and VII)

- Fundamental analysis encompasses economic analysis, stock and bond market analysis, and security analysis. The analytical function thus consists of a hierarchy of forecasts that culminate in examination and evaluation of individual industries and issues. The important considerations for the plan sponsor are the nature and depth of the research and the manner in which the research function is structured in an investment organization.

- The principal considerations in judging the timing function are: the extent to which a manager uses market timing, nature of the research supporting timing decisions, and the probable accuracy with which the manager can predict mispricing among markets for stocks, bonds, and money market instruments.

- Selection embraces determination of industry weights (and perhaps group or market sector weights, such as high growth stocks and cyclical issues) as well as selection of individual issues. The selection process uses the risk-return estimates developed by security analysts to construct portfolios designed to meet stipulated investment objectives.

- The investment portfolios that constitute the pension fund (*the* portfolio in a single manager fund) are tangible results of (1) investment objectives and strategies agreed on with the managers and (2) investment styles and capabilities of individual managers. Given a manager's style, active management is largely the process by which the manager identifies and adjusts portfolio holdings to reflect his or her conclusions as to overpricing or underpricing of individual securities, industries, sectors, and entire markets.

- Risk-return characteristics of securities are the dominant considerations in formation of portfolios. The key fact is that a difference in expected return may not be attributable to mispricing but to a difference in risk. As a result, portfolio managers carefully consider the expected return and the estimated risk in constructing portfolios to meet established objectives.

INTERNATIONAL DIVERSIFICATION

There is growing interest in foreign securities, and considerable research has been conducted on the attributes of foreign security holdings. Accordingly, for those corporate executives considering whether to diversify internationally, important factors affecting the decision are reviewed. The factors may be grouped under three major headings: benefits, deterrents, and available forms of international diversification. (Chapter VIII)

- Benefits are centered on the extent to which risk-return patterns of stocks in each national market are unrelated to those in every other national market and particularly those of the U.S. market. The evidence indicates that, at least in terms of the past, the potential has existed for decreasing the risk and improving the return of a purely domestic portfolio through international diversification.

- Deterrents are primarily political and currency risks. Sovereign nations can (and do) restrict the free flow of investment funds across their borders and otherwise constrain foreign investing. Fluctuations in rates of currency exchange can either positively or negatively affect investment results. The cost differential in terms of such factors as withholding taxes, commissions, and bid-ask spreads may also merit consideration.

- Corporations ordinarily rely on external managers in investing in foreign equity markets. To ensure spreading investments over a reasonable number of countries and issues, participation is frequently in a commingled fund, which may be either actively or passively managed.

SELECTING EXTERNAL MANAGERS

Selection of external managers is a two-step process. First, it entails determining whether to have a single or multiple manager arrangement. Second, it requires establishing a specific set of selection criteria. (Chapter IX)

● Factors weighed in deciding on the number of managers ordinarily include: size of the fund and its expected growth, extent to which reliance on a single manager subjects the fund to possible discontinuities in management or unsatisfactory performance, and such other considerations as diversification and increased involvement of the plan sponsor in the decision process.

● Many criteria are important in selecting managers. Reputation and performance record are important; however, the appraisal of a manager needs to be extended well beyond the record. It is future performance that is critical, and judgment in this regard requires careful consideration of such factors as size, professional staff, investment style, risk-return profile, and the caliber of the analytical and decision-making process.

MEASURING AND DIAGNOSING PERFORMANCE

An effective performance measurement and diagnostic analysis system provides information essential in evaluating and appraising managers, rethinking investment objectives, and revising portfolio strategy. (Chapters X and XI)

● An effective measurement system requires defined objectives and strategy, reliable and timely data, statistical methods that produce relevant measurements, and output of information in a useful format.

● Internal rate of return (dollar-weighted returns) can be used to compare performance of the total fund in terms of actuarial requirements and investment objectives. Time-weighted returns are usually more appropriate for measuring performance of individual managers. After computation, the returns should be risk-adjusted.

● The relevant time period for useful measurement requires a choice between shorter periods, providing fresher data but less statistical precision, and longer periods, providing a higher degree of statistical accuracy with the possibility of less relevancy. The generally used compromise seems to be either five years of quarterly data or three years of monthly data.

● Diagnostic analysis begins with individual securities and common group factors in examining portfolio composition. This technique has been developed because of dissatisfaction with the error ranges associated with broad descriptive statistics of bottom-line performance measurement systems.

- Diagnostic analysis divides risk into a number of categories and identifies sources of various risks on a security-by-security basis. It can be used to compare portfolio activity with a manager's stated investment style and with forecasts for individual securities. It can also be used to measure and control a fund with several managers.

CHAPTER

1 Corporate Overview

Decisions in regard to investment management of pension fund assets are now among the major decisions to be reached by corporate management. Their importance will increase significantly over the next decade.

This study is concerned with investment decisions critical to effective management of pension assets. Executives responsible for their corporations' pension funds either make these decisions in the first instance or subsequently judge them after they are made by someone else. Therefore, it is important that the executives be as fully informed as possible with respect to these decisions.

Recent investment experience, rapidly rising pension costs, the present size and continuing growth of pension assets, innovations in approaches to asset management, and fiduciary and other responsibilities resulting from the passage of the Employee Retirement Income Security Act of 1974 (ERISA) are causing corporate managers in general and financial managers in particular to consider such decisions and judgments with increased thoroughness.

Therefore, the exercise of informed judgment in regard to the following four dominant aspects of pension fund management is particularly important.

1. Setting investment objectives

2. Formulating investment strategy

3. Selecting external managers

4. Measuring and diagnosing portfolio management and performance.

Accordingly, this study is structured in terms of basic investment concepts, essential information, critical judgments, and key decisions entailed in coping with these four aspects of pension fund management as they relate to U.S. securities and security markets. The study also examines major considerations in investing in foreign securities—the international diversification of U.S. portfolios.

METHOD OF STUDY

Setting investment objectives, formulating investment strategy, selecting external managers, and measuring and diagnosing performance are complex processes. Nevertheless, they can be reduced to manageable proportions and made understandable by (1) establishing straightforward definitions of terms, (2) concentrating on those aspects of investing of particular importance to corporate action, (3) discussing basic principles in familiar terms, and (4) presenting illustrative material and accompanying analyses. These methods should make the study of maximum practical assistance to corporate decision-makers. The material is written and presented principally from the standpoint of judgments, decisions, and specific responsibilities of the financial executive or corporate pension officer.

THE INVESTMENT ENVIRONMENT

The environment in which the corporate executive exercises judgment and reaches decisions is highly dynamic. This environment needs to be brought into perspective at the outset, because the forces at work today will affect tomorrow's judgments and decisions. Accordingly, the balance of this opening chapter focuses on the following five important factors.

1. The rising cost of pension plans, the present substantial size and growth of pension assets, and the increasing importance of the return earned on pension assets

2. Secular and cyclical returns on stock and bond markets over the 53-year span, 1926-78

3. The risk-return tradeoff that underlies all investment decisions and the extent of the financial executive's involvement

4. The concepts and techniques of importance in setting investment objectives and formulating investment strategy

5. The changing regulatory climate as it relates to pension asset management.

COST OF PENSIONS AND SIZE OF ASSETS

The rapid increase in the dollar amount of annual contributions by U.S. corporations to pension funds is well-known. The same is true of the percentage of pretax profits required to meet pension costs and of the growth of pension assets. However, until the numbers are examined, the magnitude of the increases may not be fully appreciated.

The book value of private noninsured pension funds increased from $83 billion to $202 billion over the 10-year span, 1968-78.[1] This increase is equivalent to an annual average growth rate of 9.3%. Over the same period, the market value of the investment rose from $96 billion to $201.6 billion. If the market values of insured plans and separate accounts by insurance companies are included, the total investment by private plans increased from $136 billion in 1968 to $321 billion in 1978; a compound annual growth of 9.0.[2]

Profits and Contributions

The above figures reveal the growth in and the present magnitude of the total investment by private pension funds. However, they do not show the extent to which corporations have had to increase the dollar amount of their

---

[1]The span is measured from the end of 1968 to the end of 1978 and thus covers an elapsed period of 10 years. Unless otherwise indicated, annual data are year-end figures.

[2]From U.S. Securities and Exchange Commission, *Statistical Bulletin,* April 1976, July 1979 and August 1979.

Table I-1—U.S. CORPORATE BUSINESS

Profits Before Taxes and Employer Contributions to Private Pension and Profit-Sharing Funds

(Billions of Dollars)   1970–1978

	1970	1971	1972	1973	1974	1975	1976	1977	1978
Corporate profits before taxes	$67.7	$77.4	$ 91.3	$108.9	$117.3	$114.3	$147.7	$167.3	$195.8
Employer contributions to private pension and profit-sharing funds	13.0	15.0	17.8	20.7	24.2	28.1	33.1	38.6	45.0
Profits plus contributions	$80.7	$92.4	$109.1	$129.6	$141.5	$142.4	$180.8	$205.9	$240.8
Contributions as a percentage of profits	19.2%	19.4%	19.5%	19.0%	20.6%	24.6%	22.4%	23.1%	23.0%
Contributions as a percentage of profits plus contributions	16.1	16.2	16.3	16.0	17.1	19.7	18.3	18.8	18.7

Sources: Corporate profits before taxes from U.S. Department of Commerce, Bureau of Economic Analysis, *Survey of Current Business*, see Table 1.15, "Gross Domestic Product of Corporate Business." Contributions are from published and mimeographed material from Bureau of Economic Analysis, *Survey of Current Business*, see Table 6.13, "Other Labor Income by Industry and by Type."

annual contributions or the resulting impact on pretax profits. This information is set forth in compilations of the Bureau of Economic Analysis (U.S. Department of Commerce).

Table I-1 provides data for pretax profits and employer contributions to private pension and profit-sharing funds arising from domestic operations of U.S. corporations. Over the 1970-78 span, the dollar amount of contributions rose at a compound annual rate of 16.8%. Contributions as a percentage of pretax profits also increased; the 1970-73 average was 19.3% and the 1974-78 average was 22.7%. A more meaningful figure is the increased percentage that contributions were of profits before deducting contributions. They rose from 16.2% in 1970-73 to 18.5% in 1974-78.

Pension Assets

As a result of rising contributions per employee, an expanding work force, and increased coverage, private pension fund assets (including insurance company pension reserves) have grown at an impressive rate. The totals at five-year intervals over the 1948-78 span were:

Five-Year Intervals	Market Value in Billions of Dollars
1948	$ 8.9
1953	20.6
1958	44.8
1963	78.3
1968	136.4
1973	191.3
1978	321.3

Sources: Board of Governors of the Federal Reserve System, *Flow of Funds Accounts 1946-1975* and Securities & Exchange Commission, *Statistical Bulletin,* August 1979.

The massiveness of pension fund assets in the aggregate can also be seen when they are viewed at the corporate level. It can be readily demonstrated that the pension assets of individual corporations have become major pools of capital. For example, at the end of 1978 the market value of trusteed pension funds and assets held under an insured program for General Motors totaled $9.4 billion and was equivalent to 54% of the stockholders' equity. The comparable figures for General Foods at March 31, 1979, were $0.5 billion and 40% and for Du Pont at December 31, 1978, $3.0 billion and 63%.

Although the market value of private pension assets (including insurance company pension reserves) may not continue to grow at the 1958-78 compound annual rate of 11.8% or the 1968-78 rate of 9.0%, it is expected that this maturing process will still be accompanied by significant growth over the next decade or longer. Accordingly, investment management of pension assets will be an increasingly important consideration for corporate financial executives over the foreseeable future.

The cost of pension plans and the size of pension assets have reached the point that the effectiveness with which the assets are managed requires careful consideration. In this regard, the critical factors are the returns that can be expected from investments principally in stocks and bonds and the degree of risk entailed.

The amount of return sought and the degree of risk assumed in the management of a pension fund can, within limits, be influenced by the nature of securities held. However, the level of return and the related risk as they are actually experienced in security markets are beyond the control of any investment manager. An understanding of the past is helpful in anticipating the future. Accordingly, the starting point for consideration of return and risk is the past behavior of security markets.

THE STOCK AND BOND MARKETS

The behavior of the stock and bond markets is examined more fully in Chapter III. The purpose here is to provide an overview in terms of risk and return.

It is well known that investing is risky. The range of risk is substantial. Risk is the uncertainty associated with the return forecast for an individual security or group of securities; it is the likelihood of receiving a return less than that expected. For example, a significant range of returns can be realized from selling even an Aaa bond before maturity and thus encountering price changes reflecting fluctuations in interest rates. Much greater variation in return can result from cyclical swings in the market price of a common stock. Risk is also the possibility of long term or even permanent loss that comes from holding either lower quality issues (stocks or bonds) or issues that have deteriorated severely in quality (such as bonds that defaulted on their interest payments).

Since pension fund portfolios are typically characterized by diversified holdings of investment quality stocks and bonds, it is risk in the form of a possible shortfall in the realized total return (price change plus income) from that expected which is the dominant consideration here. Accordingly, in this study the term "risk" is used to indicate the likelihood of a shortfall in return from an investment over a future period.

For a specific company, risk is the result of many fundamental factors, such as competitive nature of the business, operating or financial leverage, newness and smallness of the enterprise, inadequate managerial depth, location of the business, and uncertain acceptance of the corporation's securities in the marketplace. The overall uncertainty that results from these factors tends to be manifest in the instability of the price and dividends of the company's stock; that is, the total return.

As a result, if the forecast return is within a wide range of possible returns,[3] risk is considered to be greater than if the forecast return is within a narrow range (the likelihood of divergence is limited). Accordingly, one measure of risk is the possible (expected) range of the returns. Ordinarily, the more the returns for a security have fluctuated in the past, the more difficult it is to forecast the average or level of the return to be realized from that security in the future. The fluctuations in the returns of a volatile issue would need to be sufficiently repetitive in terms of amplitude and duration to be identifiable and thus predictable for this not to be true.

The extent of differences in volatility can be readily illustrated by comparing realized stock and bond total returns over extended periods. The annual rate of total return on Standard & Poor's Composite Index of 500 Stocks

[3]In more statistical terms, the likely size of divergence from the expected result of a log normal distribution is substantial.

(S&P 500) *averaged* 11.2% over the 53-year span from the beginning of 1926 through 1978.[4] However, annual rates fluctuated widely. In terms of extremes, the maximum positive return in any one year was 54% and the maximum negative return was 43%. A more meaningful indication of volatility is the fact that in approximately two-thirds of the years, the return fluctuated between a negative 11.0% and a positive 33.4% (the variation on each side of the average return of 11.2% was 22.2 percentage points). This range of 44.4 percentage points (from −11.0 percentage points to +33.4) is wide, indicating the pronounced volatility of common stock returns. Substantial volatility exists even when the average returns for extended periods are compared. This fact is emphasized by the marked differences in the following average annual total returns (average of the rate of return for each year) for the S&P 500 over selected ten-year periods.[5]

1929–38	4.5%
1939–48	8.4
1949–58	21.5
1959–68	10.7
1969–78	4.8

In contrast, realized returns on long term corporate bonds of high quality are much less volatile. Over the 1926–78 span, the annual return averaged 4.1% and in two-thirds of the years the return fluctuated between a negative 1.5% and a positive 9.7%.[6] The value of 5.6 percentage points on each side of the 53-year average annual total return for bonds is much narrower than the 22.2 percentage points on each side of the average annual return of 11.2% for common stocks. Accordingly, as is well-known, the probability of a shortfall in the realized return from investing in common stocks is much greater than that entailed in investing in high grade corporate bonds. At the

---

[4] A distinction needs to be made between *average annual* rates and *annual compound* rates. Average annual rates are computed by summing the rates from one year to the next for a series of years and taking the arithmetic average. The annual compound rate, as used here, is the rate of growth that will produce the time series period-ending value with equivalent annual compounded percentage increments. The average annual rate will ordinarily be higher than the compound rate. For example, over the 1926–78 span the *average annual* rate was 11.2% and the *annual compound* rate of return was 8.9%.

[5] Total returns with reinvestment of dividends, from R. G. Ibbotson and R. A. Sinquefield, *Stocks, Bonds, Bills and Inflation: Historical Returns 1926–1978,* Financial Analysts Research Foundation, 1979.

[6] The annual compound rate of return for high grade, long term corporate bonds was 4.0%.

same time, as the following tabulation demonstrates, the realized average annual return on bonds can also vary significantly from one ten-year period to the next.[7]

1929-38	7.0%
1939-48	2.8
1949-58	1.5
1959-68	2.5
1969-78	6.2

THE RISK-RETURN TRADEOFF

Risk and return are the dominant considerations in investing. Given the investor's objectives, the goal of investment management is to secure the highest return for the level of risk appropriate for a specific portfolio. In other words, it is to construct and manage *efficient portfolios*.[8]

In the management of a pension fund (or any other pool of assets), the initial and one of the most critical risk-return decisions is the proportion of assets that will be put in variable income securities (typically common stocks) and fixed income securities (typically bonds and money market instruments). Although it has not always occurred in past periods, the expectation is that over a span of years the average return on stocks will significantly exceed that on bonds. The 1926-78 *compound* annual total rate of return for common stocks (S&P 500) was 8.9% (*average* annual rate 11.2%) compared with 4.0% for long term corporate bonds (*average* annual rate 4.1%). The compound total return on U.S Treasury bills (as representative of money market instruments, so-called cash equivalents) was 2.5% over the same 53-year span. Accordingly, the asset-mix decision—determining the composition of a portfolio in terms of stock/bond/Treasury bill proportions (or other asset categories)—is a critically important risk-return decision. (This and other important decisions in regard to objectives are considered in Chapter II.)

[7]Ibbotson and Sinquefield, *op cit.*

[8]In investment terminology, portfolios that provide the highest return for a given level of risk or, conversely, the lowest risk for a given level of returns, are known as "efficient portfolios."

The plan sponsor must inevitably participate in the risk-return decision in some manner. The participation may be either direct or indirect and either before or after the fact. Direct involvement before the fact is clearcut. For example, assume a situation in which the manager proposed a specific stock/bond/Treasury bill ratio to the sponsor and provides an estimate of the level of return that can be expected over a stipulated span of years together with the uncertainty or risk attached to that return estimate. The sponsor then indicates whether he or she concurs in the fund being managed in terms of the proposed asset mix. In reality, the sponsor, in deciding whether the proposed asset-mix proportions are satisfactory, is deciding whether (out of a series of alternatives) the anticipated level of return and the accompanying risk (likelihood of a shortfall in the actual return relative to the expected return) from the proposed stock/bond/Treasury bill combination constitute the best risk-return tradeoff.

In contrast, suppose the sponsor takes the position that the manager, as an investment professional, should make the asset-mix decision without the sponsor's participation. The level of return earned by the fund and the degree of risk encountered will be determined principally by the asset-mix decision (primarily the relative proportion of stocks, bonds, and Treasury bills held in the portfolio).

The sponsor will review the performance of the fund and decide whether it is satisfactory. In reaching this decision, the sponsor will typically consider the return earned by the fund and the volatility of the return including fluctuations in the market value of portfolio assets. The sponsor may also compare the level and volatility of the return with that of various yardsticks such as comparable funds and selected stock and bond indexes (such as the S&P 500 and the Salomon Brothers Bond Index).

In determining whether the performance of the fund is satisfactory or unsatisfactory, careful consideration must be given to the risk assumed and the return achieved. Accordingly, the sponsor cannot avoid the risk-return issue, although he or she may choose to exercise judgment in regard to it after the fact. In this latter instance, the plan sponsor judges results in terms of the outcome of a manager's investment decisions and actions.

Our conclusion is that neither the manager nor the plan sponsor can avoid risk-return decisions. The latter, however, may make such decisions either before (in terms of expectations) or after the fact (in terms of results) or both.

INVESTMENT CONCEPTS AND TECHNIQUES

The above discussion stresses the view that the tradeoff between risk and return is the key consideration in investment decision-making. For the financial executive and other corporate officers who have pension fund responsibilities, the risk-return decision in its most critical form relates to setting portfolio objectives. In fact, some hold that the most important and difficult task confronting the plan sponsor is deciding on appropriate investment objectives for the pension fund.

The goal is to establish a set of long term objectives that constitute an optimal matching of the sponsor's return desires and risk aversion with what is reasonably attainable in the expected investment environment over a specified span of time, such as the next five or ten years. In this manner, risk-return objectives are established that are appropriate in terms of both corporate factors and long term expectations for security markets. Objectives have always been important, but they are now at the center of a rapidly expanding research effort. This effort is centered on quantification of risk and return.

Setting Risk-Return Objectives

Much remains to be learned about both risk and return. Nevertheless the conceptual and analytical framework now exists in which these factors can be considered more definitively than ever before. As a result, the manner in which risk and return objectives for pension portfolios are defined, developed, and stated is changing significantly. This change is a radical departure from an intuitive appraisal of risk and return and specification of objectives solely in words.

The familiar statement "maximum return consistent with an appropriate level of risk" is inadequate. It conveys different things to different people. For example, what does the phrase "appropriate level of risk" actually mean?

In Chapter II, principles and procedures for setting quantified risk-return objectives are examined in depth. This development is now one of the most powerful forces for change in investment management. Accordingly, the chapter emphasizes the dominant role of risk-return objectives in portfolio decisions and thus in portfolio performance.

Definitions

No general agreement exists as to what is meant by investment objectives, investment strategy, and portfolio tactics. Each one of these terms is interpreted differently by different people. To avoid confusion, the terms as used in this study are defined as follows.

Objectives are fundamental decision criteria that can be developed at different levels of comprehensiveness. In their basic form, objectives constitute long term risk-return targets. They are developed essentially from careful consideration of the risk-return tradeoff provided by security markets. Accordingly, objectives are typically based on the estimated *average* performance over a span of years of broad indexes considered representative of the stock and bond markets. Using these expectations, *normal* risk-return targets are established. These targets can be set forth in such terms as the *normal* asset mix (stock/bond/Treasury bill ratio), level of equity diversification, quality of issues to be held, and bond maturity distribution. (They can also be stipulated in such statistical terminology as the normal beta, standard deviation, and coefficient of determination (R^2) as set forth in subsequent chapters.) As discussed below, strategic decisions by the plan sponsor provide the basis for extending these objectives into a more comprehensive set.

Strategy also pertains to the risk-return tradeoff. Essentially, it determines how actively a pension fund may be managed. Strategy needs to be viewed from the standpoint of both the sponsor and the manager. For the sponsor, strategy primarily establishes the extent to which risk in its different forms can in the short term depart from long term quantified norms or averages stipulated in basic objectives for the fund. These departures are in quest of additional return that more than compensates for the additional risk assumed.

Since investment styles and the aggressiveness with which they are employed and the resulting risk-return profiles of managers vary substantially, strategy must also embrace selection of managers. For the manager with an established style, strategy therefore determines how actively a portfolio will be managed within the constraints of that style. Thus for the manager as well as the sponsor, strategy establishes risk boundaries and return expectations. The addition of these risk boundaries and accompanying return expectations in portfolio objectives established for individual managers and in the comprehensive set of objectives for the total fund merits careful consideration by the plan sponsor.

Portfolio tactics pertain to action based on short term expectations for the economy and security markets. (The forecast period is usually not less than four quarters or more than eight.) Although tempered by projections for the intermediate term, such as the next five years, tactical decisions rest principally on forecasts of the short term. Within the ranges prescribed by strategy, tactics determine the appropriate present composition of the portfolio and therefore its current risk-return characteristics.

The Plan Sponsor's Role

As concluded above, the plan sponsor cannot avoid passing judgment on investment objectives established for the pension fund. In our opinion, it is highly desirable at the outset for the corporate executive to understand as fully as possible the long term risk and return realities of security markets and in this manner gain a more definitive understanding of what can reasonably be accomplished. Judged *solely* on the basis of investment considerations (in contrast to legal interpretations of ERISA or other statutes), it is desirable for the appropriate corporate officer (or officers) to indicate whether the proposed set of objectives appears to be satisfactory. This judgment is based on risk-return projections for security markets, appraisal of the investment manager's capabilities, financial circumstances surrounding the fund and other important corporate factors, and the plan sponsor's risk-return preferences. In our opinion, the final judgment in regard to portfolio objectives rests with the plan sponsor. Moreover, it is suggested that the objectives as finalized go beyond the basic form of only normalized standards and include the ranges established by strategy.

In actual practice, there is no clearcut delineation of the respective roles of the plan sponsor and manager in determining investment strategy for a fund. The primary consideration is the extent of the participation of the sponsor. This participation will depend on such factors as the size of the fund (or funds), number and types of managers, in-house capabilities of the corporation, desires of responsible officers, nature of the relationship with the external manager or managers, and explicitness of portfolio objectives.

The more explicit and comprehensive the objectives, the greater the precision with which the sponsor can communicate with the manager and, in turn, determine the extent of participation in portfolio strategy. In all instances, however, it is highly desirable that the corporate finance officer identify and understand the manager's investment style and the strategy that the manager will employ in seeking to accomplish portfolio objectives. This understanding is equally important in subsequent diagnosis and appraisal of the manager's performance.

The ability to make effective tactical decisions requires substantial knowledge of security markets, industries, and individual security issues. Most sponsors consider these decisions to be the province of the manager. Sponsors tend to monitor and appraise the efficacy of tactical decisions within the context of the manager's overall performance. For this reason, the present study considers setting objectives and formulating strategy in depth and gives less attention to tactics.

THE CHANGING REGULATORY CLIMATE

The manner in which investment of pension funds is regulated has undergone substantial change in recent years. Before the passage of ERISA, there was little direct federal government involvement in the management of pension fund assets and there were no federal regulatory bodies established specifically for the purpose of regulating pension fund investing. With enactment of ERISA, the federal government intervened directly both in setting standards for pension fund investing and in regulating the observance of those standards.

ERISA

So much has already been published about ERISA that additional comment in the absence of new laws or definitive court rulings would be superfluous. This study, however, is written from a point of view that assumes the outcome of several issues that are as yet unresolved. Accordingly, something must be said about those issues as they relate to positions taken in later parts of this study.

Participation under ERISA

In general terms, ERISA incorporates the following provisions relative to acting in a fiduciary capacity:

- Plan sponsors and pension fund investment managers have the same general fiduciary responsibilities as named trustees.[9]

- Pension fund assets must be managed solely for the good of a plan's beneficiaries.[10]

- Liability for fiduciary misconduct extends to individuals as well as corporations.[11]

- Exculpatory clauses and self-serving provisions incorporated into the language of pension plan instruments have no force at law.[12]

Although these provisions are clear as far as they go, they leave much unsaid. For example, the Act states that named fiduciaries have "control and management" of all assets, but that they may delegate management of such assets to someone else. In a strict constructionist sense, this could mean that they still have "control." The questions then arise as to what is "control" and how closely must plan sponsors and trustees participate in the exercise of control to perform their fiduciary duties.[13]

In regard to external management of funds, it is assumed for purposes of this study that plan sponsor participation in the investment decision-making process will at least be in (1) selection of a fund manager or managers, (2) establishment of investment objectives for the fund, and (3) evaluation of fund performance.

[9]Employee Retirement Income Security Act of 1974, Sec. 3 (21) (A).
[10]Act Sec. 404 (a) (1).
[11]Act Sec. 409 (a).
[12]Act Sec. 410 (a).
[13]See Robert C. Pozen, "The Prudent Man Rule and ERISA," *Financial Analysts Journal,* March-April 1977, p. 30.

The Prudent Man (Person) vs the Prudent Expert

ERISA contains the following language: ". . .a fiduciary shall discharge his duties with respect to the plan. . .with the care, skill, prudence, and diligence *under the circumstances then prevailing* that a prudent man *acting in a like capacity and familiar with such matters* would use in the conduct of *an enterprise of a like character and with like aims.*"[14] (Emphasis added.)

The phrase "under the circumstances then prevailing" is designed to express the intention that hindsight judgments are not relevant. "Acting in a like capacity and familiar with such matters" describes the fiduciary in his or her role as an informed member of the community of pension plan fiduciaries, as distinguished from trustees of personal trusts, foundations, endowments, and other types of funds. The standard is then positively restricted to "an enterprise of a like character and with like aims" to show that it relates specifically to a program of providing retirement income or asset accumulation for plan beneficiaries.

Legal commentators are agreed that this language is strikingly similar in spirit and intent to that of the prudent man rule found in the common law of trusts as set forth in *Harvard College v. Amory.* However, because of certain differences in language, and because of the discussion found in the *Conference Committee Joint Explanation* issued by the Congress before enactment of the legislation, several commentators have argued that the ERISA provision actually establishes a prudent *expert* rule as contrasted with the customary prudent man rule.

Supporters of the prudent expert concept have not been particularly illuminating as to what the differences are but the following ones seem germane to the consideration.

- The prudent expert might be held to higher standards than the prudent man, just as the professional fiduciary has historically been held more accountable than the individual trustee.

- The prudent expert might be expected to do a better job of achieving that which was formerly the duty of the prudent man because of greater knowledge of the

---

[14]Act Sec. 404 (a) (1) (B).

dimensions and characteristics of the investment management problem being addressed.

- The prudent man was allowed to apply subjective standards to his or her investment decision-making process, that is to look at things from the standpoint of what he or she would do under like circumstances, whereas the prudent expert should apply objective standards for pension fund investing that are as yet undefined and untested in the courts.

None of these standards presents difficulties relative to positions taken in later chapters of this study.

Diversification

Portfolio diversification for the purpose of limiting risk has long been a principal tenet of investment management. ERISA adopts this tenet by requiring pension fund investment managers to diversify portfolio holdings.[15] In addition, the Act places a ceiling on the amount of the plan sponsor's securities that can be held. Although the Act does not establish quantified standards for diversification nor state how the level of diversification should be measured and risk should be considered, it indicates that the purpose of diversification is to "minimize the risk of large losses."[16] This is an explicit recognition that some losses are inevitable: the stricture against concentration derives from the purpose of limiting exposure to large losses by spreading investments across a broad range of activities.

Before the advances in investment concepts and techniques of the last decade, diversification standards were generally neither explicit nor quantitative. They were based almost exclusively on judgment and intuition. However, recent advances, which constitute a key part of modern portfolio theory, make possible the establishment of quantified and much more explicit measures of diversification than those set forth in ERISA. The study explains in a subsequent chapter the investment and statistical concepts behind these quantified measures. With the plan sponsor rests the determination as to the extent that explicit standards of diversification will be prescribed for guidance of the investment manager.

[15]Act Sec. 404 (a) (1) (c).
[16]Act Sec. 407. See also Secs. 404 (a) (2), 408 (a), and 414 (c).

Prudence

The prudent man (or prudent expert) provisions of the Act need to be considered from two aspects: (1) prudence exercised by the pension fiduciary and (2) prudence of the investments made.

With respect to the first aspect, the Prudence Regulation under ERISA adopted June 25, 1979, states in part as follows:[17]

> With regard to an investment or investment course of action. . ., the requirements of section 404 (a) (1) (B) of the Act . . . are satisfied if the fiduciary has given appropriate consideration to . . . a determination . . . that the particular investment or investment course of action is reasonably designed, as part of the portfolio, . . . to further the purposes of the plan, taking into consideration the risk of loss and the opportunity for gain (or other return) associated with the investment or investment course of action, and consideration of the following factors as they relate to . . . the portfolio:
>
> (i) the composition of the portfolio with regard to diversification;
>
> (ii) the liquidity and current return of the portfolio relative to the anticipated cash flow requirements of the plan; and
>
> (iii) the projected return of the portfolio relative to the funding objectives of the plan.

In regard to the second aspect, another principal tenet of investment management is that individual securities should always be selected within the context of a total portfolio with specific investment objectives. Accordingly, individual securities should not be treated as independent, isolated entities in constructing and managing portfolios. The interrelationships of the individual securities within the total portfolio and the resulting overall risk-return characteristics of the portfolio are the dominant considerations. The Prudence Regulation appears to recognize and support this portfolio view, as distinguished from the security by security test of prudence that historically prevailed under the common law applicable to personal trusts.

---

[17]Issued by the Department of Labor with an extensive preamble to interpret Sec. 404 (a) (1) (B) of the Act as 29 CFR, para. 2500. 404a-1 effective July 23, 1979.

For example, if the Regulation is upheld in the courts, it would place emphasis on the risk and return characteristics of portfolios and on establishment of explicit portfolio objectives including standards of diversification.

The Department of Labor's commentary on the Prudence Regulation makes clear that the prudence of an investment decision should not be judged without regard to the role that the proposed investment course of action plays within the overall plan portfolio. Thus, "although securities issued by a small or new company may be riskier investments than securities issued by a 'blue-chip' company, the investment in the former company may be entirely proper under the Act's 'prudence' rule."[18]

ERISA and Investment Management

The purpose of this study is to provide in readily understandable terms an overview of basic investment considerations in management of pension funds. The provisions of ERISA cited above as well as others influence management of such funds.[19] In individual instances, the nature of that influence varies substantially according to the widely different interpretations of ERISA provisions by plan sponsors, investment managers, and their legal advisers. However, in no sense does the study undertake an interpretation of legal implications of the Act.

The basic issue is how deeply should the plan sponsor become involved in investment decision-making. The answer to that question is left to the plan sponsor and learned counsel. This study seeks to provide essential information on those dominant aspects of the investment management of pension

[18]See preamble to Prudence Regulation issued by the Department of Labor and adopted June 25, 1979.
[19]The strong probability exists of future changes in the enabling legislation. For example, the ERISA Improvements Act 1979 that was introduced into the Congress by Senators Williams and Javits in January would amend ERISA in important ways. Several of the provisions relate solely to matters of pension fund administration and benefits and are not germane to this discussion. There is also a provision in the proposed legislation for combining present regulatory bodies into one agency to be called "The Employee Benefits Commission." Other provisions establish minimum reserve and solvency requirements for multiple employer trusts. The latter would bear on the setting of account objectives in certain types of pension plans.

funds that, in our opinion, merit careful consideration by the plan sponsor. In this context, the premises of the study are that:

- Plan sponsors cannot avoid passing judgment—either directly or indirectly—on management of fund assets. Accordingly, there is some minimum level of involvement in matters relating to investment of fund assets.

- The "prudent expert" concept as contrasted with the "prudent man" concept does not conflict with investment principles set forth in the following chapters.

- The ERISA requirement to diversify and to "minimize the risk of large losses" is in accord with investment principles set forth in this study and the generally desirable objective of identifying and controlling risk at the portfolio level.

CHAPTER

2 Setting Objectives: The Factors

Setting investment objectives for a pension fund has always been important, but the process is now at the center of a rapidly expanding research effort. Investment managers, brokerage firms, consultants, and corporations are devoting substantial efforts to developing both the procedures and research inputs necessary to formulate explicit objectives.

The greatly expanded efforts of the last three or four years result from four principal forces:

1. The aftermath of the traumatic 1973-74 bear market experience and the communication problems that existed between sponsors and managers

2. The enactment of ERISA, with its financial requirements and impact on corporate liabilities and risks

3. The major importance of the return earned on pension assets and fluctuations in their market value, because of the present size and expected continued growth of these assets

4. The substantial body of investment knowledge and techniques now available for analyzing and specifying portfolio objectives in quantitative terms.

Why are explicit portfolio objectives so important? An answer to that question entails examining the corporate and investment factors that determine the optimum set of objectives for a specific organization.

FACTORS

The corporate finance officer or pension executive giving due consideration to fiduciary requirements under ERISA must consider two principal sets of factors in determining appropriate investment objectives for a fund. They are: (1) corporate factors, which include actuarial and liability projections for a corporation's retirement plan, the impact of these requirements on the projected financial position of the corporation, the significance of different cost patterns as affected by the nature of investments made, cash flows into and out of the fund, and the degree of risk aversion of corporate management, and (2) major investment factors, especially the risk and return aspects of security portfolios.

Corporate Factors

In setting investment objectives for a pension fund, there should be careful tailoring in terms of the cost, funding, and other financial characteristics of a corporation's pension plan. The goal is to attain an optimum balance between projected financial requirements of the pension plan, reasonable risk and return expectations for security markets, and what appears to be financially most appropriate for the corporation.

Financial appropriateness turns on a number of corporate factors. Selected factors are discussed at some length in a number of studies. In this connection, the reader will find helpful M. Leo, P. C. Bassett and E. S. Kachline, *Financial Aspects of Private Pension Plans,* Financial Executives Research Foundation, 1975; F. Pomeranze, G. P. Ramsey, and R. M. Steinberg, *Pensions,* Ronald Press, New York, 1976; and J. L. Treynor, P. J. Regan and W. W. Priest, Jr., *The Financial Reality of Pension Funding Under ERISA,* Dow Jones-Irwin, Homewood, Illinois, 1976.

A study by Greenwich Research Associates cites many of the key factors relative to a corporation and its pension plan that require specific consideration in formulating investment objectives.[1] These factors relate primarily to

[1]See Greenwich Research Associates, *Sixth Annual Report to Executives On Large Corporate Pensions,* 1978.

liabilities created by a pension plan and to financial implications for the corporation in meeting them. The following list below indicates the nature and scope of some liability and financial factors that are ordinarily considered important in setting objectives.

- Nature of the plan in terms of coverage of personnel and benefit payments

- Mortality, employee turnover, growth and composition of the work force, inflation, salary scales, interest rate, and other similar factors

- Actuarial method employed in allocating costs to particular years and implications of the method in terms of cost progression

- Funding status of the plan with respect to past service costs and vested benefits and relationship of these actuarial liabilities to the financial condition of the corporation

- Status of the corporation in such economic and financial terms as its competitive strength, growth potential, life cycle position, cyclicality, profitability, and balance sheet condition

- Liquidity needs as judged by five-year, ten-year, or longer term projections of cash flows

- Projected growth of the pension assets over a five-year, ten-year, or longer term span

- General views of senior management in regard to assumption of risk in this area.

The importance of giving careful consideration to corporate factors in setting investment objectives for a pension fund can be readily demonstrated. For example, investment objectives for a corporation with a strong financial structure, stable revenue base, high growth rate, relatively young work force, and well-funded plan might assume more risk than those for an average enterprise. The corporation could withstand interim volatility in expectation of a higher long term return. In contrast, a mature enterprise in a mature industry with an aging labor force and a weak financial position might not be expected to assume similar risk exposure.

There is also the problem of recognizing the true cost of retirement benefits in pricing products and services. A level percentage of payroll, if it can be projected, is much to be desired for financial planning, cost accounting, and profitability analysis. The greater the component of labor costs in total expenses, the greater will be the benefit of stabilizing the accrual of pension expense. Stability may, indeed, have sufficient value for these purposes to justify exchanging some expectations for higher returns for greater reliability in estimation of costs. This may be especially the case when corporate operating results tend to suffer at the same times as pension fund portfolios are likely to produce substantially below average returns.

It is generally agreed that corporate factors should receive attention in setting investment objectives for a pension fund. Consequently, for a spectrum of corporations, the expected result would be significant differences in objectives. Surprisingly, the contrary seems to be the case. Pronounced similarity rather than dissimilarity is indicated by the widespread prevalence of 60/40 as the appropriate normal stock/bond ratio. It is also indicated by the following statement by Greenwich Research Associates based on a survey of 933 corporations:[2]

> . . . our research uncovers *no* significant differences in portfolio composition due to any of the following differences: size of company; size of plan; percent of plan participants now working or retired; benefit formula; average age or length of service of plan participants; or actuarial interest rate assumption.

The focus of Chapters II, III, and IV is principally on investment factors in objective setting. Nevertheless, so that the importance of corporate factors will not be lost sight of, there will be frequent reference to corporate considerations as different investment factors are discussed. Corporate factors require the same systematic analysis and treatment that is accorded their investment counterparts. It is in this manner that they are integrated into the objective setting process and an optimum set of objectives is developed.

Investment Factors

Decisions in regard to investment management of a pension fund require careful consideration of the preceding corporate factors. Liability forecasts for the plan, projected financial flows of the corporation, the extent and nature of risks associated with all other corporate activities, and manage-

---

[2] Greenwich Research Associates, *op. cit.*

ment's views on risk aversion are all essential inputs in determining the appropriate risk-return objectives for a pension fund.

The linkage between risk as it exists in security markets and risk as it is encountered in corporate finance may be closer than generally appreciated. For example, the decision to hold variable value assets against pension liabilities is not conceptually different from the decision to leverage the financing of a new production facility through the use of debt. Both decisions entail increasing the uncertainty of the return. The conceptual transfer of risk and return criteria from corporate investment in real assets to decisions regarding pension fund investing in marketable assets (securities) may not be easy. However, some consistency of corporate management's attitude in this regard is essential to the objective-setting process.

Participation of external specialists in the objective-setting process can be helpful. However, if the specialists become the decision-makers, senior corporate management may not have the understanding and conviction necessary to hold to the resulting decisions in turbulent and adverse security markets. Accordingly, participation of senior management is highly desirable. Directors can provide important continuity and consistency in the decision process. It is essential to build into the objective-setting process those elements of stability and adaptability that are crucial to rational and consistent investment programs for pension funds.

Definition of the Investment Problem

Vague phrases such as "rates of return that can realistically be obtained without undue risk" beg the difficult questions, convey different meanings of risk aversion to portfolio managers, and often give rise to subsequent misunderstandings. There is no effective substitute for dealing explicitly with the following principal investment considerations in setting objectives for a pension fund:

- The time horizon
- Priority given to liquidity needs

- Significance of real (current purchasing power) returns compared with nominal (current dollar) returns

- Accountability of the manager

- Tolerance to variability in returns and exposure to loss (risk tolerance)

- Absolute versus relative returns.

Time Horizon. The principal aspects of time horizons are the projection period that experience indicates is practical in establishing objectives, the life span or life cycle of the fund, and the period over which performance is measured.

Given the inability to forecast with precision either future pension requirements or investment returns, time horizons of such remoteness as 30 years create an atmosphere of unreality that debilitates investment planning efforts. Experience indicates that it is more practical to set objectives in terms of expectations for the next five to ten years. Good judgment dictates setting the time horizon toward the shorter end of the range but resists permitting decisions to lapse into mercurial responses to near term developments.

Although retirement plans mature, the life span of a pension fund can ordinarily be measured in decades. Within the total span, the period over which accomplishment of a given set of objectives is sought can be related to a specific phase or stage of a fund's life cycle. At the same time, it is recognized that few corporate officers would fail to follow closely at least year-by-year performance, if not quarter-by-quarter or even monthly results. A pension fund may not have a net outflow for 25 years but the portfolio manager is acutely aware that the corporation will certainly review and monitor the status of the fund quarterly even though the sponsor may evaluate the manager's overall performance and investment capabilities on a three- to five-year basis.

The manner in which quarterly results are interpreted by the plan sponsor is particularly important. Undue emphasis on the near term may produce a response by the manager that is not in the best long term interest of the fund. Although the life span of such a pension fund is an essential consideration, the time horizon of critical importance for both the investment manager and the plan sponsor is a much shorter span (such as the next five years). Accordingly, as set forth subsequently in more detail, consideration in nearly all instances must be given to the cyclical and short run volatility of return and the significance for portfolio performance as well as to longer term aspects. The long term represents the expected average for the period. It is the norm about which the actual is expected to fluctuate.

Liquidity. Conceptually, the calculated need for liquidity in the portfolio is closely related to the period for which objectives are set. (Liquidity here describes an asset that is readily convertible to cash on short notice without material risk of loss. In a sense, liquidity management may be considered as management of cash equivalents or securities that, because of their near term maturities or other characteristics, approach cash equivalents.) A number of factors can affect liquidity. Uncertainty about future cash disbursement patterns is a legitimate consideration in determining required liquidity. For example, in some instances pension portfolios are structured to provide adequate cash flow—in the form of dividends, interest, and maturing debt issues—to meet payments to pensioners over a period of three to five years, assuming a series of adverse circumstances in regard to both security markets and ability of the corporation to make regular contributions to the fund. The purpose is to protect the fund from exposure to the consequences of forced liquidation of assets in unfavorable security markets.

The cost of liquidity across time, in terms of returns foregone, may be substantial, thus promoting the incentive to seek arrangements that will meet such requirements at minimum cost. Certificates of deposit, participation in liquid asset pools, securities containing the right to accelerate maturity, and repurchase agreements are examples of such arrangements.

Real and Nominal Returns. Return objectives are typically expressed in nominal (current dollar) rates of return. Because dividends, and interest, and profits from the sale of securities are received in current dollars, the return is usually stated in these terms. If liabilities or spending needs are also in nominal terms, no adjustment is required. On the other hand, if productivity of the investment pool is measured in real terms (command over goods and services), objectives must either include an estimated allowance for inflation or be set in real terms. Historically, this distinction has not been significant in the United States but it becomes significant in periods characterized by two-digit or even near two-digit inflation. Determining whether the nominal or real rate of return is applicable is part of the definition of the investment problem. (A recently developed "index income contract," while subject to certain limitations, links a guaranteed return with the Consumer Price Index.[3])

Accountability. The manner in which results are measured and judged and responsibility is assigned for them also constitute essential features of the investment management problem. Accordingly, the terms of this accounting must be carefully specified as one of the dimensions in establishing objectives.

Risk Tolerance. The term risk means different things to different people. A meaningful consideration of risk tolerance therefore requires a common interpretation of "risk." Risk may be defined as the degree of uncertainty attached to an expected outcome; it is the likelihood of the actual outcome being less than the predicted outcome. In a total return sense, risk has two principal aspects.

One aspect is the uncertainty regarding the return that will actually be realized over the intended holding period for a portfolio. With the exception of 90-day Treasury bills, certificates of deposit, and a few other short term instruments of the highest quality, all securities embody some degree of uncertainty or risk.[4] Thus, it is possible to realize a significant range of returns even from a U.S. Treasury bond if it is sold before maturity and price changes reflecting fluctuations in interest rates are encountered. Much greater variation in holding period returns ordinarily results from cyclical swings in the market price of an equity issue.

The other aspect of risk is the possibility of long term or even permanent loss that comes from holding issues (stocks or bonds) that have deteriorated in quality. For such issues, the best that can be anticipated is partial recovery of the market price in the next cycle.

The aspect of risk examined first is the uncertainty inherent in a total return prediction. Forecasting the average rate of return and the amplitude of fluctuations in return (with this dispersion around the average preferably measured for a portfolio in terms of its standard deviation) will provide in

---

[3]See "Aetna Develops $100 Million 'Index Income Contract' for Ford," *Pension and Investments,* October 23, 1978, p. 1.

[4]In a strict sense, it can be held that only Treasury bills are risk-free. However, the degree of risk in certificates of deposit, bankers' acceptances, and prime commercial paper is sufficiently low to warrant their inclusion.

explicit terms the probable range of future returns over the time horizon selected. Developing these forecasts is a difficult but important task.

Fluctuations in returns (insofar as they relate to market prices of principal holdings) can be reduced by increasing the proportion of liquid assets—such as short term, high grade fixed income issues—in the portfolio. However, this can be an expensive method of reducing return volatility. Moreover, unless the proportion of the fund in liquid assets is substantial, the effect of such asset-mix change can be more than offset by the composition of the portfolio's equity portion.

The plan sponsor's tolerance to risk relative to the level of expected returns needs to be determined as specifically as possible. For any given level of risk, the goal is to construct a portfolio that will provide the maximum expected return. (It should be emphasized that while liquidity may produce the desired stability of return, it may fall far short of the acceptable level of return.)

In relating return objectives to exposure to loss, the question is whether realization of losses on individual securities, although constrained by substantial portfolio diversification or even offset by total portfolio gains, creates problems of accounting or fiduciary responsibility. Temporary depreciation in a portfolio because of a transient cyclical decline in the price of high quality investments may be acceptable, if it is not too severe or too extended. On the other hand, the apparently permanent loss resulting from ownership of securities that have deteriorated in quality, such as Penn Central bonds and stock, causes acute embarrassment. Accordingly, the degree of tolerance to such losses from deteriorated or lower quality securities must be carefully evaluated in setting portfolio objectives. This evaluation is independent of the judgment as to whether expected return differentials are adequate premiums for accepting the additional exposure to loss.

Absolute versus Relative Returns. Return objectives are increasingly being stated in absolute rates of return. These are based on projections for the next five or ten years of the *average* return on stocks, bonds, and Treasury bills. In using these absolute numbers, it is recognized that (1) they are best guesses as to the average return over a span of years and (2) actual return in any one year may depart substantially from the expected average. The expected extent of year-by-year departures is indicated by the predicted annual standard deviation of the return, and the uncertainty attached to the projected average return is indicated by the standard deviation for the period. Use of relative returns is more appropriate in judging the actual performance of a fund. The following discussion of risk and return will amplify the role of absolute forecasts in objective setting and portfolio decision-making.

RISK-RETURN DETERMINATION

Risk and return are the key considerations in making investment decisions and thus the factors of overriding importance in setting objectives. It is important to determine (1) realistic risk-return expectations over a prescribed time horizon—the period for which objectives are set—for a given fund, (2) whether price appreciation and yields will be comparable to or significantly different from those indicated by past experience, and (3) whether variability of returns in response to cyclical and other influences will be greater or less than in the past.

These difficult determinations are necessary inputs to rational objective setting and portfolio decision-making. It is possible to make the determinations intuitively and specify the risk-return objectives for a fund in words. However, it is much more desirable to examine and appraise risk and return more precisely through use of analytical and statistical techniques and to state objectives quantitatively.

The manner in which risk-return objectives for pension funds are developed and stated is changing significantly. A pronounced departure from the traditional intuitive appraisal of risk and return and specification of objectives solely in words is taking place. The move is toward appraising risk and return within a formal, systematic framework and specifying them in quantitative terms.

Increased knowledge of the past and advances in concepts and techniques are increasingly allowing development of more internally consistent and meaningful risk-return projections. These explicit projections will bring, among other changes, significantly improved communication between pension executives and investment managers.

Both sponsors and managers will examine and appraise in more definitive terms the risk-return tradeoff produced by different asset mixes. Estimates, assumptions, and methods underlying the level of risk and return expected for a fund with a given stock/bond mix will be set forth and agreed to by the manager and the sponsor. Corporate executives will more fully understand the probabilities concerning fluctuations in market value and total return.

Throughout the decision process, research-based judgments will replace those based principally on intuition. The result should not be the exercise of less judgment but rather the exercise of more fully informed judgment within a more effectively structured process. The general principles that underlie this process merit careful consideration.

General Principles

Strictly speaking, it is impossible to *analyze* the future. It is the present and the past that are thoroughly analyzed. The results are then used in developing informed and intelligent forecasts as to the future. Irrespective of the diligence and capability of analysts, the future return on an investment (except in the case of risk-free securities) cannot be predicted with certainty. There is a range, or series, of possible returns from any investment, and there are varying degrees of likelihood attached to each estimated return.

Modern investment practice employs statistical techniques in examining and interpreting the range of estimated returns for an investment portfolio and the likelihood (probability) that each estimate in the range will be realized. Since actual returns (outcomes) are uncertain, the important considerations are the probabilities attached to the forecast returns.

Two aspects of modern investment practice are considered in the pages that follow. The first aspect relates to measuring *past* variability and other return characteristics of individual securities and portfolios and providing techniques that assist in forecasting in quantitative terms the future risk-return behavior of securities and portfolios. The second aspect is use of a resulting array of quantified risk-return forecasts for portfolios ordinarily with different stock/bond/Treasury bill combinations to make possible more effective communication between plan sponsors and managers in establishing definitive investment objectives.

The uncertainty of the future return on an investment portfolio can be described by estimates of the probability (or chances, such as four chances out of twenty) of achieving different predicted rates of return. This approach is also a useful method for considering alternative possibilities when setting objectives.

The approach may be readily illustrated. Assume that an analyst is asked to estimate the average return over the next five years for a well-diversified portfolio of common stocks. The analyst states that his or her best guess—most probable return—is 12% and that it is unlikely that the return will average below 6% or above 18%. As set forth below, the analyst then indicates his or her opinion as to the likelihood (probability) that each estimate in the range will be the actual return.[5] Typically, the analyst would assign a high probability to the best guess (12%) and a low probability to the minimum (6%) and maximum (18%) estimates. For purposes of the illustration: (1) take the above hypothetical range of predicted returns (6% to 18%) and divide it into a number of symmetrical subintervals,[6] (2) estimate for each subinterval the probability (or chances) that the actual return will be in the interval, (3) array the predictions and their probabilities in tabular form, and (4) present the results graphically. Table II-1 and Chart II-1 represent a probability distribution. All of the probabilities sum to 1 (100%), because the distribution includes all the potential returns.

The data in Table II-1 provide the framework used in formalizing and quantifying the expected return and risk of an investment portfolio. Probability distributions provide an effective way of describing an entire range of possible outcomes from holding an investment portfolio. They reflect the average level of return expected (in this instance 12%) and, by their spread (6% to 18%), the riskiness.

In developing sales, expense, and earnings forecasts for a company, the *starting point* is an analysis of the company's past experience. In a similar

[5]The analyst subjectively estimates the probability that the actual return will be in the subinterval of the range implied by the specific return prediction.

[6]The number of possible outcomes included as clearly more than would be necessary in actual practice. They have been used in this instance to illustrate a more complete profile of a probability distribution.

Table II-1—HYPOTHETICAL PROBABILITY DISTRIBUTION OF PORTFOLIO RETURNS

Average Continuously Compounded Rate of Return over the Next Five Years	Probability of Occurrence	
	Chances Out of 20	Percentage
18%	1	5%
16	2	10
14	4	20
12	6	30
10	4	20
8	2	10
6	1	5

manner, the spread and shape of distributions of past returns constitute essential starting points in assessing the probability distribution of future returns. In other words, the actual frequency with which different returns occurred in the past (the frequency distribution of past returns) provides a useful yardstick in considering future probabilities. Past distributions should be modified to the extent it is expected that (1) future returns are likely to be

CHART II-1—HYPOTHETICAL PROBABILITY DISTRIBUTION OF PORTFOLIO RETURNS

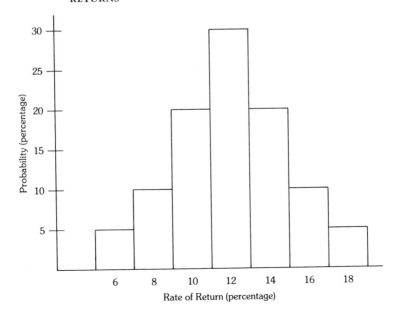

more or less risky (the spread of the distribution will be increased or decreased) than those experienced in the past and (2) the future average level of the return will be higher or lower. From a statistical standpoint, the methodology is straightforward. However, in the final instance, the estimation of future risk for an individual company rests on analytical judgment.

In recent years, there has been substantial statistical analysis of returns over extended past periods. The result is increasing evidence that the frequency distribution of compound rates of return earned on a well-diversified portfolio of common stocks reasonably representative of the stock market (and on the typical individual common stock) has approximately the shape of a normal distribution. This is the well-known bell-shaped curve; it is roughly illustrated in Chart II-1. The center or central tendency of a normal distribution and the spread or dispersion of returns about that central tendency can be accurately described by two numbers: the average or expected mean return (12% in Table II-1) and, as a measure of the "closeness" of the other returns to the average, the standard deviation. One standard deviation measures the return range (the distance on each side of the average) within which actual returns should lie about two-thirds of the time.

The compound rates of return for well-diversified equity portfolios across time tend to be lognormally distributed. As a result, the probability distribution of forecast compound returns for such portfolios will broadly conform to the bell-shaped curve of a normal distribution. A normal distribution has two advantages. First, the range or dispersion of future returns can usually be more readily predicted. Second, it is necessary only to forecast the average (mean) return and the probable range of return based on, say, one standard deviation to describe the entire pattern of future probabilities and thus summarize a considerable amount of important information. For example, the probability distribution described earlier for a hypothetical portfolio is roughly normal. The average or mean return is 12%, and the standard deviation is about 3%. Accordingly, these two figures indicate that about two-thirds of the time the return on the portfolio would be between 9% and 15%.

Building a probability distribution of future returns for the stock market (e.g., S&P 500) usually entails setting forth in numerical terms a range of economic and related security market scenarios. Illustrative economic scenarios could be high inflation, moderate inflation, stable growth, low growth, and so forth. The fact that each scenario would have significantly different implications for pension liabilities as well as security markets and thus asset returns is obvious. The investment consequences of these scenarios can be observed in the risk-return sensitivity of stocks and bonds to different assumptions about the long term outlook.

In the final instance, the plan sponsor must develop a reasonable degree of conviction as to the probabilities associated with various economic and security market scenarios and act accordingly in deciding on risk-return objectives for a fund. These are neither easy nor avoidable decisions. As pointed out in Chapter I, the sponsor cannot sidestep the risk-return decision. Judgment must be exercised either at the time the objectives are established or subsequently in appraising the risk-return performance in terms of the manager's decisions. In either instance, conclusions must be reached about the investment environment and appropriate risk-return expectations for the fund.

The plan sponsor may well find it inappropriate to undertake inhouse the substantial task of forecasting the economy and security markets. In this regard, the investment manager or selected external consultants can be of major assistance.

The past requires in-depth analysis and interpretation as a starting point for formulation of expectations as to the future, but mechanical extrapolation as a forecast of the future is hazardous. Careful consideration needs to be given to existing and emerging social, political, and economic forces of change that can be expected to affect interest rate levels, common stock risk premiums, and variability of returns.

Chapter III examines in some detail the development of risk and return forecasts for interest rates and the stock market.

Subjective Determination

Establishment of definitive risk-return objectives requires choosing among alternatives. Giving due consideration to fiduciary responsibilities, this choice depends on the attitude toward risk of the plan sponsor (as represented by the finance officer, pension executive, members of the board, or other appropriate corporate decision-makers) as well as on financial circumstances surrounding a fund and the estimated range of returns for the security markets. Accordingly, even if the expected financial conditions and pension fund liabilities and requirements were identical for two corporations, it does not necessarily follow that corporate executives in the respective corporations would reach identical risk-return decisions.

Because attitudes are largely psychological, investment objectives are the product of subjective determinations. Nevertheless, modern investment technology provides both a conceptual framework and procedures for developing informational inputs that make it possible to set objectives more systematically and more explicitly than does the still too frequent use of intuition. This is important because explicit objectives are essential guides for the asset manager in reaching investment decisions that—given the difficulties of predicting the future—meet as closely as possible the requirements and preferences of the plan sponsor.

The preceding section ("General Principles") sets forth statistical procedures that make feasible the quantification of subjective risk-return estimates. These estimates are ordinarily developed for the stock market (as represented by a selected composite index such as the S&P 500), bond market (as represented by an index such as the Salomon Brothers High Grade Corporate Bond Index), and risk-free money market instruments (such as 90-day Treasury bills). These assets can then be combined in different proportions.

Through simulation techniques, it is possible to (1) develop for a plan sponsor a spectrum of risk-return estimates for portfolios with differing asset-mix combinations and (2) demonstrate over selected periods (e.g., one year, two years, five years, ten years) the significance of resulting levels of variability and return on a given fund. In this manner, simulation makes it possible for the corporate executive or executives to perceive the probable annual and cumulative effects of different combinations of securities on the revenue produced by a fund, its market value, and the degree of risk assumed. In view of the importance of simulations in the objective-setting process, Chapter IV reviews several representative systems for simulating asset returns and their related risk.

Subjective risk-return estimates and simulations do not ensure either a surprise-free future or wise decisions. However, carefully developed estimates and well-designed simulations should result in information-based decisions that are both superior to and more stable than those derived principally from intuition. Moreover, decisions formulated in this manner make possible fuller consideration of such other important matters as meeting the requirements of ERISA and appraising the impact of funding on corporate finances.

When the plan sponsor designates out of a spectrum of stock/bond/Treasury bill simulations the risk-return tradeoff that under normal conditions is considered preferable, explicit risk-return objectives can be set for a fund in numerical terms that quantify the expected level of return (average over a span of years) and specify the variability of return. For example, assume that (1) the expected return for bonds is 9% and the annual standard deviation is 7%, (2) the respective numbers for stocks are 14% and 22%, (3) for Treasury bills they are 6.5% and 4%, and (4) the selected stock/bond/T-bill ratio is 60/30/10. On the basis of these expectations, the return objective would be 11% [(.60 × 14%) + (.30 × 9%) + (.10 × 6.5%) = 7.8% + 2.7% + 0.65% = 11.15%] and the risk objective as represented by the standard deviation would be approximately 16%.[7] In other words, two-thirds of the time the return would be expected to be between +27% (11% plus 16%) and −5% (11% minus 16%).

Optimal Passive Objectives

The risk-return combination decided on in the foregoing manner is—for the specific sponsor—optimal in terms of long term levels of return for primarily stock and bond markets[8] and the expected standard deviation of the returns of each market. The relative levels of return are projected norms. They represent the returns expected if stock and bond markets are appropriately priced relative to one another. Moreover, stock and bond portions are based on well diversified indexes considered to be representative of those markets.

The data inputs to risk-return determinations are therefore based on passive management. The passive nature of the management results from

[7]For ease of discussion, this calculation makes the simplifying assumption that there is no covariance between stock, bond, and Treasury bill returns.

[8]Although at times the amount of Treasury bills or other money market instruments may be substantial, the normal holding is usually modest, such as 10%. Accordingly, the principal holdings are stocks and bonds and thus stock and bond markets are the "primary markets." Moreover, such modest proportions of liquid assets have little effect on portfolio return volatility.

two facts: (1) no selection is entailed because stock and bond indexes were used to represent the two markets and (2) no timing is entailed because the stock/bond (and Treasury bill) ratios are held constant throughout the projection period.

The procedures described in this chapter are essential to formulation of a set of investment objectives for a pension fund. The asset-mix and risk-return ratios determined in this manner represent the optimum passive set of objectives. However, a majority of pension fund portfolios are actively managed; that is, both selection and timing are entailed. Accordingly, to provide for active management, further amplification of objectives is necessary. However, this additional step is not discussed until Chapter V, "Determining Strategy," because further consideration must first be given to developing basic risk-return forecasts and to asset allocation (Chapters III and IV).

REVIEW AND REVISION OF OBJECTIVES

The foregoing has emphasized that objectives should be based on long term expectations. These expectations pertain to projections for the business enterprise and the pension plan, as well as security markets. At the same time, however, investment objectives of a fund should be subject to change as long term expectations change.

Although important modifications can result from major changes in the financial position of the company or the plan itself, the changes will more frequently be in terms of revised projections for security markets. These revisions should result from significantly changed projections for key factors bearing on the relative attractiveness of the markets and returns expected from them. Such factors include average rates of growth in output for the economy, inflation, and corporate profits. The risk aspect of security market projections could also be revised as a result of changed views as to the amplitude of business and stock price cycles, volatility of interest rates, and related factors. Clearly, investment objectives should not be "cast in concrete." They must be modified when *significant* changes occur in expectations.

Although the term "significant" is subject to interpretation, it suggests the undesirability of frequent and minor changes. Establishment of definitive objectives eliminates ambiguity and vagueness and provides a basis for effective sponsor-manager communication and understanding. If changes are too frequent, they may prove to be both confusing and self-defeating.

SUMMARY

Although this study is concerned with investment management of pension funds, Chapter II stresses the importance of corporate factors in setting investment objectives. It also stresses that participation of senior management in setting objectives is highly desirable. In this manner, corporate management can have the understanding and conviction necessary to hold to resulting decisions in turbulent and adverse security markets. Finally, there is no effective substitute for dealing with such principal investment considerations as the priority given to liquidity needs, tolerance to variability in returns and exposure to loss, and absolute or relative returns.

CHAPTER

3 Setting Objectives: The Risk-Return Forecasts

The dominant consideration in investing is what will happen in the future; not what occurred in the past. Accordingly, portfolio objectives are based on forecasts of the future. This chapter covers stock and bond market forecasts essential to establishing specific risk-return objectives for a pension portfolio. Specifically, the chapter examines (1) the role of forecasting in objective setting, (2) the historic risk-return behavior of security markets in terms of returns actually attained over the last half century and volatility of those returns, (3) the general nature of the forecasting process, and (4) a summary set of illustrative projections.

ROLE OF FORECASTING

Long term expectations for stock and bond markets are basic ingredients in setting portfolio objectives. Such expectations ordinarily culminate in forecasts of (1) the average total rate of return (based on both price changes and income) over the projection span and (2) the degree of uncertainty (risk) attached to the predicted outcomes. In other words, a plan sponsor needs to base decisions on the appropriate asset mix for a fund (predominantly the stock/bond proportions) on the estimated *average* rate of return for each asset class over the forecast period and on the probable extent to which the return actually realized in any year might depart from that estimated average (the risk factor).[1]

Estimating future returns and risk requires determining, analyzing, and appraising past variability of returns from stock and bond markets and modifying that past variability to the extent that knowledge of the present and judgment about the future dictate.

In view of the substantial price inflation in recent years and other factors, extrapolating long term past nominal rates of return is subject to serious reservations. A review of the behavior of rates of return on stocks and bonds over an extended period is, however, the logical next step in considering the portfolio objective-setting process. For common stocks, this review provides price, total return, variability of rates of return, and stock risk premium (the stock return differential over fixed income securities) benchmarks that are essential inputs in developing estimates of future returns and the variability of those returns. It also provides perspective and insight for readers who will not actually make such projections but will examine and appraise the projections of others.

STOCK MARKET RETURNS

Stock Market Indexes

Stock market indexes are the most convenient means for a long term examination of the behavior of the "market." A number of indexes can be used, including the Dow-Jones Averages, NYSE Composite Index (New York Stock Exchange), and the Value Line Index. However, because of the wide-spread use of the Standard & Poor's Composite Index in research studies and in performance measurement, the following analysis of historical common stock data is based on that index. A number of important studies of stock returns covering all or most of the last five decades are available.

---

[1]In this connection, a wide range of actuarial methods exist for smoothing realized annual fluctuations in the total return of a portfolio and thereby reducing the impact on the current expense of a pension plan.

Accordingly, the examination of returns in this study covers prinicipally the span from 1926 through 1978.

The S&P 500 consists of 400 industrial (including AT&T), 20 transportation, 40 utility, and 40 financial stocks. The percentage price changes are weighted by the total market value of the outstanding shares of each stock. The broad sample base, use of market weights, and relative interpretive ease make the S&P 500 a useful representative index. Standard & Poor's defines the price index "as a 'base-weighted aggregative' expressed in relatives with the average value for the base period (1941-1943) equal to 10."[2]

Stock Prices

The rate of return for common stock depends on both price changes and dividend payments. Over most extended past periods, dividends have constituted the major portion of total return. However, as a result of pronounced price changes, over short periods these changes frequently dominate the return factor. For example, if the S&P 500 had been purchased at 92.06 at the beginning of January 1970, the dividend yield in 1970 would have been 3.4%. Over the entire span from 1970 to 1974, dividend payments grew at an average annual compound rate of 2.6%. Accordingly, if it had been possible to sell the S&P 500 fives years later on December 31, 1974, at exactly the purchase price, the annual compound rate of return would have averaged 3.7% (assuming that dividends increased 2.6% in each year over the entire five-year period and that dividend yield is calculated on the purchase price). However, instead of ending the period at 92.06, the price of the S&P 500 had declined to 68.56 by the end of 1974 (equivalent to a compound annual decline of −5.7%), as a result using the actual price compound annual total return would have been −2.4%.[3] Accordingly, in determining the amount to invest in stocks, careful consideration must be given to their price (and thus return) volatility. The starting place for this consideration is the record.

---

[2] *Standard & Poor's Statistical Service, Security Price Index Record*, 1978 Edition, Standard & Poor's Corporation, p.3.

[3] Assumes reinvestment of dividends.

Chart III-1—STANDARD & POOR'S 500 COMPOSITE STOCK INDEX

Average Annual Price
1926–1978

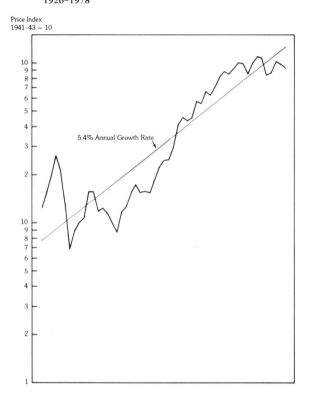

Price Index
1941–43 = 10

5.4% Annual Growth Rate

The average annual price index of the S&P 500 over the 1926–78 period is plotted in Chart III-1. (Semilog paper is used so that proportional changes in prices can be compared across time.) The familiar long term upward sweep in stock prices and the violent stock price gyrations, particularly in the early years, should be noted. To demonstrate the irregular and inconsistent upward movement of prices over the 53-year span, a trend line has been statistically fitted to the annual price data. Although the trend line accurately represents the mean for the data (the total amount by which actual prices are above the mean and the amount by which prices are below the mean are equal), the extent and duration of the departures from the line establish that the line and, therefore, the 5.4% compound annual growth rate in prices for the period is of little significance, either as a yardstick of extended periods of the past or in today's environment as an indicator of the future.

Within the 1926-78 span, significantly different price performances occurred over lengthy periods. As a result, compound annual rates of increase in prices that would have been realized over these periods were greatly different. To illustrate this fact, two types of period analyses are undertaken.

The first analysis shows the effect of starting with the full 53-year period and arbitrarily reducing the span by ten-year intervals (to 43 years, 33 years, and so forth) to a final 13-year period. The results are as follows.

Period	S&P 500 Compound Annual Growth Rates[4]
1926-78	5.4%
1936-78	6.8
1946-78	6.7
1956-78	3.7
1966-78	0.5

[4]Growth rates are calculated from least squares regressions of the logarithms of the average of each year's daily closing prices.

The second type of analysis is based on the view that the 53-year span can be divided into four relatively distinct periods: 1926-49, 1949-56, 1956-68, and 1968-78. The price characteristics of each period are summarized below.

1926-49

The 1926-49 period encompasses a 23-year span of violent gyrations in the stock market. It ends with a cyclical trough that became, with only limited interruptions, the beginning of a 20-year secular rise in stock prices. It encompasses the excesses of the late 1920s, the Great Depression and turbulence of the early 1930s, and World War II. As a result of the 1926-29 bull market, the subsequent devastating deflation, and impact of the war, stock prices declined more than they rose and the compound annual rate of decrease in the S&P 500 price index over the 23-year period averaged −0.4%.

1949-56

Over the 1949-56 interval, the price increase averaged 16.2% per year and far exceeded that for any similar period, except the 1921-29 span. In considerable part, this increase was attributable to a major reevaluation of earnings, in the form of a marked increase in the capitalization rate, such as the price/earnings (P/E) ratio. With only a slight pause in 1953, the price rise was sharp and continuous throughout the period.

1956-68

Although the rate of increase was substantially lower from 1956 to 1968 than during the 1949-56 span, this 12-year period experienced a pronounced upward swing in stock prices with only modest bear markets. The compound annual rate of increase was 7.2%.

1968-78

Marked stock turbulence characterized the 1968-78 period. It was dominated by the two most severe bear markets of the postwar era. The recovery subsequent to the 1974 bear market was substantial but insufficient to push the 12-year growth rate above zero. Therefore, in marked contrast to the two preceding postwar periods, there was a slight downward drift in prices for the 1968-78 period that averaged -0.1%.

The pronounced difference in price performance from one postwar period to the next raises serious questions in regard to predicting the future by simply assuming a replication of the past. The historic record provides an essential starting point but projection of a future average rate of increase in stock prices requires exercise of judgment supported by careful research.

Stock Price Cycles

In appraising past price movements and predicting a future *average* rate of increase, careful attention should be given to the magnitude of historic stock price movements. One method is to examine the extent to which price fluctuates about computed trend lines that represent average annual rates of change for selected past spans of years. This method is illustrated by Chart III-1 and by the discussion above of the wide departures from the trend line. The greater the fluctuations about the trend, the less meaningful is any average of the past as an indication of the future.

Another method for appraising common stock price variability is to measure the amplitude of stock price cycles. Cyclical amplitude may be measured in terms of the percentage decline from a peak to a trough or the percentage increase from a trough to a peak. The results of measuring separately each cyclical downturn and upturn for the S&P 500 are set forth in Table III-1. The important consideration is whether the amplitude of the cycles or swings is changing. Table III-1 shows that the respective 1968–70 and 1973–74 declines of 29% and 43% significantly exceeded those for any other bear markets since 1937–42. However, the most recent decline of 16% in 1976–78 is more in line with previous postwar declines.

The percentage decline in a bear market or increase in a bull market is determined in part by the level from which either started. For example, although accompanied by the Great Depression, the percentage decline in 1929–32 was partly the result of eventual realization of the magnitude of excesses of the 1921–29 bull market. Likewise, the amplitude of the 1932–37 recovery was to a considerable degree attributable to the severely depressed level of the economy in 1932 and the excesses of the 1929–32 bear market. To avoid these potential distortions, a method for measuring the amplitude of a full cycle was developed.

A full cycle may be measured peak-trough-peak or trough-peak-trough. Since the fourth quarter of 1974 and the first quarter of 1978 represent the two most recent cyclical troughs, it is appropriate to measure the amplitude of a full cycle in terms of trough-peak-trough analysis. Table III-2 shows that the cyclical amplitude declined, although erratically, until the 1957–60 cycle and then increased over the next four cycles. The price amplitude over the 1970–74 cycle (84%) was much greater than those of the four preceding cycles (the four cycles averaged 50%). The amplitude of the cycle from the fourth quarter of 1974 to the first quarter of 1978 (54%) is less than

Table III-1—STANDARD & POOR'S 500 CYCLICAL PRICE AMPLITUDE PEAK-
TROUGH AND TROUGH-PEAK PERCENTAGE CHANGES

Monthly Data 1921–1979

	Value	Peak-Trough Percentage Change	Trough-Peak Percentage Change
T 1921 Aug.	6.45		
P 1929 Sept.	31.30		385%
T 1932 June	4.77	−85%	
P 1937 Feb.	18.11		280
T 1942 Apr.	7.84	−57	
P 1946 May	18.70		139
T 1947 May	14.34	−23	
P 1953 Jan.	26.18		83
T 1953 Sept.	23.27	−11	
P 1956 July	48.78		110
T 1957 Dec.	40.33	−17	
P 1959 July	59.74		48
T 1960 Oct.	53.73	−10	
P 1961 Dec.	71.74		34
T 1962 Oct.	56.17	−22	
P 1965 Jan.	93.32		66
T 1966 Oct.	77.13	−17	
P 1968 Dec.	106.50		38
T 1970 July	75.72	−29	
P 1973 Jan.	118.40		56
T 1974 Dec.	67.07	−43	
P 1976 Sept.	105.45		57
T 1978 Mar.*	88.82	−16	
P 1979 Aug.*	107.36		21

*The March 1978 and August 1979 figures constitute the subsequent low and high to date. Whether they constitute a cyclical low or high cannot be determined at this time.

two-thirds of the 1970–74 amplitude and close to the above four-cycle average.

Measurements of the amplitude of stock prices *after the fact* is not a difficult assignment. However, interpretation of cyclical amplitudes and

Table III-2—STANDARD & POOR'S 500 CYCLICAL PRICE AMPLITUDE
MEASURED TROUGH-PEAK-TROUGH

Quarterly Data 1932–1978*

1932II–1942II	201%
1942II–1949II	109
1949II–1953III	68
1953III–1957IV	74
1957IV–1960IV	41
1960IV–1962III	43
1962III–1966IV	58
1966IV–1970III	56
1970III–1974IV	84
1974IV–1978I	54

*In accordance with the technique developed by the National Bureau of Economic Research for measuring business cycles, the value of the cyclical peaks and troughs are indexed relative to the average of quarterly values within the cycle. The difference between the index value of the peak and troughs are then summed to find the full cycle amplitude. Quarterly price data (calculated as an average of monthly data) are used in lieu of monthly figures for purposes of later comparison with earnings and dividend data, which are available only on a quarterly basis.
Source: Calculated from data in Standard & Poor's *Trade and Securities Statistics.*

analysis of cyclical relationships in terms of economic and financial factors are tasks of substantial magnitude.

Determinants of Stock Price Movements

Stock price movements are determined by changes in expectations; that is, by changes in what is expected to happen to such factors as economic activity, earnings, dividends, inflation, and interest rates (as well as by what actually happens). Furthermore, as is clear only in retrospect, if such expectations embrace either substantial errors of judgment or are accompanied by undue fear, greed, or other powerful emotions, they create bull and bear markets that are subject to excesses. Stock price movements represent the summation of investors' opinions about, enthusiasm for, or fear of key determinants of stock prices. Thus the amplitude of stock price cycles is determined by the extent to which people *change* their expectations, primarily in regard to earnings, dividends, the capitalization rate (discount rate for dividends or the multiplier for earnings), and the factors that impact on each of these.

Earnings per Share

Note from Chart III-2 that the annual earnings per share (EPS) for the S&P 500 over the 1926–78 span increased at a compound annual growth rate of 5.6%. As in the case of stock prices, the cyclical departures of earnings per share from the trend line were substantial over the 53-year span. The relative fluctuations of earnings and stock prices cannot be compared cyclically, because their cycles do not coincide sufficiently. This fact is not surprising. Stock price movements are based on expectations and thus usually (but not always) lead by several months changes in the profitability of business. Nevertheless, both logic and empirical research establish the cause and effect relationship between earnings and stock prices. Moreover, Charts III-1 and

Chart III-2—STANDARD & POOR'S 500 COMPOSITE STOCK INDEX

Earnings Per Share
1926–1978

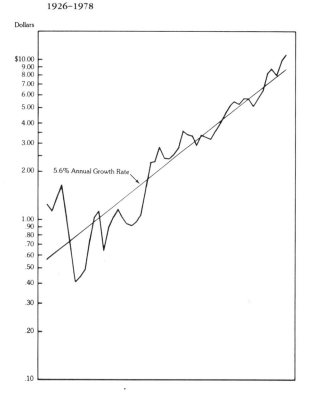

III-2 show that in general sharp changes in prices are associated with sharp changes in earnings.

Since stock prices represent the summation of investors' analytical and emotional opinions about key determinants of stock prices, the amplitude of stock price fluctuations is understandably greater than that of any single factor such as earnings. To illustrate this fact, the compound growth rates for the S&P 500 were computed for the foregoing four time periods. Note from the following tabulation that the period growth rates are much more stable for earnings than prices.

Period	Earnings per Share Compound Annual Growth Rate	Price Compound Annual Growth Rate
1926–49	2.4%	−0.4%
1949–56	5.3	16.2
1956–68	5.8	7.2
1968–78	8.9	−0.1

Price/Earnings Ratios

Either earnings or dividends may be capitalized. Today there is a decided move toward capitalizing dividends through discounting the expected dividend stream for the market (e.g., the S&P 500) to derive its present value or through using the expected dividend stream to estimate the rate of return implicit in the current price of the market. Although analysts have always given substantial attention to estimating dividends, the pronounced increase in capitalization of dividends by investment managers has resulted in more analytical effort being devoted to forecasting dividends. However, up to this point, use of P/E ratios as multipliers to capitalize earnings remains the more familiar and more generally used capitalization technique.

Historic annual P/E ratios for a stock market index or an individual issue are typically computed by dividing the average price for the year by the EPS for the year. The gyrations of annual P/E ratios of the S&P 500 over the 1926–78 span are shown in Chart III-3. The wide fluctuations in the P/E ratio over the 53-year period result principally from (1) the inherent cyclicality of

Chart III-3—STANDARD & POOR'S 500 COMPOSITE STOCK INDEX

Price/Earnings Ratio
1926–1978

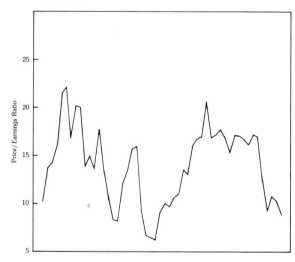

earnings of most corporate enterprises; (2) marked changes in investor expectations as to the future level, growth, and stability of corporate earnings and as to the proportion of the earnings that will be paid out in dividends; and (3) in recent years, pronounced changes in the returns available from principally fixed income securities.

The first two points have already been discussed, and their role in stock price movements is well recognized. It is necessary to add only that, although earnings fluctuate substantially from year to year and from cyclical peak to trough, expectations as to future earnings are considered by some to be more volatile than the subsequent reality. To the extent that earnings expectations are excessively high in periods of prosperity and low in recessions, price movements will tend to be exaggerated and P/E ratios, when computed from actual earnings, will also be exaggerated.

The third point—the impact of substantial changes in the return obtainable from alternative investment vehicles—is not as familiar. The rate at which earnings (through a P/E ratio or multiplier) are capitalized is not determined solely by the growth and stability of earnings and the cash dividend payout ratio. (The same comments apply to the discount rate for dividends.) Investing takes place in a world of relative returns. It is also a world of relative risk. The only way in which the attractiveness of the expected return for an investment can be appraised is by relating it to expected returns on viable investment alternatives, giving due consideration to risk. This risk-return tradeoff is continuously taking place in security markets. For this reason, in valuing the stock market, consideration must be given to the return available on such alternative investment vehicles as risk-free Treasury bills or high grade corporate bonds.

Over the 1926-78 span, there have been sweeping changes in P/E ratios for the stock market. The period of the early 1930s was so distorted by the exceedingly low earnings of the Great Depression that, even when related to low stock prices, it produced relatively high P/E ratios.

The 1940s were dominated by World War II, the early postwar recovery, and a recession that caused wide cyclical swings in P/E ratios. In the 1950s and 1960s, annual P/E ratios ranged from approximately 6.5x in 1950 to nearly 21x in 1961. In the 1970-78 span, in part because of marked inflation and significantly increased interest rates, P/E ratios fell from more than 17x to below 8x. If prices at cyclical peaks and troughs were employed rather than annual price data, the amplitude of the price swings and P/E ratios would have increased further.

Today, inflation is perhaps the prime mover of stock prices. Inflation impacts directly on stock prices primarily through its effect on corporate profits and the interest rate. Accordingly, inflation, profits, and the interest rate merit principal considertion in forecasting (1) average total return on stocks over a span of years and (2) probable variability of annual returns about that average.

Dividends per Share

The S&P 500 dividends per share are plotted annually from 1926 through 1978 in Chart III-4. In recent years, the percentage of earnings paid out in the form of cash dividends has declined significantly. For example, the payout ratio averaged 67.0% over the 1935-46 span and 51.5% over 1947-70 but only 44.5% over the 1971-78 period. Principally as a result of this decline,

Chart III-4—STANDARD & POOR'S 500 COMPOSITE STOCK INDEX

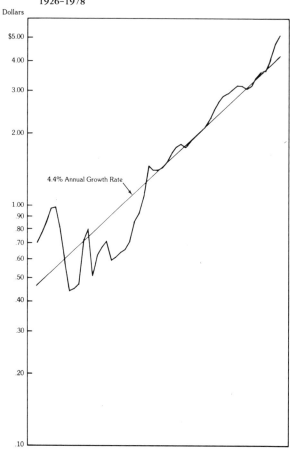

Dividends Per Share
1926-1978

the compound annual growth rate for dividends per share over the 1926-78 period was 4.4%, compared with 5.6% for EPS. After the volatile 1926-49 period (due in part to the Depression and World War II), dividends per share began to exhibit a steady upward trend. Although there were some years in which dividends declined, they were few and infrequent. Therefore, the 1950-78 period can be characterized as one of steady growth in dividends per share.

The variability of the S&P 500's dividends per share has been statistically measured over the 1926-78 span. For this 53-year time interval, it was well below that for both the S&P price index and EPS. This greater relative stability would be expected because of corporate management's general desire to avoid cutting cash dividends in periods of cyclical downturns.

Since common stock dividends are much more stable than common stock prices, dividend yields (annual cash dividend divided by average annual price) must be more volatile than dividends. Chart III-5 graphically shows this fact. Over the first three decades, 1926-54, dividend yields fluctuated widely about a plateau well above 5%. The 1926-54 average was 5.5%.

From 1954 through 1973, the amplitude of fluctuations was much less than in the earlier period and the plateau was sharply lower (1954-73 average 3.5%). Over much of this period prices moved up rapidly, the dividend yield was exceedingly low, and P/E ratios for a number of years fluctuated narrowly about a level well above that encountered before (at least for more than 50 years). Subsequent experience has brought a pronounced change in both P/E ratios and dividend yield.

The most severe post World War II decline in stock prices that began in 1973 and extended throughout most of 1974 combined with a continued

Chart III-5—STANDARD & POOR'S 500 COMPOSITE STOCK INDEX

Dividend Yield
1926-1978

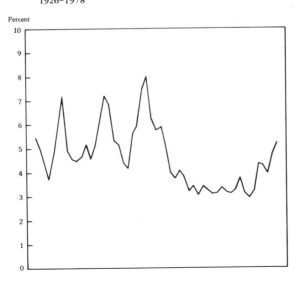

increase in cash dividends to produce a sharp rise in dividend yield. The subsequent recovery brought prices back close to their former level. However, during the 1973–78 period, dividend yield fluctuated about an average level of 4.3%, well above the 1954–73 average of 3.5%. This rise was the result of a growth in dividends of 8.6% over the 1973 to 1978 period, compared with 4.5% during the 1954–73 span.

Although the 1973–78 average dividend yield was 4.3%, it still remained significantly below the 1926–54 average of 5.5%. In spite of the recent improvement in the S&P 500 dividend yield, the comparative yield on Moody's Composite corporate bond series was far greater.

Period	Average Annual Corporate Bond Yield	Average S&P 500 Annual Dividend Yield
1926–54	4.0%	5.5%
1954–73	5.4	3.5
1973–78	8.8	4.3

How can the lower 1973–78 dividend yield be reconciled with the corporate bond return during the same period?

One possible answer lies in the payout ratio. Over the 1926–54 span, cash dividends averaged 70% of earnings but in the 1954–73 span they averaged only 54%, and in the 1973–78 span they averaged only 42%. This lower payout means that if the rate of return earned by corporations on the book value of their common stock is maintained the lower payout will produce a higher growth rate in earnings and in turn in dividends.[5] Furthermore, present tax laws make the capital gains to be expected from this growth more attractive than dividend income for tax paying investors. For tax free investors, such as those in pension funds, there is no distinction between appreciation and dividend income.

----

[5]For example, if a corporation earns on average 14% on its common stock equity and grows solely through retained earnings, a payout of 70% would leave only a little more than 4% of earnings to grow on whereas a 40% payout would leave more than 8%.

Returns on Common Stock

Keeping in mind the cyclical fluctuation in stock prices over the 53 years from 1926 through 1978, the general character of price movements for the entire span and for selected subperiods, and the impact of price variability on total return, the next step is to examine the record of common stock returns. Several studies of historical returns exist, but the two most widely used are by Fisher and Lorie, which covers the period from 1926 through the first quarter of 1975, and by Ibbotson and Sinquefield, which covers the 1926–78 span.[6] Both studies develop compound annual rates of return for common stocks but are somewhat different in method, sample selection, and sample weights. Fisher-Lorie used equally weighted investments in all New York Stock Exchange (NYSE) stocks with the weights equal as of January 1926. Ibbotson-Sinquefield used market-weighted investments in the S&P 500 with the investment updated monthly.

The results of the two studies are not significantly different. Over the 1926–74 span, Fisher-Lorie calculated an 8.0% compound annual growth rate for total common stock returns with reinvestment of dividends, and Ibbotson-Sinquefield obtained a modestly higher return of 8.5% for the same period. Because the S&P 500 is more familiar than the NYSE series and because more recent data are available, the discussion below is confined to the Ibbotson-Sinquefield study.

The compound annual rate of return including reinvestment of dividends for the S&P 500 over the 1926–78 period was 8.9%. This return is based on purchasing the S&P 500 as of January 1926, reinvesting dividends (assuming no taxes or commissions), readjusting the portfolio monthly, and selling out in December 1978. If dividends had not been considered, the compound annual return attributable solely to price appreciation would have been 3.9%.

This total return figure for 1926–78 represents the compound annual rate of return for 53 years, but use of this figure as the most probable estimate

[6]One of the first studies by Lawrence Fisher and James H. Lorie was "Rates of Return on Investments in Common Stock: The Year-by-Year Record, 1926–65," (*Journal of Business*, Vol. 41, No. 3, July 1968, pp. 291–316.) This study was updated in April 1970 and again in 1975. Roger G. Ibbotson and Rex A Sinquefield's most recent study is entitled *Stocks, Bonds, Bills and Inflation: Historical Returns (1926–1978)*, Financial Analysts Research Foundation, 1979.

during the next five to ten years is highly questionable. The past is usually an imperfect predictor of the future, and, in the final instance, forecasts must be based on the estimator's best judgmental appraisal of the future, taking full advantage of an understanding of past and present levels and trends in returns as well as the current environment.

Instability of common stock returns is to be expected but the extent of past volatility may be greater than most recognize. Comparison of average holding period returns for all one-, five-, ten-, and twenty-year periods over the 1926–78 span shows an extremely wide range of returns. Averaging these period returns naturally decreases the range of returns as the number of years in the holding period rises. However, the tabulation below shows that the range of returns even for ten-year holding periods was such that one ten-year holding period return was double that of the average of all the ten-year periods in the 1926–78 time span and the return for another ten-year period was actually negative.

Holding Period	Arithmetic Mean of Period Returns	Range of Period Returns
1 year	11.2%	−43.3% to 54.0%
5 years	8.8	−12.5 to 23.9
10 years	9.9	− 0.9 to 20.1
20 years	11.1	3.1 to 16.9

Considerations in Forecasting the Stock Market

In developing forecasts of the stock market, forecasts of earnings, dividends, and a capitalization rate are the essential ingredients. Earnings and in turn dividends must be related to both cyclical and secular forecasts for the economy. (Illustrative forecasts are set forth later in this chapter.) Accordingly, near term (cyclical) and long term (secular) macroeconomic forecasts are needed as bases for estimating future growth and cyclical fluctuation of earnings and dividends.

Forecasting the capitalization rate for earnings or dividends is the next step in the valuation process. Because valuation of securities takes place in a world of relative returns and relative risks, the risk-return tradeoff between common stocks and investment alternatives is a key consideration. The starting point is analysis and appraisal of present and past return and risk differentials between classes of assets in the security markets. Returns on stocks are more uncertain (more risky) than returns on high grade fixed income securities. Accordingly, the common stock investor is entitled to a risk premium and will invest in common stocks only in anticipation of it.

Investment theory has provided the conceptual structure for considering the risk premium in valuing common stocks, and empirical research has provided extensive data for analyzing past relationships. Therefore, a more systematic and structured approach exists for estimating the risk differential for common stocks and selecting a capitalization rate for the stock market. The result should be more fully informed judgment, which hopefully will produce better decisions.

RISK PREMIUM

The purpose of this section is to consider the record and examine the choices available in forecasting the risk premium.

The Record

Three points in regard to the historic record of holding period returns on common stocks and fixed income securities should be stressed. First, the record always measures outcomes; that is, what was realized rather than what was expected. Moreover, as everyone recognizes, outcomes can depart widely from expectations. For example, no rational investor would have purchased common stocks in January 1968 in the anticipation that over the next ten years the realized annual compound return with reinvestment of dividends (3.6%) would be significantly less than that for U.S. Treasury bills (5.6%).

Second, statistical tests indicate that annual common stock risk premiums tend to follow a random walk. This fact is not suprising. The findings of a number of studies conclude that stock prices over the short run move in a random fashion—a random walk. In a random walk, each subsequent price change is independent of all previous price changes.

Third, as amply demonstrated in the above section, stock prices and returns on common stocks are highly volatile.

To formulate quantified portfolio objectives and make meaningful portfolio decisions, it is necessary to develop explicit return projections for common stocks, bonds, and Treasury bills. This task, as it relates to common stocks, cannot be accomplished without reaching a conclusion as to the appropriate risk premium for stocks over either Treasury bills or high grade corporate bonds. The question is how to do this.

Alternative Forecasting Methods

Four alternative courses of action can be considered. The first is to assume that a long term average of the past is the best estimate of the long term future. For example, it might be concluded that the future will replicate the experience of the past 53 years; therefore, the appropriate equity risk premium for the future is the 1926–78 average. However, in predicting the future, long term averages of the past need to be used with more care than might initially be anticipated. The following examples are illustrative.

- The addition of one or two years can result in a surprising change in the long term risk premium (based on compound annual rates of return):

Period	Equity Risk Premium over Treasury Bills	Equity Risk Premium over High Grade Corporate Bonds[7]
1926–74	6.1%	4.7%
1926–76	6.7	5.0
1926–77	6.3	4.7
1926–78	6.2	4.8

[7]Although theory suggests use of the default-free T-bill, we prefer to use the premium over high grade corporate bonds because bonds are the more appropriate long term investment alternative to stocks, for comparative purposes, whereas Treasury bills are typically held for liquidity or other reasons.

- Average equity risk premiums over Treasury bills for extended past periods, for the most part, would not have been effective forecasts of premiums for future five or ten-year periods:

Past Period	Equity Risk Premium over Treasury Bills	Actual Risk Premium	
		Next Five Years	Next Ten Years
1926–55 (30 years)	9.1%	6.2%	8.0%
1926–60 (35 years)	8.6	9.9	3.8
1926–65 (40 years)	8.8	−2.0	−2.3
1926–70 (45 years)	7.5	−2.5	—

The second course is to select a specific past period that is considered to be closely representative of the expected future. Although it may well be that a future five- or ten-year period will approximate some past period, identification of such an historic period before the fact is almost impossible. The difficulty arises in part becaue security markets are continually evolving and changing. For example, consideration needs to be given to the fact that institutional trading is a larger factor in the stock market than ever before. Accordingly, even if future economic conditions replicated those of an identifiable past period, there is no assurance that future market responses would be the same as in the past.

The third alternative is to use the past as a starting point and modify it to whatever extent and knowledge of the present and judgment of the future dictate. This judgment should rest on an appraisal of overall environmental factors as well as economic considerations. Over the next five to ten years, the impact of revision of tax laws, international competition, governmental regulations, inflation, and other factors bearing importantly on the business and investment climate could be substantial.

Any single average drawn from the past will be a fragile starting point. One alternative available to those seeking to draw useful information from the past is to select an historic range for the risk premium that appears to bracket a reasonable spread. On the basis of economic, political, and other expectations bearing on the riskiness of both bonds and stocks, one can identify a specific risk premium within that range.

The fourth alternative is to conclude that the past is not a guide to the future. Some investors hold that high grade bonds should be purchased instead of stocks because equities over the foreseeable future may not provide a higher return (risk premium) than high grade bonds. This view is based on the fact that recent holding period returns have been higher for bonds than for stocks, and in some instances (as noted earlier) even the returns for T-bills have been higher. The issue becomes the extent to which one accepts the basic logic behind the operation of security markets in a free economy: that risk-averse investors will seek a higher return from more risky investments than from less risky ones.

In spite of the experience of the last decade, it is our opinion that across time the logic of security markets will prevail and be evidenced in realized return differentials between more risky and less risky markets. Accordingly, valuation of the stock market should be based on a risk premium over fixed income securities. In a later section of this chapter, procedures for forecasting stock market returns are discussed. First, consideration needs to be given to forecasting interest rates because these predictions must precede forecasts of stock market returns.

FORECASTING INTEREST RATES

One well-known measure of interest rates is the yield to maturity on Moody's Aaa Corporate Bonds. Annual yields for the 1926–78 span are shown in Chart III-6. Rates were pegged at low levels during World War II and until March 1951. The sharp and extensive rise in yields subsequent to 1965 principally reflects the impact of a substantial increase in inflation. For example, when the price level (as measured by the overall index for all goods and services in the United States—the GNP deflater) was rising at less than 1.5% per year in the early 1960s, long term bond yields were 4.5% or lower. In the mid-1970s, as the inflation rate approached 5.5%, corporate bond yields reached 8.5%. A four percentage point increase in the rate of price inflation was roughly matched by a four percentage point rise in corporate bond yields. The so-called Fisher effect (named after Irving Fisher, a famous economist) describes the theoretical relationship between interest rates and inflation.

Near the turn of the century, Fisher first explained how interest rates in the marketplace (nominal rates) adjust to changes in the amount of inflation anticipated by lenders and borrowers. Fisher's basic principle is that a market

Chart III-6—MOODY'S Aaa CORPORATE BOND YIELDS

Annual Data
1926–1978

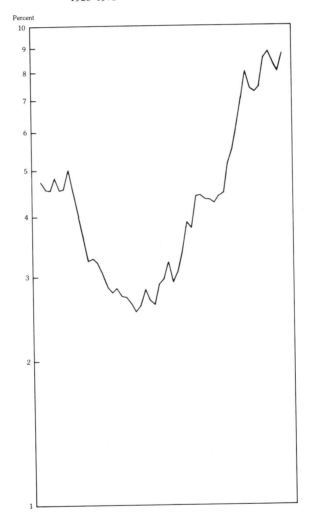

interest rate consists of two parts: a real rate and an adjustment for anticipated inflation.

Before the mid-1960s, this theory was not generally accepted by practitioners. Forecasters implicitly assumed that the nominal (market) rate and the real rate were equal (primarily because they anticipated little or no inflation).

Interest rates were ordinarily expected to fall during business recessions and to rise during business expansions. Therefore, a forecast of business conditions was the usual starting point for a forecast of interest rates.

When the Board of Governors of the Federal Reserve System (the Fed) became more active in trying to stabilize the economy in the early 1950s, interest rate forecasters came to expect monetary authorities to reinforce the cyclical pattern in rates by pushing interest rates down to cure recessions and by pushing them up in times of excessive expansion to curb inflation. Accordingly, forecasters devoted much of their time to predicting the Fed's interest rate policies. In view of the importance of the U.S. Treasury in the money and capital markets, forecasters also tried to estimate the impact of the Treasury's financing requirements on current and future interest rates. Attention was therefore focused on cyclical changes in business investment spending, Fed operations, Treasury borrowing, and other factors expected to influence the supply of and demand for funds.

By the late 1960s, inflation was rampant and both forecasters and practitioners realized that inflation expectations drove a wedge between the real rate and the nominal rate. No longer could it be assumed that the nominal rate and the real rate were the same. The Fisher effect was "rediscovered," and interest rate forecasters began to search for ways to cope with the inflation factor. The key problem became how to measure the rate of inflation anitcipated by lenders and borrowers.

It is not the purpose of this study to undertake a technical analysis of different methods for estimating inflation expectations and for forecasting interest rates. Rather, the purpose is to set forth the broad concepts and principal factors that are considered in developing the forecasts.

Forecasts of nominal interest rates (future market rates) attempt to separate the forces that affect inflation expectations from those that affect the real rate. (The real rate is what lenders receive and borrowers pay after adjusting for actual inflation.)

Changes in inflation expectations are generally considered to account for most of the changes in nominal interest rates. Accordingly, as set forth above, beginning in the mid-1960s interest rate forecasters devoted particular attention to developing techniques for estimating inflation expectations. This is a difficult task, because inflation expectations cannot be measured directly.

There are two principal approaches to overcoming this handicap. One is to assume that investors base their expectations of future rates on past rates. Some forecasters therefore use an exponentially weighted moving average of past rates as a predictor of future rates. The other approach assumes that those active in the financial markets do not restrict themselves to information on past inflation in forming expectations as to future inflation and interest rates. Rather, it assumes that investors have powerful incentives to use any relevant information available.

Accordingly, one of the major issues currently dividing forecasters is how to forecast inflation most effectively and thus to predict future inflation expectations of lenders and borrowers. Putting aside the differences in points of view, it can be said that in total a substantially expanded number of factors are being assessed. The spectrum of factors includes the unemployment rate; changes in productivity; changes in the output of agriculture, energy, and other basic industries; general business conditions; changes in the money supply and other Fed actions; federal deficits; and the international balance of payments.

Another set of factors analyzed by some forecasters is summarized in estimates of the supply of and demand for credit. In this connection, use may be made of the Fed's flow of funds accounts, which provide extensive historic data on the supply and demand situation.

If the market rate of interest consists of a real rate and an adjustment for anticipated inflation, the question then is how to determine the real rate.

Unfortunately, the real rate of interest (like inflation expectations) cannot be observed directly. One way to measure it is to subtract an estimate of expected inflation from the nominal market rate to derive an estimated real rate. However, some hold that the real rate is determined by variables that change slowly. These include such factors as the return on business assets and the public's time preference for money as reflected in the real savings rate.

Therefore it is generally considered that changes in inflation expectations are much more important than changes in the real rate in forecasting market (nominal) rates of interest. As a result, some contend that a forecaster would generally not be far wrong if a constant real rate were assumed in short term forecasts and attention concentrated on inflation expectations. This would become less true as the forecast periods were lengthened. Another important consideration in long term forecasts will be whether over the projection span inflation is expected to be reduced from its present high level and by how much.

FORECASTING STOCK MARKET RETURNS

In forecasting the stock market, the principal purpose is to determine its attractiveness relative to investment alternatives—basically fixed income securities. The manner in which this comparison can be effectively made is in terms of a common denominator—expected returns. Accordingly, nearly all forecasting methods seek to develop return predictions for the market.

There are two primary methods for forecasting market returns. One method is to estimate a value for the stock market (e.g., S&P 500 or some other well-known index). The estimated return may then be derived through (1) relating the estimated value to the prevailing market price, assuming a specific period over which price will converge with value and thus obtaining an appreciation rate (if the market price is below estimated value); (2) forecasting the dividend yield based on current market price; and (3) combining these two rates to secure a total return estimate.

The other method for forecasting market returns is to estimate the return directly. This estimate is typically made by using a projected stream of dividends to derive the implicit rate of return from the current price.

Irrespective of the method used, it is necessary to decide whether the expected return for the stock market is attractive relative to the expected return from the selected fixed income alternative. This decision entails determining whether the extent by which the forecast stock market return exceeds the fixed income market return (the risk premium) is adequate. The risk premium impinges in some manner on nearly all methods for forecasting the stock market. Accordingly, particularly as noted in the following review of discounted cash flow (DCF) and implicit return methods, it is essential that careful consideration be given to the risk premium.[8]

Discounted Cash Flow Method

The discounted cash flow (DCF) method[9] is based on the concept that the value of a share of common stock—and thus, in turn, the stock market—is equal to the present value of the stream of cash dividends that the investor expects to receive. This stream is usually projected over an extended time span; theoretically, it is to infinity. However, because of the discount factor, the significance of estimates beyond 25 or 30 years is limited. Valuation models of this type typically use simplifying assumptions as to future growth beyond the first five to ten years.

The discount rate is ordinarily the product of two estimates: (1) the forecast of the return for Treasury bills, or long term high grade corporate bonds (such as Moody's Aaa corporates), or some other fixed income series and (2) the desired risk premium for investing in stocks.

For example, assume for illustrative purposes that the return on Moody's Aaa corporate bonds over an extended future period is forecast at 8% and that a common stock risk premium of 5% is considered appropriate. On this basis, 13% is the rate at which the projected stream of dividends should be discounted to obtain the estimated present value of the stock market (S&P 500). As the price of the S&P 500 drops below this estimated value, the expected total return rises and stocks become increasingly attractive. Contrariwise, as the price of the S&P 500 rises above the estimated value, the expected total return declines and stocks become increasingly unattractive.

Implicit Return Method

An alternative approach is to forecast a stream of dividends (in the same manner as the preceding method) and determine the discount rate that will

---

[8]The historic return differential between stocks and fixed income issues and alternative methods for forecasting this differential (risk premium) are discussed earlier in this chapter.

[9]Also known as the dividend discount method or model (DDM).

produce a present value equivalent to the prevailing market price. This derived discount rate may be viewed as the total return implicit in the current price. A primary consideration in determining whether that return is attractive will be the differential over the return expected from the selected fixed income security.

Using the foregoing standards, to the extent that the implicit return exceeds 13% (given an assumed bond return of 8% and a risk premium requirement of 5%) the market becomes attractive. To the extent that the market return is less than 13%, it is unattractive. Thus, the forecast return for the chosen fixed income security and the selected risk premium for the market create the standard for appraising the attractiveness of the stock market.

Price/Earnings Ratio Method

Discounted cash flow methods are based on the valuation of dividends. Although there is a clearcut move toward discounting dividends, capitalization of earnings is still widely used.

It is generally held that changes in investors' earnings expectations are more important than changes in dividend expectations in determining at least short term changes in price. Furthermore, as noted earlier, price changes can swamp dividends in determining realized returns over five-year periods or even longer. This fact is critical because the appraisal of the performance of pension fund managers is typically geared to a three- to five-year span. For these reasons and because dividends have their source in earnings, arguments can be advanced for evaluating the market by capitalizing earnings.

There is no earnings multiplier method that constitutes a strict counterpart to the dividend present value method. However, those who use the multiplier approach need to consider a company's present dividend policy and the possibility that it may change both in forecasting the growth rate in earnings and selecting a capitalization rate (multiplier). Accordingly, an earnings multiplier method may be logically substituted for discounting dividends, because the choice of a multiplier should be dependent on the estimated growth and stability of earnings, cash dividend payout ratio, and expected return on fixed income issues.

Typically, the multiplier selected is based on an analysis and appraisal of past P/E ratios and on such adjustment as considered necessary for past mispricing and for expected departures from the record in terms of growth in earnings, payout ratio, and other factors cited above. The return expected from this valuation process would be derived from the anticipated appreciation resulting from the expected convergence of the prevailing market price and the estimated value plus the current dividend yield.

Price to Book Value Method

To provide a cross-check on the foregoing methods, an entirely different concept based on book value may be employed. The principal argument ordinarily advanced in support of this approach is that book value is much more stable than earnings and therefore provides a more consistent factor against which to compare price. It is to be noted, however, that significant variations can occur in book value as a result of changes in the companies constituting the S&P series, inflation and accounting adjustments, and other factors. Moreover, in recent years there have been wide fluctuations in the price/book value relationship. As a result, this method is typically viewed as a rough cross-check.

SUMMARY SET OF ILLUSTRATIVE FORECASTS

The role of macroeconomic forecasts in developing security market predictions is summarized below. The preceding methods for forecasting interest rates and the stock market are also illustrated with selected, key economic series.

Macroeconomic Forecasts

Macroeconomics deals with the economy as a whole in terms of such aggregate series as employment; the nation's output of goods and services by major categories; monetary and fiscal policy; expenditures by consumers, business, and government; inflation; and the flow of commerce with other nations.

Macroeconomic forecasts provide a consistent framework within which to analyze and project (1) developments in stock and bond markets, (2) the outlook for sectors of the economy and industries, and (3) prospects for sales and earnings of individual companies. By outlining the expected environment in which to appraise the outlook for interest rates, earning, and valuation of the stock market, economic forecasts constitute the foundation for setting portfolio objectives.

Macroeconomic forecasts are of two types: cyclical and secular. Cyclical forecasts typically consist of predictions for the next four to eight quarters. However, some organizations make cyclical forecasts as far out as five years. Cyclical forecasts tend to concentrate more on the path and level of aggregate demand and its relationship to the nation's supply capacity.

Secular forecasts are essentially trend (growth rate) projections that usually cover spans of five, ten, or even more years. These long term projections reveal primarily the results of underlying determinants of economic growth, structural change, and inflation. They generally encompass an analysis of the nation's output potential—its ability to produce goods and services—and thus are supply oriented.

The emphasis placed on cyclical or secular forecasts by a manager can vary somewhat depending on the investment style employed and on the extent to which reliance is placed on timing in contrast to selection. For example, an organization stressing timing will probably devote significantly more time to cyclical than to secular forecasts. In contrast, a high growth manager investing in large capitalization stocks can be expected to devote more attention to secular forecasts. However, irrespective of timing or style, secular projections are growing in importance because (1) establishment of quantified portfolio objectives requires long term return estimates for markets and (2) increased use of DCF common stock valuation models requires long term forecasts of dividends (and thus earnings) for companies.

It is highly desirable that the plan sponsor be familiar with and understand the general nature of economic forecasts and assumptions that support the risk-return projections for stocks and bonds used in setting portfolio objectives. This understanding is particularly important in increasing the effectiveness of communication between plan sponsor and investment manager. It provides the basis for interpreting and discussing significant changes in the outlook for the economy and, in risk-return forecasts for stocks and bonds.

Bond and Stock Market Forecasts

Since portfolio objectives are based on expected average returns over a span of years, the primary concern is with the long term outlook for the U.S. economy. Long term projections are available in substantial detail together with monetary, fiscal, and other public policy assumptions that underlie them. To avoid a lengthy analysis of the details and the underlying assumptions, the following discussion is confined to the examination of three key economic series that dominate stock and bond market projections. They are: real GNP (the quantity of goods and services produced in the United States), inflation (rate of increase in the GNP deflator), and nominal (current dollar) GNP.

Although individual long term forecasts available from external sources usually cover various projection spans and have different beginning and ending years and although the range of results is substantial, the compound rates of increase over approximately the next ten years currently tend to cluster within the following ranges:

Real GNP	3.0%–3.5%
Inflation	4.0 –6.0[10]
Nominal GNP	7.1 –9.7[11]

Assume for purposes of this illustration, that the most probable:

- Annual growth rate of real GNP is 3.25%

- Rate of increase in inflation (in terms of the GNP deflator) is 5.0%

- Annual growth rate in nominal (current dollar) GNP is 8.4% ($1.0325 \times 1.050 = 1.084$).

Another key series contained in the set of economic projections is the aggregate amount of corporate profits after taxes. Although cyclical swings will be wide, assume that on average the growth in corporate profits will keep pace with the 8.4% annual growth in nominal GNP.

---

[10]The 4% to 6% range was based principally on a survey of forecasts at the beginning of 1978. At the end of 1979, prevalent thinking about the next ten years would appear to be more in the 7% to 9% range. Inflationary expectations for the next decade have changed greatly in less than two years.

[11]The real GNP and inflation rates are not additive but rather compound on one another.

There is considerable debate as to the appropriate number for the real rate of interest. However, the real rate for long term, high grade corporate bonds probably lies between 2% and 4%. If 3% is arbitrarily taken as the appropriate rate and the assumed inflation rate of 5% is added, the long term return on corporate bonds would be forecast as 8%.

A set of predictions for the bond market as a whole would require predicting the term structure of interest rates. Because of the simplified nature of this example and because the return on corporate bonds will be used in developing a discount rate for the stock market, this illustration is not carried beyond the long term coporate bond rate.

The next step is to forecast the risk premium for common stocks. If it is assumed that existing inflation, regulatory constraints, and other factors have created a business environment subject on average to as much uncertainty as that which prevailed over most of the last five decades, a risk premium in the 4% to 6% range might be employed. On this basis, a return expectation of 12% to 14% for stocks might be taken as appropriate relative to an 8% long term bond yield. If 13% is assumed to be the most probable figure, it becomes simultaneously the appropriate return expectation for the stock market and the discount rate to be employed in valuing the projected stream of dividends.

Dividends have their source in earnings; therefore, long term forecasts of earnings and dividends provide the next essential inputs to a valuation of the market. Earnings forecasts for the stock market may be developed in a number of ways. One approach is to relate EPS for the S&P 500 directly to corporate profits after taxes for all U.S. corporations (as compiled by the Bureau of Economic Analysis of the U.S. Department of Commerce and used in connection with the national income accounts).

A much more thorough approach is to probe the relationship of EPS to total corporate profits by securing aggregate income statement and balance sheet figures for the 500 companies constituting the S&P series[12] and

---

[12]Alternatively, aggregate income statement and balance sheet data can be used for the S&P 400 industrial companies because there tends to be more financial statement consistency among these companies than between these companies and utilities and financial institutions.

analyzing the following relationships across time:

> Sales to GNP
> Net income to sales
> Net income to corporate profits

On the basis of an analysis of these relationships, it may be concluded that, because of dilution in EPS resulting from issuing additional shares, the growth rate for EPS of the S&P 500 might slightly lag that for total corporate profits.

Compared with a growth rate of 8.4% for corporate profits, a more appropriate number for EPS might be close to 8.0%. However, if, as generally expected, the cash dividend payout ratio were to rise from about 40% to 50% over the next several years, the long term growth rate for dividends would approach 8.5% compounded annually.

In December 1978, the S&P 500 was selling at 95 and dividend forecasts for the year tended to cluster about $5.15. Accordingly, on this basis, the current dividend yield was 5.4%. If the future growth in dividends were to average the assumed 8.5% and the price were to rise proportionally, the total return would average 13.9% annually. This return would be slightly in excess of the "appropriate" or target return of 13% set forth above.

SUMMARY

Risk-return forecasts for security markets are essential inputs in setting objectives for pension funds. The corporate executive therefore needs to be familiar with (1) the role of forecasting in objective setting, (2) the historic risk-return behavior of security markets, and (3) the general nature of the forecasting process.

Giving full consideration to corporate factors, those officers responsible for setting pension fund objectives must base their decisions principally on the expected *average* rate of return for each asset class (stocks, bonds, money market instruments) over the forecast period and on the probable extent to which the return realized in any year might depart from the average. Thus, forecasts of security markets play a key role in setting investment objectives.

The impressive characteristics of particularly the common stock market, as reflected in the S&P 500, over the last 53 years (1926-78) are the pronounced differences in rates of return over extended periods and in the amplitude of stock price cycles. Accordingly, instability of common stock returns is to be expected. This is the primary reason why stock returns should provide a substantial risk premium over fixed income securities. At the same time, it must be recognized that the total return on bonds is also subject to volatility, although ordinarily much less than that for stocks.

Forecasting interest rates and common stock returns is always a challenging assignment. It is particularly difficult at present because of the current two-digit inflation and the uncertainty as to the probable level over the next five or ten years. Nevertheless, forecasts of the future must be made and alternative methods exist for undertaking this task.

CHAPTER

4 Setting Objectives: Asset Allocation

Determining the appropriate risk-return tradeoff is the dominant consideration in setting investment objectives for most pension funds. The allocation of a fund among stocks, bonds, and money market instruments (with stocks and bonds being by far the principal holdings) is the primary determinant of the amount of risk assumed and return earned.[1] The asset allocation decision is therefore critically important.

The risk-return decision clearly entails a tradeoff because, up to a point, investors will assume additional risk if the expected additional return more than compensates for the added risk. Accordingly, in reaching an effective decision, information as to the expected risk-return characteristics of different stock/bond/money market instrument (as typified by Treasury bills) combinations can be most helpful. Given a range of stock/bond/Treasury bill proportions, the plan sponsor can appraise in specific terms the risk-return characterisitcs of alternative asset mixes. In this manner, the combination of risk and return that appears to suit the circumstances most appropriately can be chosen. The circumstances, of course, include the previously discussed fiduciary responsibility and corporate factors as well as expectations for the security markets.

The risk-return decision may be expressed only in terms of minimum and maximum asset proportions (e.g., stock minimum 40%, bond maximum

---

[1] As cited in the Preface, over the 1974-78 span an average of 90.5% of private noninsured pension funds were invested in these securities.

40%, and Treasury bills 20%; stock maximum 80%, bond minimum 20%, and Treasury bills 0%). However, more typically, the decision is summarized in terms of a normal ("preferred" or "target") asset mix (e.g., 60% stocks, 30% bonds, 10% Treasury bills). It is that mix which, under *normal* circumstances,[2] is expected to offer the most appropriate combination of risk and return.

In view of the importance of the asset mix decision and the number of factors that must be considered in reaching it, various procedures have been developed to understand and quantify the risk-return tradeoff. The following discussion is principally in terms of the stock/bond ratio, since the proportion ordinarily invested in Treasury bills is limited to about 10% or less.

SIMULATIONS

Simulation techniques are particularly applicable in reaching an asset-mix decision. The plan sponsor needs to determine the effect of changes in the stock/bond ratio on the expected level and volatility of a portfolio's return (risk). For example, because riskier securities are expected to provide higher returns, it can generally be expected that increases in the common stock proportion of a portfolio will be accompanied by increases in the expected return as well as risk. Conversely, as the bond (less risky) proportion is increased, the reverse will ordinarily be true.

To illustrate, assume (as in Chapter III) that the forecast average annual return for common stocks over the next five years is 13% and the annual standard deviation 22% and that the corresponding forecasts for high quality corporate bonds are 8% and 7%. Using solely these rough assumptions, a portfolio consisting of 80% stocks and 20% bonds would have an expected return of 12% and a standard deviation of about 18%. (As set forth below,

---

[2]"Normal" in the sense that this stock/bond/Treasury bill ratio would be held if the expected returns for stocks and bonds were considered to be in their normal relation to one another after allowing for the risk differential. The normal asset mix is usually accompanied by minimum and maximum limits.

cross correlation and serial correlation must be considered in addition to the expected risk and return of each asset class.) In contrast, if the stock and bond proportions were 40%/60%, the expected return would be reduced to 10% and the standard deviation to approximately 10%.

Simulations can be run using different sets of forecasts of returns, standard deviations, and any other necessary factors for each class of assets. They can be run taking the asset mix through the full range of 100% stocks and no bonds to 100% bonds and no stocks or through limited portions of this range. Likewise, simulations can be run using narrow or wide differencing intervals, such as changes of five percentage points (from a stock/bond mix of 100/0 to 95/5) or ten percentage points (100/0 to 90/10).

The simulations are ordinarily based on the expected performance of highly diversified (so-called passive or index) portfolios, such as those represented by the S&P 500 and Salomon Brothers High Grade Bond Index. This approach is a logical initial step, because, through using indexes, the results are indicative of the general levels of risk and return expected in each market. However, the results are based on *passive* management, in terms of representative cross-sectional samples of the stock and bond markets. Accordingly, depending on the nature and extent of the *active* management to be employed and the resulting additional risk-adjusted return expected, the risk and return forecast from passive management would be subject to adjustment. Such an adjustment would need to be tailored to the specific situation. Accordingly, the following discussion is based on the use of stock and bond market indexes.

Simulation systems differ in three principal regards:

- Procedures for simulating risk and return
- Level of detail regarding cash flows
- Nature of results provided in decision-making summaries.

These aspects of simulations are dealt with in turn, and the manner in which selected representative systems treat each aspect is briefly described.

PROCEDURES FOR SIMULATING RISK AND RETURN

Required Inputs

Two points stressed in Chapter II are critical to the discussion in this chapter. First, for nearly all securities, it is uncertain whether the expected return or a lower (or higher) return will actually be realized. Because of the possibility of a shortfall in the return or even a loss, most securities are risky. For this reason, estimates of risk as well as return are essential inputs in a simulation model. Second, the frequency distribution of continuously compounded rates of return earned on a well-diversified equity portfolio (e.g., industry and company weights are closely comparable to those of the S&P 500) when plotted approximates a normal (bell-shaped) distribution. As a result, only the expected (mean) return and standard deviation of return need to be specified to establish the likelihood of various outcomes for a given portfolio over a specified span of time. (The mean represents the central tendency of the distribution, and the standard deviation is an effective measure of the dispersion of returns about the mean.)

Risk and return forecasts for each asset class must be included in a simulation. However, forecasts used by representative simulation systems may be developed by significantly different methods. One approach is to employ historic data and to extrapolate this past experience into the future on the assumption that the past contains a representative sample of future possibilities. Other approaches use historic data as a base and, modifying and adjusting the past for existing and emerging forces and factors, develop expected returns and standard deviations and thus probability distributions.

In developing risk and return estimates for each asset class, it is important to consider cross correlation and serial correlation. Cross correlation refers to the fact that returns from some assets are correlated with contemporaneous values of returns from other assets. For example, in a year in which bond returns are high, stock returns are more likely to be high than low. In a simulator using probability distributions, specific estimates of relevant cross correlations must be incorporated in the program. In a simulator using historic data, it may not be necessary to specify explicitly such cross correlations since they are implicit in the actual historic data. Thus, any procedure that uses actual returns from different assets in the same historical year automatically incorporates an historic degree of cross correlation.[3]

Serial correlation refers to the fact that for some assets returns are correlated through time. For example, in the year following a year of high Treasury bill returns, Treasury bill returns are more likely to be high than low. Either an assumption must be made about the behavior of such returns over time or actual historical years must be used in sequence to capture this phenomenon. Serial correlation is particularly evident in Treasury bill returns and the rate of inflation. It is much smaller for stock and bond returns and is usually ignored.

Representative Systems

Some systems use historic returns almost exclusively; others generate returns wholly from probability distributions derived in part from analysis of the past and in part from projections of the future; and others fall between these two ends of the spectrum of possible approaches.

One service using historical returns directly is that provided by the Frank Russell Company. It uses annual returns for stocks (S&P 500) and bonds (S&P High Grade Index) for the period from 1900 through 1979. All available historic periods are considered equally likely for any future period of years. Thus, if a ten-year horizon is being considered, the projected return is assumed to be that from 1900 through 1909, or that from 1901 through 1910, and so forth for every ten-year period over the 1900–79 span. The return for each of the 70 possible periods is assumed to be equally likely to represent the actual future return.

The other end of the spectrum is represented by a probability-distribution approach used by Wells Fargo Investment Advisors. An expected return and standard deviation of return (based on an analysis of the past and a forecast of the future) are specified for stocks, along with an expected return and standard deviation of return for bonds and a degree of correlation between

---

[3]It is to be recognized, however, that the extent to which cross correlation actually exists over the forecast period may be different from that which existed over the selected historic period.

the two returns. The range of values (the probability distribution) at the end of a specified holding period resulting from investing a dollar at the beginning of the projection period, assuming a given stock/bond mix (with frequent reallocation to maintain the desired proportions by market value), can be computed directly.

Wilshire Associates employs a similar set of assumptions concerning the behavior of stock, bond, and Treasury bill returns, but uses Monte Carlo simulation to deal with a broader range of possible contribution or withdrawal policies (the name for the simulation comes from the analogy between the method used to obtain simulated outcomes and the results of playing at the Casino in Monte Carlo). To generate a specific "pseudo-history" of, say, ten years of bond and stock returns, a computer is instructed to select at random values for each year from underlying assumed probability distributions, taking into account an assumed degree of cross correlation. In this manner, any desired number of such pseudo-histories can be obtained; each is considered equally likely. When enough have been constructed to represent the range of possible outcomes adequately, the process is terminated.

Models that include inflation or Treasury bills should cope with serial correlation in some manner. Moreover, the difference between current inflationary expectations and the historic rate of inflation requires some adjustment if historic returns are to be used. The Russell Company deals with this issue by raising all historic bond and stock returns an amount equal to the difference between expected future inflation and past historic inflation.[4] Others simply use real returns (that is, total return less actual inflation) in their simulations. Still others explicitly model the behavior of inflation and Treasury bills.

In a widely cited study,[5] Ibbotson and Sinquefield used both historic data and simulations to generate inflation and Treasury bill returns with an estimated degree of serial correlation built into the procedure.

The basic estimates of current and future rates of inflation and Treasury bill returns were imputed from the current term structure of interest rates for

[4]To accommodate assumed differences in risk premiums, the spreads between bond and stock returns are sometimes altered as well.

[5]R. G. Ibbotson and R. A. Sinquefield, *Stocks, Bonds, Bills and Inflation: The Past (1926-1976) and the Future (1977-2000),* Financial Analysts Research Foundation, 1977.

U.S. government bonds, thus representing market expectations at the time (December 31, 1976). To the Treasury bill rate, there were added the following:

- Maturity premium to provide the return on long term government bonds
- Default premium to provide the return on high grade corporate bonds
- Risk premium to provide the return on common stocks.

A similar approach that employs simulation exclusively is that of the Boston Company. A closely related procedure has been used at Stanford University, the Ford Foundaton, and Wells Fargo. Degrees of serial correlation and cross correlation are assumed explicitly, and Monte Carlo procedures are applied to obtain pseudo-histories for any desired number of years.

LEVEL OF DETAIL REGARDING CASH FLOWS

Systems differ considerably in the amount of detail with which the particular cash flows relevant to a client are simulated.

At one end of the range lie analyses that assume that an initial investment is left to compound for a stated number of years, with no further contributions or withdrawals from the fund. This approach has been used in some instances by Wells Fargo Investment Advisors and was also employed by Ibbotson and Sinquefield.

The other end of the range is represented by analyses that incorporate all the details of a pension fund, beginning with such records as employees' ages, work histories, and salaries. Specific actuarial procedures used to determine contributions are included, and effects of simulated returns on amounts contributed are taken into account in the analysis. Projected corporate growth is used to predict contributions and withdrawals associated with new employees. Mortality and turnover tables are also used. Such analyses are provided by both Wilshire Associates and the Boston Company.

Between these two ends of the range lie a great many possibilities. Two issues are relevant: how much detail should be incorporated and which aspects should be included. There are many examples of such intermediate approaches. Simplified approximations of pension fund contribution or withdrawal patterns have been employed by Wells Fargo, the Russell Company, and others. In some cases, the amounts contributed are assumed to be unaffected by the actual returns on the portfolio; in other cases, a feedback between returns and contributions is incorporated.

Generally, the more detailed the simulation of a fund's characteristics, the more expensive the analysis. The goal is to find a level of detail that provides an appropriate balance between the benefit of more realism and its cost.

NATURE OF RESULTS IN
DECISION-MAKING SUMMARIES

Most simulation systems can produce massive amounts of output. The challenge is to distill out a limited set of results that can help the decision-maker choose an appropriate normal asset mix.

A major problem is the difficulty of comprehending multiperiod uncertainty. For example, in some pension fund simulations, both the contribution for each of the next ten years and the value of the fund at the end of ten years are uncertain. Although the uncertainty associated with each of these eleven numbers (ten annual contributions plus the terminal value of the fund) can be displayed and understood by the decision-maker, it is almost impossible to deal adequately with the relationships among the eleven values. For example, is a lower than average contribution in year 3 likely to be followed by a higher than average contribution in year 4 or vice versa? No one has found an effective way to make answers to questions of this type easily understood, and most simulation services do not try.

Chart IV-1 shows one output from a simple simulation provided by Wells Fargo Investment Advisors. The value of $1.00 invested in a mix of 70% stocks and 30% bonds after ten years is plotted on the horizontal axis, with the likelihood of each possible value plotted on the vertical axis. In this simulation, it is assumed that there are no contributions or withdrawals during the ten-year period. The figure is but one of many in a "picture book." The other figures show results for different horizons and different stock/bond mixes. Study of such a "book" assists in selecting an appropriate mix.

CHART IV-1—WELLS FARGO MODEL

Probable Value in Ten Years of $1.00 Investment

Probability

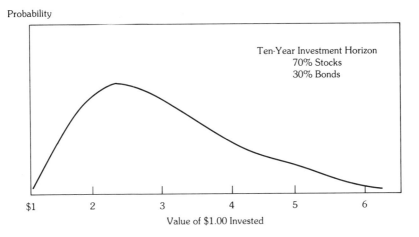

Ten-Year Investment Horizon
70% Stocks
30% Bonds

$1   2   3   4   5   6

Value of $1.00 Invested

CHART IV-2—IBBOTSON AND SINQUEFIELD MODEL

Probable Real Values Over 24 Years of $1.00 Invested

1977–2000

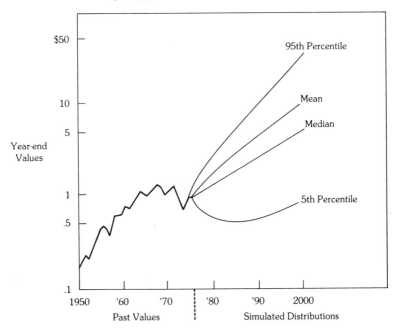

$50

10

5

Year-end
Values

1

.5

.1

1950   '60   '70   '80   '90   2000

Past Values   Simulated Distributions

95th Percentile

Mean

Median

5th Percentile

Note: All values in Chart IV-2 are plotted using a ratio (logarithmic) scale.

Chart IV-2 shows a somewhat different display, which indicates the real value of a portfolio invested solely in common stocks, assuming no withdrawals or contributions. The value in 1976 is assumed to be $1.00. Values for the 26 years before 1976 are based on historical results for the S&P 500. Values for the next 24 years are based on the simulation study by Ibbotson and Sinquefield. For each year after 1976, four values are shown:

1. The mean: a weighted average of all possible values, using probabilities as weights

2. The median: the "50-50" value; the actual amount is as likely to be above as it is to be below this

3. The 95th percentile: only a 5% chance that the actual value will exceed this

4. The 5th percentile: only a 5% chance that the actual value will be less than this.

Ibbotson and Sinquefield also provide a chart for a fund invested solely in long term bonds. For choosing an overall stock/bond mix, similar charts would be needed for other combinations.

CHART IV-3—FRANK RUSSELL CO. MODEL

Probability of Different Stock/Bond Proportions Meeting Required Return in Ten Years

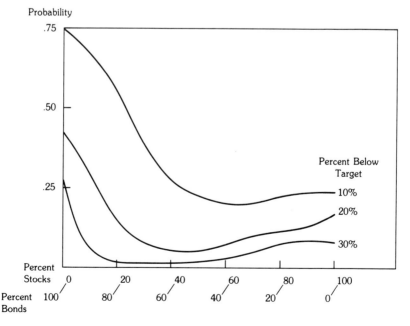

Chart IV-3 shows a set of results from another simulation entailing no contributions or withdrawals. In this analysis, provided by the Frank Russell Company, each point on the horizontal axis represents a different stock/bond mix. For each mix, a simulation was used to determine the probabilities of various values of the fund in ten years. The client's actuary based the contributions on an assumption that the fund would earn 6% per year — leading to an expectation that each $100 currently in the fund would be worth $179.08 in ten years. The top curve in the figure shows the probability that the value could be more than 10% below this target (i.e., below $161.17). The middle curve shows the probability that the value could be more than 20% below this target (i.e., below $143.26), and the bottom curve the probability that the value could be more than 30% below this target (i.e., below $125.36).

Charts IV-4 and IV-5 show some of the output provided in a detailed simulation of a pension fund performed by Wilshire Associates. Chart IV-4 shows ranges of the sum of annual costs over the next ten years for six

CHART IV-4—WILSHIRE ASSOCIATES MODEL

Probable Sum of Annual Costs by Tenth Year Different Stock/Bond/Treasury Bill Proportions

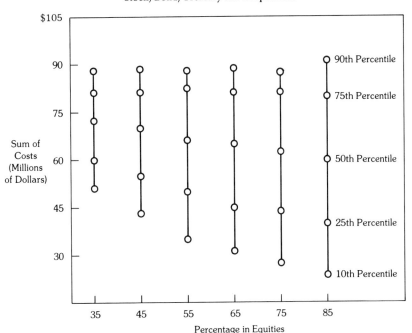

CHART IV-5—WILSHIRE ASSOCIATES MODEL

**Probable Market Values of Fund in Tenth Year Different
Stock/Bond/Treasury Bill Proportions**

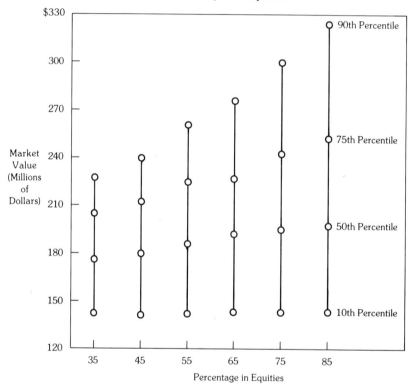

stock/bond/Treasury bill mixes. Chart IV-5 shows the ranges of the fund's market value at the end of the tenth year for the six mixes. The median (50th percentile) value is shown, along with the 90th, 75th, 25th, and 10th percentiles.

Chart IV-6 provides another example of output from a detailed pension fund simulation as done by the Boston Company.[6] Here the projected values of vested and total liabilities 20 years hence are compared with the likely values of the fund's assets at the time, calculated for different stock/bond

---

[6]Currently, the Boston Company model includes the impact of inflation (both anticipated and unanticipated) on pension fund liabilities and assets.

CHART IV-6—BOSTON COMPANY MODEL

Pension Plan Asset Value and Liabilities in 20th Year

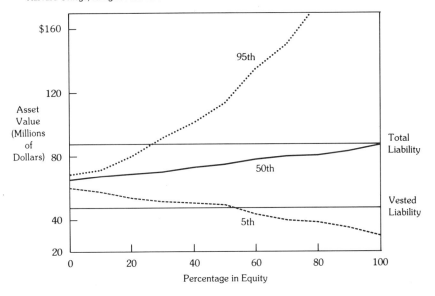

mixes. The median (50th percentile) is shown, along with the 95th and 5th percentiles.

As the preceding survey indicates, many approaches to asset allocation are available. None is obviously best for every possible situation. Moreover, most decisions warrant an analysis more or less tailored to the specific case in question. It is doubtful that a complete general purpose set of projections can be produced.

CHAPTER

5 Determining Strategy

In practice, no generally accepted and clearcut distinction exists between investment objectives and investment strategy. For this reason, Chapter I presents working definitions of these two terms (as well as of portfolio tactics). Chapter II expands on the definition of investment objectives and emphasizes that objectives typically represent a plan sponsor's long term views on such key factors as the optimal stock/bond mix, risk-return goals, and portfolio diversification requirements. Accordingly, as defined in this study, investment objectives in their basic form constitute designated risk and return norms—expected average relationships over a span of years.

In reality, these norms constitute expected results from passive management. Recognition of this fact is important because the major portion of the fund will probably be actively managed. As a result of active management, the composition of the fund and its risk-return characteristics will at times depart from those specified in the basic set of objectives. From the standpoint of the plan sponsor, the extent and nature of these departures are determined by strategy. Accordingly, strategy determines the extent to which portfolios will be actively managed. Moreover, the results of certain strategic decisions may well be added to investment objectives in their basic form to create a more comprehensive set of instructions to managers.

STRATEGY AND ACTIVE/PASSIVE MANAGEMENT

The reasoning behind the above statement can readily be clarified by reemphasizing three facts set forth earlier. First, risk-return objectives for pension funds are typically based on the expected performance of markets for stocks, bonds, and money market instruments. Broad indexes considered reasonably representative are used for stock and bond markets. Treasury bills are ordinarily used as a basic measure of money market instruments. Second, using these expectations, normal stock/bond/Treasury bill mixes are determined. Third, by establishing objectives in this manner, the implication, whether stated or not, is that the objectives can normally be met by *passive management* of highly diversified portfolios constituting representative cross sections of the two major asset classes, stocks and bonds, and by buying and holding Treasury bills.

The following discussion focuses on use of stock and bond indexes. An alternative, but much less generally used approach, is to create what might be termed a "baseline portfolio." This portfolio would be so tailored in terms of both asset mix and securities comprising the holdings of stocks, bonds, and money market instruments that it is expected to meet risk-return objectives of a pension fund on a buy-and-hold basis.

Passive management is characterized by a buy-and-hold approach to investments, low turnover ratio, and maintenance of prescribed normal asset proportions. Under these circumstances, strategy is almost nonexistent. It will principally entail conforming the portfolio to any changes that occur in the composition of the indexes employed and reestablishing the stock/bond/Treasury bill ratio to compensate for cash inflows or outflows and for differential price movements of the asset classes.

The differential price movements may be readily illustrated. Suppose that the normal asset mix *at market value* is set at 60% stocks, 30% bonds, and 10% Treasury bills. It is highly unlikely that the market prices of these three classes of securities will move so closely in tandem that the 60/30/10 ratio will still exist, say, one year from today. Accordingly, rebalancing will be necessary.

In contrast, *active management* of portfolios entails departures from the normal risk-return relationship. At times, active management requires reducing diversification within an asset class, increasing the common stock portion and reducing the fixed income portion (bonds or Treasury bills) and thus increasing risk. At other times, active management requires increasing diversification and reducing the common stock portion and increasing the fixed income portion and thus reducing risk. In changing the portfolio risk, the manager considers that (1) at the moment markets are incorrectly pricing stocks, bonds, or money market instruments as asset classes, groups of stocks or bonds, or selected individual issues and will subsequently correct this mispricing and (2) when additional risk is assumed, the expected additional return will adequately compensate for the change in risk.

Active management uses selection to change the composition of primarily the common stock and fixed income portions of portfolios (i.e., changing the diversification within each asset class) and market timing to change the asset class proportions (i.e., the stock/bond/Treasury bill relationships). Under these circumstances, portfolio strategy plays a critically important role, because strategic decisions determine the extent to which portfolio components will deviate from the norms established by investment objectives. Accordingly, strategy needs to be conceived of fundamentally within an active management context.

SELECTION AND TIMING

In view of the dominant roles played by selection and timing in active management, the pronounced differences in those roles needs to be clearly distinguished. Selection entails changing the composition of principally the common stock and fixed income holdings of a market portfolio to take advantage of estimated mispricing in the marketplace. The following discussion is principally in terms of stocks, but, as discussed later in this chapter, analysis and appraisal of bonds in terms of such factors as maturity, quality, and sector (e.g., federal government issues, public utility, industrial, financial, and other corporate bonds, and dollar denominated foreign bonds) also constitute an important part of the selection process. Selection of money market instruments does not require consideration in this study, because the process is directly comparable to that entailed in the short term investment of liquid corporate funds, a process with which the corporate finance officer is intimately familiar.

Selection is a two-stage process. First, it requires identification of those securities that are considered to be overpriced and underpriced. Security analysts ordinarily undertake industry studies as an integral part of examination of companies and valuation of their common stocks. Accordingly, the selection function encompasses stock groups as well as individual issues.

Second, selection seeks to take advantage of this appraised overpricing or underpricing by increasing or reducing the market weights of issues currently in the portfolio (on either a group or individual basis) or by adding new issues. This selection is *internal* to the stock (and bond) portion of a portfolio and creates holdings different from those of a fully diversified equity market portfolio. Because of the changes in diversification resulting from these "differential holdings," the composition of the equity portion of the portfolio will be different from that of the market index. As a result, it is to be expected that neither the price nor total return performance of the equity portion will any longer replicate that of the market index (S&P 500).

The timing function is more difficult to delineate. It can be argued with validity that timing exists at every decision level—stock and bond markets, market sectors, industries, and individual issues. Nevertheless, because of its distinctive character, *market timing* may be distinguished from all other forms of timing. Market timing entails changing the asset mix (the portfolio stock/bond/Treasury bill ratio) but not the composition of the holdings.[1] Accordingly, one approach to timing requires market analysis, which seeks to determine when the markets for stocks, bonds, and money market instruments are overpriced or underpriced relative to one another. Market timing is therefore *external* to the stock and bond holdings of a portfolio. If the stock holdings were identical to those of a market index at the outset, they would still be identical after timing either reduced or increased the stock portion relative to bonds.

Keeping in mind the manner in which portfolio objectives are ordinarily set and the nature of the two primary functions performed by investment management, the next step is to reach some conclusions as to the fundamental risk-return characteristics of passive and active management.

PASSIVE MANAGEMENT

To simplify the present discussion, assume a pension fund comprising only stocks and bonds. (This assumption is not far from reality, because under

---

[1]Market timing may also entail changing the beta of the equity portion of a portfolio. Thus, the beta might be increased if a market rise were expected and reduced if a market decline were anticipated.

normal conditions money market instruments would be about 10% or less of the portfolio.) Assume further that the stock portion replicates the stock market and the bond portion replicates the bond market and that the S&P 500 stocks and the Salomon Brothers High Grade Corporate Bond Index (or any other stock or bond series) are used as proxies for the two markets. Under these assumptions, the only type of risk in the portfolio reflects the inherent risk-return characteristics of the two markets (market risk).

Passive management does not alter the long term or normal risk-return ratio established by the fund's objectives. It seeks to avoid both selection and timing and thus it makes no bets against either market. Accordingly, passive management does not change the composition of the stock and bond holdings or the stock/bond proportions. Conceptually, it is the same as a buy-and-hold approach. As a result, passive management neither increases nor reduces the risk level of a portfolio.[2]

From a return as well as a risk standpoint, passive management seeks to perform in an equivalent manner to some clearly identified, objective standard that is considered appropriate to the investment assignment. In fact, it seeks to replicate the performance of the standard. This goal of equivalence (or replication) for passive management is in sharp contrast to active management's goal.

ACTIVE MANAGEMENT

Active management seeks to exceed a prescribed standard. Accordingly, on the basis of perceived mispricing, it changes the risk-return ratio from the long term average or normal level specified in the fund's basic objectives.

---

[2]In reality, absolutely passive management over an extended period is unlikely for four reasons. First, with the passage of time, there may well be a need to modify the projected long term levels of return and risk for the pension fund and thus to revise the stock/bond ratio initially established. Second, a change in the financial situation of a plan sponsor may require a change in the stock/bond ratio. Third, if there is a close holding to published stock and bond indexes, revisions in the composition of the indexes by their creators will require corresponding adjustments in the actual holdings of the portfolio. Fourth, the stock/bond ratio is almost always established in terms of the market value of the fund. The market prices of the indexes do not move in lock-step; therefore, from time to time, it will be necessary to reestablish in some manner the prescribed stock/bond ratio.

This action is in the form of timing or selection or a combination of the two. It is in this manner that active management bets against the market.

Market timing is based on an expected difference between the near term relationship in the markets and the forecast long term average return relationship used in setting the portfolio's objectives. Timing changes the portfolio beta (amount of market risk) by changing the portfolio mix in terms of asset classes. It increases or reduces the stock portion of the fund and conversely reduces or increases the bond portion. For example, when the expected additional return on stocks more than compensates for the expected additonal market risk, the stock portion of a portfolio would be increased above the average or normal level. When the reverse is expected, the stock portion (and, in turn, market risk) would be reduced below the average level. As noted earlier, market timing that shifts only the stock/bond proportions does not change the composition of the stock holdings or the composition of the bond holdings.

In contrast, selection changes the composition of the stock holdings by overweighting some industries and companies relative to their market weights and underweighting others. This overweighting and underweighting creates nonmarket risk, which exists in two forms. One form is the risk attributable to those common factors that affect the returns for homogeneous groups of securities and industry groupings. It is termed "extramarket covariance." For example, the prices and returns of individual stocks constituting such groups as growth stocks, oil stocks, electric utilities, or drug stocks generally tend to move together; that is, they covary.

The other type of risk is that attributable to factors that affect only a single stock. It is termed "specific risk." For example, a product failure, an ineffective marketing strategy, loss of a key executive, or a lawsuit can materially affect the fortunes of an individual company.

Thus, through changing the relative weights of stock groups, industries, and individual issues from those existing in a market index, selection adds extramarket covariance and specific risk to a portfolio. In other words, the stock holdings are not as well-diversified as they formerly were and, to this extent, additional risk is assumed.

In conceptual terms, the marked contrast between active and passive management is clear. One seeks to replicate—to provide a risk-return performance equivalent to that of a predetermined standard. The other seeks to outperform—to provide a risk-return performance that exceeds that of a predetermined standard.

The Risk-Return Tradeoff under Active Management

As set forth earlier, investment objectives in their basic form are derived principally from the use of market indexes, long term risk-return estimates for those indexes, and passive management. Therefore, the objectives set forth the optimal long term risk-return tradeoff within that context. However, the foregoing has shown that relative to this optimal long term risk objective, active management at times entails assumption of increased risk in the pursuit of increased return. It is the expected additional return that warrants the additional risk. At other times, it may entail a reduction of risk below the long term optimum because expected returns are considered inadequate. Accordingly, although objectives in their *basic form* are an essential first step, they typically provide only partial guidance in determining the risk range within which active management can operate and the resulting return expected from assuming additional risk.

It is in connection with determining the optimum risk-return tradeoff within an active management context that the role of strategy for the plan sponsor becomes clear. Strategic decisions determine the optimal departures from the risk parameters established by objectives in their basic form.[3] To make these determinations, data needs to be examined and informed judgments must be reached on:

- The additional return that can be expected from active management relative to the additional cost

- The probability of attaining the additional return (the degree of uncertainty or risk entailed)

- The manager (or managers) that are considered capable of producing the

---

[3]These decisions are optimal on the basis of the sponsor's or manager's (or both) expectations for the security markets.

expected additional return and the amount of additional risk that will be assumed in seeking the additional return. In the case of a multimanager pension fund, the development of risk-return profiles and judgments on a manager-by-manager basis will be desirable, particularly if the managers have different styles.

Major Equity Investment Styles

A key consideration in judging risk-return characteristics of an active manager is the investment style employed. Major styles of active bond management are discussed in the next section of this chapter.

Classification of common stock investment styles is a difficult but necessary undertaking. Only in this manner can meaningful comparative risk-return profiles be developed.

Discussions with a substantial number of managers indicate that market timing ordinarily cuts across investment styles. Accordingly, irrespective of the style employed, a manager could attempt substantial or limited market timing. For this reason, it is considered that the dominant identifying characteristics of an equity investment style are the extent and nature of diversification of common stock portfolios and the manner in which diversification is managed.

The traditional means for appraising diversification characteristics of a portfolio is to compare its structure with that of a market standard, such as the S&P 500. This approach has two major advantages. First, it is easy to compute and compare the company, industry, and sector weights of a portfolio with similar statistics on the composition of the market standard and then appraise in these general terms portfolio risk implications of the differences. Second, portfolio stratification of this type benefits from its tangibility and ready comprehension. For example, everyone can observe and interpret to some degree the implied risk and return significance of having double the market weight in cyclical stocks, small growth stocks, the drug industry, or IBM and underweighted representation in other sectors of the market, industries, or companies.

Certain generic features characterize most investment styles. Using these features as the basis for distinguishing between styles, it is possible to group most investment managers into four major categories: diversified, undiversified, rotator, and module manager.

Diversified Managers

The diversified category of managers may be identified principally through two basic tests. First, the organization will "play the entire keyboard." In other words, all industries of investment significance will be held and the manager will have no strong and continuing bias toward any single industry or sector of the market (e.g., high growth stocks or income stocks). The second test is that the normal industry holdings of a portfolio will be at the market weight when the manager considers the outlook for the industry to be neutral. As a result, when the manager is bearish on an industry, less than the market weight is held; when the manager is bullish on an industry, more than the market weight is held.

Managers in this category consist principally of two types. One type is characterized by investment organizations that because of their limited research capability or other reasons wish to restrict the amount of exposure to extramarket covariance and systematic risk of the portfolios under management. The other type is characterized by substantial organizations that have adequate research capability but believe there is no persistent market inefficiency for any sector of the market or any major industry or group of industries. Accordingly, the strategy is to monitor closely the relative investment attractiveness of all industries and then, depending on the degree of conviction, overweight or underweight those industries that are considered to be underpriced or overpriced.

The first type of manager will ordinarily undertake limited departures from the normal risk-return relationships set forth in the portfolio's objectives. Changes in asset mix and diversification will typically be modest. Accordingly, limited changes are to be expected in the portfolio's beta and standard deviation. Likewise, the amount of extramarket covariance and specific risk assumed would be limited.

The second type of diversified manager may employ both timing and selection to change substantially the normal asset mix and level of diversification of the fund. Accordingly, risk-return profiles for managers in this category could vary greatly.

Undiversified Managers

The undiversified manager category encompasses every type of specialist manager whose portfolios have a strong continuing bias toward a chosen sector or sectors of the market. Examples include organizations that concentrate their investment activities in such major sectors of the market as large capitalization growth stocks, small capitalization growth stocks, venture capital investments, quality oriented stocks, special situations, income stocks, or low P/E stocks. The portfolios of pure specialists should never—either across time or at any point in time—reflect a shift to a different bias (e.g., from large capitalization growth stocks to income issues or to major cyclicals).

The primary argument for concentrating investments in a given sector (or sectors) of the market is the particular expertise possessed by the manager and thus the ability to produce an above average risk-adjusted return. Accordingly, if the sector (or sectors) on which a specialist organization centers its attention is considered to be unattractive, one would not expect the portfolio to be shifted to other sectors of the market. Rather, the pure specialist organization would be expected to play only that part of the "keyboard" for which it possesses special talents.

The range of risk-return profiles for managers in this category will be substantial. However, it is inevitable that across time the nonmarket risk (extramarket covariance and systematic risk) in their portfolios will be substantially higher than that for diversified managers.

Rotator Managers

Managers in the rotator category lie between the diversified and undiversified managers. In certain respects, the rotator is similar to the diversified manager because the organization (1) moves across all sectors of the market and all industries ("plays the entire keyboard") and (2) has no continuing bias toward any sector of the market or industry. However, the rotator is significantly different from the diversified manager in that the rotator would not usually consider the market weight of a sector or industry to be the neutral position. The rotator may not choose to hold any securities in a sector or industry unless it is appraised as attractive.

Although the true rotator has no persistent bias, at points in time, this type of manager's portfolios might have such pronounced growth, income, or other tilts that they appear comparable to the concentrated portfolios of specialist managers.

In risk terms, the portfolios of a rotator will probably fall between those of the two preceding categories. Typically, one can expect the nonmarket risk assumed to exceed that of a diversified manager, but to be less than that of the specialist.

Module Managers

Module[4] managers represent a new approach to investment management. To date, this approach has not been used widely enough to permit generalizations about it. A module consists of a group of stocks that from their economic, financial, or other characteristics can be considered comparable from an investment standpoint. Some illustrative equity modules would consist of high growth stocks, income stocks, special situations, or foreign issues.

If an investment organization had a full set of modules, it could create portfolios concentrated in any major sector of the market or covering all sectors. Thus, it would be possible for the manager to be in the specialist, diversified, or rotator categories. For example, in a given instance, a manager could be a specialist through limiting a portfolio to a single module, such as high growth stocks. In contrast, he or she could be a diversified manager

[4]The term "module" is used in the sense of an individual, self-contained unit representing a sector of the market that can be combined with other units to equal the total market.

through combining all of the equity modules at approximately their market weights or a rotator through shifting substantially the proportions of a portfolio invested in different modules.

In view of this possible multiple style approach to investing within a single management organization, the style determination would rest more with the needs and desires of the plan sponsor than with the manager. In other words, the amount of emphasis on a selected module or group of modules would be determined principally by the sponsor. For a plan sponsor with a number of managers, it would depend primarily on the nature of a particular manager's modules and the manner in which the sponsor wanted a stipulated portion of the fund managed. Depending on the nature and extent of the modules developed by an investment organization, it could be playing the entire "keyboard" or only selected portions of it. The extent to which timing is entailed would depend on the manager's capabilities and the desires of the sponsor.

The risk profile of a module manager as such is impossible to delineate, primarily because experience is exceedingly limited. Also the potential variation from manager to manager could be enormous depending on the nature of the modules employed, the sponsor's desires, and the manager's capabilities. It is clear, however, that individual modules should have risk-return characteristics related to the market sectors from which they were drawn. A manager's objective in constructing and managing each module would be to have it outperform its peer group on a risk-adjusted basis.

ACTIVE/PASSIVE BOND MANAGEMENT

Bonds mature whereas common stocks do not; therefore, it is not possible to conceive of passive management for bonds in terms identical to those for stocks. Some active management cannot be avoided in a portfolio that is preordained to change with the passage of time. Nevertheless, relatively passive management can exist in one of three forms: an index fund that seeks to replicate a selected market index, a "baseline" bond portfolio,[5] or bond immunization. Active management could embrace one or more of several different approaches to changing the composition of a bond portfolio.

[5]This terminology was developed by M. L. Leibowitz.

Passive Management

Bond Index Funds

At the present time, several bond index funds are either in the formative stage or operational. One that is ready to become operational may be taken as illustrative. It has been constructed to track closely the Salomon Brothers Composite Corporate Bond Index. The objectives of the fund are to provide customers "with a cost-effective approach for allocating a portion of their pension plan's portfolio to the long term fixed income market and to utilize a widely recognized Index of that market . . . ."[6]

The Salomon Brothers Index consists of issues representative of utility, industrial, and financial sectors initially offered with a maturity of 1990 or later, a quality rating of A or above, and an outstanding par amount of at least $25 million.

The bond index fund developed to track the Salomon Brothers Index is based initially on a "statistical sampling technique." Those sectors of the Salomon Brothers Index that are closely correlated are combined and issues representative of these combined sectors are selected. As a result of the sampling technique, it is expected that when it becomes operational, the performance of the bond index fund will be "within plus or minus .85% on an annual basis at the outside limit" of the index.

Baseline Portfolio

Although the concept underlying the baseline portfolio is straightforward, it merits some discussion. Given currently agreed on expectations in regard to the future, the basic concept is to construct a portfolio that is considered to meet a pension fund's long term fixed income objectives most satisfactorily.

[6]Wells Fargo Investment Advisors, *Wells Fargo Index Fund Quarterly Report,* March 31, 1978.

To illustrate, assume that the fixed income portion of a fund is expected to constitute an assured long term source of income in nominal dollars. Given the risk averse nature of this objective, assume further that the baseline portfolio considered most appropriate has the following risk characteristics:[7]

- Well-diversified portfolio of high grade issues

- Principally long term maturities

- High level of call protection.

The performance of this passive portfolio might be significantly different from that of a bond index because the portfolio has been tailored to fit the objectives of the pension fund. Nevertheless, once the tailoring has been done, management remains passive in the sense that there are no departures from the baseline portfolio to take advantage of any perceived mispricing in the market place.

Immunization

Another form of bond management that conceptually may be put in the passive category is the immunized portfolio. The term "immunization" is applied to bond portfolios that are constructed to attain a designated level of total return irrespective of subsequent changes in interest rates.[8] How can this be done?

The yield to maturity on a bond is based on three sets of payments to the bondholder: (1) coupon payments, (2) payment of principal at maturity, and (3) the return from the reinvestment of the coupon income. Because of fluctuations in the interest rate in the marketplace over the life of a bond, there is no assurance that the reinvestment income ("interest-on-interest") necessary to produce the designated level of total return will be earned.

There are two contrary forces at work in the return earned on a bond. Putting aside credit risk and thus assuming the receipt of coupon payments, changes in interest rates can affect only the reinvestment income and the

---

[7]This example is based on M. L. Leibowitz, *Goal Oriented Bond Portfolio Management*, Salomon Brothers, 1978.

[8]For a fuller discussion, see M. L. Leibowitz, *Bond Immunization*, Salomon Brothers, 1979.

market price of the bond. Moreover, the effect is contrary: if the interest rate rises, the reinvestment income will increase but the market price of the bond will decline. If the interest rate declines, the reverse will be true.

Given a bond's coupon and maturity, there must be some point in time when the reduced reinvestment income and the increased market price of a bond exactly offset one another (or when the reverse occurs). Frederick Macaulay in 1938 developed the concept necessary to calculate this point and called it the "duration" of a bond.[9] The calculation is based on the present value of a bond's stream of payments.

Through determining the duration of a bond—an intermediate point in its full life—it is possible to attain a level of return that will be unaffected by changes in the interest rate for the stipulated period. This approach to bond management can be relevant when it is important for an investment (a bond portfolio) to attain a given asset value by the end of a designated time interval. Accordingly, it may be applicable in constructing a bond portfolio that is to meet specified pension liabilities.

Immunization, therefore, entails selecting a portfolio of bonds that in the aggregate has an average duration as long as the specified pension liabilities that are being funded by the portfolio. This subject merits consideration by the thoughtful reader well beyond what can be covered within the confines of this study. There are negative as well as positive considerations. For example, problems exist in finding bonds with durations approaching those of pension liabilities. Moreover, immunization restricts the possibility of additional return under favorable interest rate conditions. On the other hand, the approach provides the basis for active bond management if that is desired. In this connection, one writer states:[10]

> Knowing how far we are from an immunized position gives us both a measure of our vulnerability to a change in the general level of interest rates and a base from which to plan investment strategy if we have a definite opinion on which way the general

[9]F. R. Macaulay, *Some Theoretical Problems Suggested by the Movements of Interest Rates, Bond Yields, and Stock Prices in the United States Since 1856,* National Bureau of Economic Research, 1938.

[10]D. Don Ezra, "Immunization: A New Look for Actuarial Liabilities," in *The Theory and Practice of Bond Portfolio Management,* Institutional Investor Books, New York, 1977, pp. 151-52.

level of interest rates is going to change. For example, if we expect interest rates to fall, we should arrange for our assets to be longer than our liabilities, for then the value of the assets will increase by more than the value of the liabilities when interest rates fall.

Active Management

Since the term "active bond management" can mean many and significantly different things, it is important that the corporate pension executive have some appreciation for alternative approaches to active management and thus have a basis for considering the manner in which the bond portion of the corporation's pension fund is being managed.

Active bond management is a relatively new phenomenon. One writer suggests that it "is little more than ten years old."[11] From the standpoint of pension fund investing, it has been only in the last decade that fixed income securities have regained some of their past stature. For example, bonds (U.S. government securities and corporate and others) fell from more than 50% of the total market value of assets of private noninsured pension funds at the beginning of the decade of the 1960s to 25% by the close. However, a reversal occurred and by the end of 1978, bonds exceeded 33% of the total.[12]

Active bond management can take a number of forms. However, generally speaking, there are four broad categories of style: yield pick-up, substitution, sector spread, and rate anticipation.[13] The following paragraphs summarize these representative approaches. It will be seen that the level of risk and potential returns are not the same for all approaches.

Yield Pick-up

In the so-called pure yield pick-up, the objective is to replace a bond currently in the portfolio with one that is similar in quality and certain other

[11]Peter L. Bernstein, *The Theory and Practice of Bond Portfolio Management,* Institutional Investor Books, New York, 1977, p. 9.

[12]Computed from Securities and Exchange Commission, *Statistical Bulletin,* Washington D.C., July 1979, Table AN-322.

[13]For a thorough discussion see S. Homer and M. L. Leibowitz, *Inside The Yield Book,* Prentice-Hall, Inc., Englewood Cliffs, New Jersey, 1972; also M. L. Leibowitz, *Trends in Bond Portfolio Management,* Salomon Brothers, New York, 1979.

characteristics but offers a higher contractual return over the life of the bond. These shifts in the portfolio are for the sole purpose of securing an immediate increase in return. This increase can be in the form of a higher current coupon or higher yield to maturity or both. Opportunities for shifts of this type result in part from various accounting and other constraints against realizing book losses. This category of active bond management is concerned with the longer term outlook and thus requires careful consideration of the expected interest rate on reinvested interest, quality of the issue, and call protection, because it typically entails lengthening the maturity to secure the highest yield.

Substitution Swaps

A substitution swap entails switching from a bond currently held to another that, except for price, is practically identical in such pertinent characteristics as coupon, maturity, quality, and marketability. The fact that the bond acquired is conceptually a "perfect substitute" for the bond results in the term "substitution swaps." The objective is to take advantage of a transient discrepancy (momentary aberration) in price that is expected to provide a gain either in the form of price appreciation or higher yield to maturity. Substitution swaps are typically closed by a reversal into the original issue.

The possibility for swaps of this nature results from temporary market forces that briefly cause such price discrepancies among bonds of equivalent value. Substitution swaps entail almost no risk if there is "true substitution," but the increase in return will usually be modest. Accordingly, these swaps must be repeated frequently if they are to have a significant impact on a portfolio's return across time. The result is considerable emphasis on short term trading and limited gains in an area of the market that has become highly competitive. For this reason, it is doubtful that substitution swapping alone can be an adequate basis for active bond management.

Sector Spreads

The sector spread form of active management shifts funds from one sector of the bond market to another to take advantage of spreads. The market sectors can be differentiated by quality, coupon, issuer, and type of issue. For example, issues would consist of federal, state, and municipal governments; public utilities; industrial corporations; foreign dollar bonds; and so forth. The sector spread approach requires identifying yield spreads among sectors of the market that represent temporary departures from normal relationships. Shifts of this nature are riskier than substitution swaps and thus require considerable professional competence. However, they can offer an opportunity to shift significant portions of the portfolio and thus have the potential of substantially affecting the overall performance of a portfolio.

Rate Anticipation

As the name implies, the rate anticipation form of active management is based on an anticipated significant change in the overall level of interest rates. Although there are several ways to gain from anticipated interest rate changes, the principal one is to shorten or lengthen maturities depending on the nature of the expected change. For example, maturities would typically be shortened if higher long term yields were expected. If successful, rate anticipation swaps are considered the "most productive bond portfolio action."[14] Since return and risk are usually closely related, this form of active management is—as might be expected—the riskiest.

The magnitude of these shifts in maturities can be substantial, accordingly timing is a critically important factor, particularly for a long term fund such as a pension fund. Double-digit inflation and other economic and political factors and a significant increase in the number of organizations actively seeking to forecast and take advantage of interest rate changes are making effective rate anticipation shifts increasingly difficult.

STRATEGIC DECISIONS

This chapter emphasizes the fact that a number of strategic decisions are essential to management of a pension fund. Some of these decisions may be delegated but others must inevitably rest with the plan sponsor. To bring

---

[14]M. L. Leibowitz, *Trends in Bond Portfolio Management,* p. 14.

these decisions into focus, they are grouped in five categories:

- Active/passive management
- Aggressiveness of active management
- Number of active managers
- Nature of active management
- Control of flows to managers.

Active/Passive Management

The first step in formulating the strategy for a pension fund is to decide on the respective roles of active and passive management. The basic issue is the proportion of the fund that will be actively managed. Experience to date indicates that the total fund or by far the majority of it will be generally actively managed. However, a tendency remains to include a modest amount of passive management. Clearly, this strategic decision must be made by the plan sponsor—there is no one else to make it.

The decision may take another form in that the sponsor may select a manager and let the manager make the decision. However, in this instance, the selection of the manager in itself represents the decision. For example, if the specific manager chosen does not believe in passive management in any form or to any extent, the sponsor by selecting this manager indirectly decides to have only active management.

Aggressiveness of Active Management

If the past is a guide to the future, it can be expected that at least the major portion of a pension fund portfolio will be actively managed. Thus, the next strategic decision is the extent to which the risk-return tradeoff decided on in establishing the fund's basic investment objectives will be modified. The only reason for deciding on active management is the conclusion that assumption of additional risk and cost will be more than compensated for by additional return. Accordingly, there must be an adjustment of the risk-return tradeoff to make this possible.

Number of Active Managers

The number of active managers and the nature of active management are closely linked. Although the two are treated separately for clarity of exposition, either decision obviously cannot be made as if it were entirely independent of the other. The overriding consideration in determining the number of managers is the size of the fund. The considerations in regard to a single or multiple manager are discussed more fully in Chapter IX. At this point, two general comments are appropriate. First, in the single manager situation, it is possible to delegate much more strategic decision-making to the manager because that manager has an overview of the total fund. Second, in a multiple manager situation—particularly if there are distinctive differences in investment styles—it is not possible to delegate such decision-making. Coordination and control of this decentralized management of portions of the fund must rest with the plan sponsor or with an organization specifically designated to undertake this task.

Nature of Active Management

The pronounced differences in various forms of active stock and bond management are set forth earlier in this chapter. It is emphasized that differences in the resulting risk-return profiles can also be substantial. Accordingly, the plan sponsor must give careful thought to procedures and practices employed by managers as well as to their records and capabilities. It is in this manner that managers are selected who can be expected to provide the results anticipated.

Asset Flows to Active Managers

In the single manager case, the allocation of new monies presents no problem. All inflows must obviously go to that manager. However, in the multiple manager situation (again with different investment styles), the decision is more difficult. For example, suppose that there are three equity managers and one fixed income manager. Does this mean an arbitrary allocation of one-fourth of the fund to each? Such an action would appear questionable. Presumably, the fixed income manager will receive the amount determined by the asset-mix decision reached in establishing the fund's investment objectives in their basic form. The issue then arises as to how the balance will be allocated among the three equity managers with different investment styles and thus probably with different risk-return profiles. Another issue is, how will it be determined that, given risk-return characteristics of the four managers, aggregate results for the pension fund can be expected to meet the investment objectives. Clearly, a number of strategic decisions must be made.

SUMMARY

Investment objectives in their basic form typically constitute designated risk and return norms—expected average relationships over a span of years. They are the results anticipated from passive management. It is important that this fact be recognized because the major portion of most pension funds will probably be actively managed. Under active management, composition of the fund and its risk-return characteristics will at times depart from those specified in the basic set of objectives. Strategy determines the extent and nature of these departures and the extent to which portfolios will be actively managed.

CHAPTER

6 The Investment Process: Analysis, Timing, and Selection

Corporate officers responsible for their corporation's pension fund must understand the basic principles on which the investment process rests. This understanding is essential for three primary reasons. First, the selection of an external manager solely on the basis of the manager's past performance record is questionable. In fact, in judging future performance it is generally considered desirable to accompany an examination of the record[1] with an appraisal of the effectiveness of the manager's analytical and decision-making process and the caliber of professionals operating it. If the process and the people are to be appraised with reasonable competence, the corporate officer must have in mind the basic considerations in structuring the investment process.

Second, to decide on appropriate objectives for individual managers, it is necessary to understand procedures, practices, and policies employed by each manager.

Third, to appraise fully differences in the performance of managers, it is necessary to consider and understand operational differences in their styles and strategies.

---

[1] In undertaking this examination, it is important that the standards used in measurement and diagnosis of the record be appropriate in terms of the manager's specific style.

Chapter V discusses the fact that active management seeks to outperform a predetermined passive standard. For these reasons, Chapters VI and VII provide an overview of the basic investment functions that, irrespective of the manager's style, underlie the active management of investment funds. A tight chain of logic follows from the goal of active management to outperform. This logic is the basis for each major step and function in the investment process. Accordingly, clear understanding of both the logic and its sequence makes possible an understanding of the investment process.

The chain of logic is as follows:

1. There is mispricing of securities in the marketplace that is large enough to be identified and determined with sufficient accuracy to take advantage of after defraying management and transaction costs.

2. Mispricing occurs at three levels: classes of securities (security markets), groups of securities (both homogeneous groups and industries), and individual securities.

3. Identification and estimation of mispricing can be accomplished through fundamental analysis.

4. Market timing seeks to take advantage of mispricing at the security class level (security markets).

5. Selection seeks to take advantage of mispricing at the group and individual security level.

6. Results of timing and selection are brought together in constructing and managing portfolios.

7. The aggressiveness with which timing and selection are employed in management of portfolios should be determined by investment objectives of the portfolio, strength of the mispricing evidence, and forecasting accuracy and organizational efficiency of the manager.

These seven points provide the general structure for Chapters VI and VII. Chapter VI considers the much debated issue as to whether mispricing exists, reviews major aspects of fundamental analysis, and examines the nature of timing and selection. Chapter VII discusses construction and management of portfolios. It examines the procedures and practices that govern the use of timing and selection to design and manage portfolios that conform to and seek to meet specific risk-return objectives.

FUNDAMENTAL ANALYSIS

Much of the balance of this chapter discusses fundamental analysis and its key role in investment management. This emphasis is based on two important considerations: (1) the opinion that mispricing of securities exists in the marketplace and that analysis is an essential and economically justified part of the decision-making process and (2) the fact that effectiveness of timing and selection decisions depends on the accuracy of the predictions developed by fundamental analysis.

The Challenge to Fundamental Analysis

It must be recognized that U.S. security markets are intensely competitive. It is not easy to outperform the market. In fact, there are those who hold that securities are so *efficiently* priced in U.S. markets that after allowance for transaction costs it is impossible across time to outperform the market. The exponents of this point of view are known as adherents of the strong form of the *efficient market hypothesis* (or theory). Although this view, as it relates to fundamental analysis, is contrary to the position taken in this study and although there is mounting evidence in support of our position, the theory has received sufficient prominence to warrant examination. Furthermore, the corporate officer should be knowledgeable with regard to principal arguments relating to it.

Research dealing with the efficient market hypothesis has predominantly centered on common stocks and the performance of common stock portfolios. Accordingly, throughout this chapter, the discussion concentrates on the active management of equities. Efficient market theorists contend that the stock market is efficient primarily because (1) the number of informed participants is large, (2) transaction costs are low, and (3) information is well and quickly diffused. The term "efficient" is used to mean that information is rapidly and appropriately reflected (impounded) in security prices. This rapid and, presumably, appropriate price response results when experienced investors promptly analyze and react to new information that is "widely, quickly, and cheaply available."

The hypothesis in its so-called strong form holds that, since current prices already reflect what is knowable and relevant in regard to a security, it is difficult—if not impossible—to identify common stocks that are significantly overpriced or underpriced. Accordingly, the efficient market hypothesis challenges fundamental analysis, which seeks to value securities for the purpose of identifying overpriced or underpriced issues.[2] The hypothesis holds that there will be no returns attributable to the analytical effort and, as a result, no returns attributable to either timing or selection.

Although the strong form of the hypothesis is an extreme assertion, it has some general plausibility. There are a large number of competent security analysts, and there are no entry barriers to analyzing and investing in securities. As a result, considerable in-depth research is centered on companies of investment consequence.

The implications of the strong form for fundamental analysis are subject to much controversy. The critical issue is whether the potential exists for differential gains from analytical skills. It is true that substantial evidence

[2]The hypothesis also challenges technical analysis. Its so-called weak form holds that future price movements do not follow predictable patterns but, instead, follow a "random walk." In a random walk, each subsequent price change is independent of all price changes. (A tossed coin is a familiar example of this kind of process, since the coin has no memory and the chance of its showing heads next time is independent of the past sequence of heads or tails.) In the context of stock prices, this suggests that it is not helpful to use past changes in stock prices to predict future changes.

Statistical tests have found only the most tenuous relationships between price movements in successive time periods. This evidence of the unrelated nature, or independence, of successive returns through time is reinforced by studies of the lengths of runs of price changes in the same direction. The lengths of runs observed are consistent with the random walk theory.

Tests have also been conducted to determine whether particular trading rules, based on price series, would result in improved performance—such as filter rule. Under this procedure, for example, a stock is bought when its price advances a specific percentage above a previous low and is sold when it declines by the same or different percentage below a previous high. There is no evidence that, after transaction costs, this kind of trading rule can earn returns in excess of those from a naive approach, such as buy and hold. The same is true of a number of other technical theories.

The overall conclusion that may be drawn from these studies is that although there is some evidence of nonrandomness in the price series of security returns, it appears to be insufficient for purely technical approaches alone to increase returns consistently after allowance for transaction costs.

exists for two findings: (1) stock prices are highly responsive to new information and changes in investor expectations and (2) it is difficult for any select group of investors consistently to outperform the market over a span of years after adjusting for risk. In light of this evidence, some hold that undertaking fundamental analysis in the attempt to outdo the market is a waste of resources.

This study recognizes that the efficient market hypothesis in its strong form is clearly a challenge to fundamental analysis, but does not concur in the view that the analytical function is an uneconomic activity.[3] The findings of research on the efficient market hypothesis establish that the market is highly competitive and that careful consideration needs to be given to the manner in which fundamental analysis is structured and used in investment management. However, it is our considered opinion that fundamental analysis has an important role, for the following reasons:

- Fundamental analysis is needed, even according to extreme believers in the efficient market, to keep the market "efficient." It is also needed to evaluate risk in individual issues, because an extrapolation of past measures of risk is an imperfect indication of future risk.

- Certain aspects of the strong form need considerably more empirical support before the evidence can be accepted as conclusive. Recent information, however, appears to be to the contrary and raises more doubts about the strong form.[4]

- The market may respond promptly to obvious information, but it may respond more slowly to results of unique, complex, more thorough, or longer time horizon analyses of obvious information.

- There is some question whether access to all information is simultaneous or whether at times larger numbers of investors may not have made the same error

[3]There is also the so-called semistrong form of the efficient market hypothesis. It maintains that stock prices are efficient with respect to *generally known* information. Accordingly, it holds that knowing and acting on what is known by most others would typically not produce a portfolio return better than average for the level of risk assumed. This form does not present the same challenge to security analysis as the strong form, because it does not exclude the contribution that can come from effective in-depth analysis.

[4]For example, see Clinton M. Bidwell III, "A Test of Market Efficiency: SUE/PE," *The Journal of Portfolio Management,* Summer 1979; Bruce D. Fielitz and Myron T. Greene, "New Evidence of Persistence in Stock Returns," *The Journal of Portfolio Management,* Fall 1978; and Robert M. Lovell, Jr. "Whose Efficient Market?" *The Journal of Portfolio Management,* Winter 1977.

of judgment (such as being too bullish or too bearish) and thus caused possible substantial mispricing in the market.

- There is evidence that institutional analysts are able to make stock price forecasts containing some predictive power. Recognition of this fact is important.[5]

- The difficulty in outdoing the market lies primarily in the margin of error entailed in the required sequential chain of forecasts of variables subject to unexpected shifts and shocks, the high sensitivity of common stock valuation models to minor errors in growth and other forecasts, and at times in vagaries of the market (in the form of lengthy price departures from expectations based on reason and representative past experience).

The foregoing analysis of the efficient market hypothesis leads to the following major conclusions:

- There is a definite role for fundamental analysis in investment management, but its specific nature, scope, and form must be carefully structured to the needs and capabilities of each investment organization.

- Effectively structured fundamental analysis of above average quality has the potential of producing above average returns. Forecasts of the future will always be subject to considerable uncertainty. Thus complete accuracy is obviously not possible. What can be expected from tightly structured analysis by capable people are consistent results and effective ranking of securities in terms of their attractiveness.

- U.S. security markets are intensely competitive (principally because of the large number of capable professional organizations competing in them); therefore the extent of above average returns will probably be modest over time. Nevertheless, the cumulative effect of this return differential on large pools of capital, such as pension funds, can be substantial. (A differential of 1% per year will increase the value of the fund by 28% in 25 years with reinvestment of the return.)

- Fundamental analysis provides input essential in judging both the risk and return entailed in timing and selection decisions.

---

[5]For example, see K. P. Ambachtsheer, "Profit Potential in an 'Almost Efficient' Market," *The Journal of Portfolio Management,* Fall 1974; also K. P. Ambachtsheer and J. L. Farrell, "Can Active Management Add Value?", *Financial Analysts Journal,* November–December 1979.

Perspective

Fundamental analysis includes a hierarchy of forecasts. The reasons for these forecasts and their important roles can best be explained in the more familiar terms of common stock investing.[6] The nature of fundamental analysis in common stock investing is determined primarily by the basic or underlying determinants of value. In this regard, two major points are to be made:

- In conceptual terms, the investment value of a stock is determined basically by the current "normal" level, growth, and stability (variance or risk) of earnings[7] and the "normal" payout rate.[8] Since stability is judged in terms of earnings rather than dividends, since the payout rate is considered in predicting the growth of earnings, and since earnings are the source of dividends, all of these forecasts are necessary irrespective of the valuation method employed. The forecast of earnings is the first priority. However, it is important that the analysis give full consideration to dividends.

- Investing takes place in a world of relative values. In fact, investing might be defined as the discipline of comparative selection. To be comparative, analysis of individual companies, projection of earnings and dividends, and selection of capitalization rates must all be part of a structured, consistent, and orderly process.

The sales, operating expenses, and earnings of all but a few companies depend on the overall business and earnings environment. Moreover, the price movements of few stocks are unaffected by the sweeps of bull and bear markets. Accordingly, if comparative selection is to be rational, appraisal of

---

[6]A portion of Chapter III is devoted to forecasting the stock market and, in this connection, to explaining the role of macroeconomic forecasts. To provide an overview of the full scope of fundamental analysis and the interrelationship of economic, stock market, and security analysis, an expanded examination of macroeconomic and stock market forecasts is included here.

[7]The determination of stability embraces an appraisal of all of the factors of variability that make it difficult to predict the normal level, secular growth, and cyclical volatility of the earnings of a company.

[8]In this manner, the future stream of dividends as well as the stream of earnings is provided. At a given point in time, the actual payout rate may differ from normal. In the case of a high growth nondividend-paying stock, it is the capacity to pay dividends (the potential payout rate) that the investor is buying. In predicting the payout rate, analysts usually consider the company's expected cash flow as well as earnings.

individual issues requires the use of consistent projection methods for the economy (including its major sectors), total corporate earnings, and the stock market as well as for per share earnings, dividends, and capitalization rates for specific issues.

The capitalization rate for the stock market and individual common stocks cannot be determined in isolation. Consideration must be given to the return available on alternative investment vehicles, such as risk-free Treasury bills or high quality corporate bonds. These alternative returns must be compared and appraised even if capitalization rates are derived from current prices.[9] Neither the expected holding period return for the market as a whole nor for individual issues can be meaningfully appraised apart from the returns on fixed income securities—the principal investment alternative.

Economic analysis and stock market analysis thus provide the forecasts that constitute the essential underpinning for security analysis. Accordingly, fundamental analysis as it applies to common stock investing consists of:

- Economic analysis—development of macroeconomic forecasts and prediction of aggregate corporate profits

- Stock market analysis—derivation of value estimates from macroeconomic forecasts and appraisal of the market in terms of the cyclical relationship of stock market indexes to economic variables

- Security analysis—examination and appraisal principally of industries and individual issues.

Economic Analysis

Economic analysis is essentially concerned with developing forecasts for the total economy. These aggregate (macroeconomic) forecasts provide a consistent framework within which to analyze and project: (1) developments in stock, bond, and other security markets; (2) the outlook for broad sectors of the economy and individual industries; and (3) the outlook for sales and

---

[9]For example, it is possible to determine that discount rate (which constitutes the return for the investor) that will result in a present value equal to the current price. However, it is still necessary to appraise the relative attractiveness of this return.

earnings of individual companies. By defining the expected environment in which to appraise the outlook for interest rates, earnings, and valuation of equities, economic forecasts constitute the foundation for comparative appraisal and selection of investments.

This section considers first the factors concerned with short term, cyclical forecasts (four to eight quarters) and second those related to longer term secular projections (five years or longer).

Cyclical Forecasts

Short term economic forecasts are predictions of the quarterly cyclical path of business activity, prices, expenditures, and incomes over a horizon of typically four to eight quarters. Short term forecasts concentrate on the path of aggregate demand and the relation of aggregate demand to the nation's supply capacity (output potential). These forecasts also predict cyclical changes in the composition of demand and income.

At one extreme, short term economic forecasters may work within a largely judgmental and informal framework. At the other extreme, they may rely primarily on the structure imposed by an econometric model that predicts sectors of the economy and components of expenditures and incomes through a formal system of equations. Most short term forecasters use some combination of judgment and formal econometric modeling.[10]

Considerable uncertainty surrounds any predicted path of business activity, inflation, and major expenditures and incomes. Therefore, it is exceedingly valuable in establishing investment tactics to assess the probability associated with a particular economic forecast through considering and appraising possible alternative forecasts. In addition to the assumptions underlying the probable path of the economy, different assumptions that would result in alternative paths and therefore different forecasts of business activity, inflation, corporate profits, and interest rates should be considered.

[10]V. Zarnowitz, "Forecasting in Economics: State-of-the-Art, Problems and Prospects," *The Study of the Future: An Agenda for Research,* The Futures Group, Inc., Glastonbury, Conn., 1974, p. 32; R. A. Kavesh and R. B. Platt, "Economic Forecasting," *Financial Analysts Handbook I,* Chapter 33, Dow-Jones Irwin, Inc., Homewood, Illinois, 1975.

In addition, it should be determined how these alternative paths affect the outlook for individual components of demand such as consumer durable goods, housing construction, and business investment.

The ultimate usefulness of short term economic forecasts in investment decisions lies not only in their predictions of probable economic events, but also in their predictions of how the economic environment might deviate from the probable outcome. This fact suggests that forecasts which encompass alternative cyclical paths (with some assessment of the probabilities) will find increasing application in coping with the uncertainties of the future.

Secular Forecasts

Most longer term forecasts are fundamentally secular or trend projections revealing principally the results of underlying determinants of economic growth, structural change, and inflation. For three principal reasons, the focus differs from that of short term forecasts of the cyclical path of the economy. First, the cyclical path (the course of the economy year by year) over a span as long as five years is highly uncertain and it is doubtful that it can be predicted with meaningful accuracy. Second, underlying forces of change may have little effect on the economy over the short term but can have substantial effect over the longer term. Third, the supply capacity (output potential) of the economy does not change significantly over the year term[11] but can be increased substantially over the longer term. Accordingly, short term forecasts primarily emphasize demand, whereas longer term projections emphasize the growth of the nation's output potential and are thus supply oriented.

In determining which factors to consider in preparing longer term economic and financial projections, the first step is thorough appraisal of the underlying forces of change that are expected to affect the growth and structure of the economy over the projection span. In this connection, it is necessary to consider domestic social forces and international political and economic developments. Careful analysis of these factors brings to the forefront the

---

[11]The output capacity of a nation can be temporarily reduced by energy shortages, labor strikes, and social unrest.

complex interaction of social, political, and economic forces that are important in determining (1) governmental, monetary, fiscal and regulatory policy
(the climate within which business operates) and (2) the position of the United
States in major international markets. Analysis and appraisal of underlying
forces of change provide a foundation for specific long term estimates of the
economy and security markets.

Forecasting Corporate Profits

Forecasts of aggregate corporate profits are critical inputs in developing
forecasts for the stock market and in judging the profit environment in which
individual industries and companies will operate.

Different methods may be used in forecasting profits. For example, one
approach relates total profits to such key economic variables as changes in
current dollar GNP and in current and past rates of capacity utilization.
Another derives corporate profits from forecasts of the level of total business
output, the ratio of price to unit labor cost in the business sector, and the
unemployment rate. An alternative method relies on detailed sales, cost, and
profit data provided by the Department of Commerce. Forecasting by this
last method promotes a thorough consideration—item by item—of the
economic variables that affect corporate profits.

Stock Market Analysis

In valuing the stock market (typically the S&P 500 although other indexes
can be used), fundamental analysis follows a logical and sequential step
process. It begins with macroeconomic projections, particularly aggregate
corporate profits. It then moves progressively to forecasts of earnings per
share (EPS) for the selected stock index, estimates of the dividend payout
rate, and selection of a capitalization rate. On the basis of these inputs, an
estimated *investment value* is developed for the stock market index.

In contrast to the foregoing extensive analytical process, short cut methods
have been developed for predicting price movements of the stock market.

These methods predict stock prices directly either from observable (past and present) economic data and trends or from forecasts derived from these data. In this manner, the methods bypass the analytical and valuation process.

A structured method for accomplishing a specific task or undertaking is in reality a model. Accordingly, to distinguish the two types of approaches, the former are termed "market valuation models" and the latter "market price models." These models are discussed briefly below. Because the analysis and valuation approach is much more widely used, it is given more attention.

Market Valuation Models

Forecasts of earnings per share need to be made in terms of secular growth projections as well as near term estimates. The secular projection should cover a span of years. To accomplish this projection, earnings in the current year need to be estimated on a normalized as well as an "actual" basis. These EPS forecasts should be derived within the context of the preceding sets of macroeconomic forecasts. In this manner, the EPS forecast for the stock market will be consistent with the total economic outlook.

There are a number of methods for forecasting EPS for a stock market index. Three methods are described here. First, EPS can be related to aggregate profits of the companies constituting, say, the S&P 500 or to total corporate profits as reported by the Department of Commerce (or to both).

Second, aggregate sales for the 500 companies can be developed and related to GNP. By analyzing the relationship of profits after taxes to sales and the relationship of EPS to aggregate profits of the 500 companies, an estimate of EPS can be developed within the context of this sales-profit margin approach and the foregoing cyclical and secular projections for the U.S. economy.

Third, EPS may be based on an analysis of rates of return on book value. It is well known that book value is a historic figure while earnings are expressed in current dollars. For this and other reasons, the return on book value is necessarily rough. Nevertheless, it provides a cross check with the results of the other two methods. (Chapter III provides an examination of earnings for the S&P 500 over the 1926–78 span.)

The proportion of a corporation's earnings that is paid out in cash dividends depends primarily on management's judgment in regard to (1) expected financial requirements of the corporation resulting from growth in sales, asset expansion, and other factors; (2) expected profitability (including cash flow); (3) the degree of access to capital markets and the cost of externally raised capital; and (4) past dividend policy. (Chapter III provides an analysis of dividends for the S&P 500 over the 1926–78 span.)

Corporate executives are thoroughly familiar with the factors that determine the dividend policy of an enterprise. The same logic applies in estimating cash dividends for a stock index. Accordingly, these determinants do not require elaboration here.

The next step is to consider selection of a capitalization rate for valuation of the market (a specific stock index). In selecting a capitalization rate, different approaches and different projection spans can be employed. However, certain broad principles are applicable, irrespective of the valuation method employed.

The rate at which earnings are capitalized through use of a P/E ratio or dividends through a discount rate is a function of (1) the level, growth, and stability of earnings; (2) the cash dividend payout ratio; (3) the expected return from investment in a selected fixed income security; and (4) a risk premium. It is not necessary to explain why the stock of a company with substantial stability and growth in earnings and a high payout should have a higher capitalization rate than one with less stability, growth, and payout. However, the relationship of the capitalization rate to the yield on fixed income securities merits consideration.

Alternatively, if the stream of dividends is projected sufficiently far into the future, the stream may be used to derive from the current price the implicit rate of return; the rate that equates the present value of expected dividends to current price. The procedure for deriving this rate is discussed further in the section dealing with individual common stock issues.

As noted in Chapter III and earlier in this chapter, investing takes place in a world of relative returns and relative risks. As a result, there is a continuous tradeoff between risk and return. It is in this manner that return differentials in security markets are determined.

There is difference of opinion as to the interest rate standard to be used and certainly as to the amount of risk premium to be added in arriving at a capitalization rate for the stock market. In regard to the interest rate standard, some use the expected Treasury bill rate (risk-free rate)[12] and others use the rate for new issues of Aa bonds (typically public utility issues) or seasoned Aaa corporate bonds (typically industrials) and so forth. In regard to the appropriate risk differential for common stocks, an extensive record of the realized return on stocks, bonds, and Treasury bills (as set forth in Chapter III) is now available. The selection of a risk premium begins with the record and then rests on careful appraisal of current trends and on the exercise of considerable judgment. The capitalization rate for stocks is therefore the total of the forecast interest rate level (using the selected standard) plus the chosen risk premium.

Market Price Models

Many methods have been developed for predicting price movements of the market directly from economic data and trends or from forecasts and judgments derived from these data. The methods range from simple decision rules to econometric models. The methods relate changes in stock prices to changes in such economic variables as the money supply, real money stock, real GNP, and the GNP deflator.[13]

A broad conclusion can be drawn; a number of models designed to predict stock prices fit past data well. When estimated stock prices are compared with actual prices over the sample period, the accuracy can be impressive. However, when required to predict prices into the future, models may predict well at times and poorly at others. This result may be attributed, at least in part, to unstable relationships. Nevertheless, there is merit in studying the

---

[12]Use of the risk-free rate ties more closely to the capital asset pricing model. On the other hand, it is debatable whether Treasury bills are the most realistic investment alternative to stocks.

[13]See, for example, B. W. Sprinkel, *Money and Markets: A Monetarist's View,* Richard D. Irwin, Inc., Homewood, Illinois, 1971; M. W. Keran, "Expectations, Money, and the Stock Market," *Federal Reserve Bank of St. Louis Review,* January 1971; "Forecasting Stock Prices," *Journal of Portfolio Management,* Winter 1975; R. A. Crowell, *Stock Market Strategy,* McGraw-Hill Book Company, New York, 1977, Chapter 5; and B. W. Sprinkel and R. J. Genetski, *Winning with Money,* Dow Jones-Irwin, Homewood, Illinois, 1977.

relationships developed by these models to gain as much insight as possible and, perhaps, in using their results as cross checks. The amount of work and difficulties entailed in the market valuation approach are both substantial. Nevertheless, it is questionable whether analysis and valuation of the stock market should be bypassed and complete reliance placed on short cut methods.

Security Analysis

Security analysis operates at the stock group level as well as the individual issue level. Stock group research is in the form of industry studies and homogeneous group analyses.

Stock Group Research

Industry studies are the traditional province of the security analyst. The analyst ordinarily combines information from the economist's macroeconomic outlook and his or her own appraisal of both industry fundamentals and individual company prospects to form an industry forecast. This method is typically a judgmental approach in which there is neither formal linkage with the economy (although regression analysis may be employed) nor formal linkage with other industries.

With the advances in economics, statistical modeling methods, and computers, and the establishment of extensive machine-readable macroeconomic data banks, considerable effort has been devoted to seeking out econometric linkages between selected macroeconomic variables (such as GNP, consumer expenditures, and personal income) and sales, expenses, and profits of individual industries. The focus has tended to be on building individual industry models on an industry-by-industry basis. However, attempts have also been made to construct large blocks of industry models for the purpose of ranking industries and cross checking industry totals against the macroeconomic forecasts.

Industry studies are essential because an appraisal is needed of the specific business environment in which a group of companies will probably operate to reach effective investment decisions at the industry level and to analyze and appraise more effectively the outlook for individual companies in that industry. However, the problems are substantial.

Definition of industries is a critical step in constructing a framework for industry analysis. First, the industries must encompass companies or product lines that are relatively homogeneous and are broadly sensitive to the same factors in the economic environment. However, the expanding number of multi-industry companies increasingly complicates this task. Moreover, there may be "broader than industry factors" (besides the market factor) that affect earning power and common stock returns. In addition, relationship patterns may be unstable in successive cycles. Second, both classification and composition of industries must be useful to security analysts in examining and forecasting company performance. Third, consistent data for industry sales, profits, and, if possible, costs must be available or must be constructed. It is also important that the data be current because significant industry changes can occur rapidly. Fourth, the total coverage of industries should be sufficiently diverse that industry rankings reflect a meaningful array of investment alternatives.

Continuing progress can be expected from this effort, but it is possible that the major contribution of econometric industry models to security analysis lies in the fact that the modeling and forecasting process brings the economist and security analyst closer together. The advantages are threefold: (1) security analysts consider explicitly the economic factors that impinge on their industries, (2) analysts examine industries relative to one another in the context of the expected economic environment, and (3) the economic forecast benefits from the economist's interaction with analysts who have detailed knowledge of sectors and industries.

Recent research has sought to segment the market into "homogeneous stock groups" (sometimes called "pseudo-industries"). Such groups as growth, stable, cyclical, and oil stocks have been analyzed. As suggested by the category titles, some of the homogeneous groups differ markedly from traditional industries. Another approach is to group companies by economic sector, for example, consumer durable goods, consumer nondurables, and residential construction.

Homogeneous groups have practical significance for the portfolio manager and the security analyst in terms of share price behavior. For example, if significant homogeneous group effects exist in a portfolio, simply holding a large number of stocks may not be sufficient to bring nonmarket risk down to acceptable levels. To attain those levels, it may be necessary for the portfolio manager to diversify across homogeneous groups. Contrariwise, if the strategy is to have a portion of a fund assume considerable nonmarket risk in anticipation of a higher return, the manager may choose to concentrate his or her efforts on a specific group and manage a portfolio with a specific tilt, such as high growth stocks.

For the security analyst, identification of a group of companies that react to changing economic conditions in a broadly similar manner may be helpful in forecasting such key factors as sales, costs, or earnings. The present level of research in this area is modest. In view of the potential, it will be surprising if the research effort does not increase.

Individual Common Stocks

As discussed earlier in this chapter, it is our opinion that mispricing does occur in the U.S. security markets. Moreover, it is of sufficient dimension that above average analytical talent can identify and estimate the mispricing with enough accuracy to provide a basis for achieving an above average return.

The fundamental nature of the activity termed "security analysis" is to estimate the return obtainable from holding specific securities and in this manner identify overpriced and underpriced issues. To accomplish this task, security analysis undertakes examination and appraisal of individual companies.

The manner in which the earning power and dividend-paying capacity of individual companies are analyzed has not changed significantly over the last two decades. Although computers have provided assistance in massaging numbers, techniques for analyzing the record of sales, expenses, earnings, and dividends of a company remain for the most part unchanged. The same is true for the analysis of a company's balance sheets to determine the financial condition of the enterprise and its strengths and weaknesses.

Corporate finance officers are intimately familiar with the examination of corporate financial statements. Moreover, for the most part, the techniques are standard and are set forth at some length in a number of textbooks on investments. Accordingly, those techniques are not covered in this study. It is principally the structuring and scope of the analytical effort that the corporate officer will wish to probe in discussions with prospective and perhaps existing managers. In this connection, there are three areas in which significant changes are taking place: conditional forecasting, specification of risk, and valuation models.

As a result of the findings of modern financial theory, advances in economic and econometric models, and progress in decision theory, there have been significant developments in conditional forecasting and specification of risk.

Conditional forecasting entails explicit recognition of the fact that sales and profits of almost all business enterprises and market values of their shares are to some degree affected by (conditional on) external factors. Accordingly, the security analyst's sales, expense, earnings, and value predictions (when value is estimated by the analyst) for a company constitute in reality the resultant summation of a series of predictions. In other words, company predictions that are affected significantly by the outlook for external factors—principally the economy and the stock market—should be conditional on explicit predictions of those external factors.

Specification of risk is the new dimension of security analysis.[14] If portfolio objectives are stated in risk and return terms and if the extensive risk-return conceptual framework provided by theory is to be employed effectively in meeting portfolio objectives, it is essential that the risk inherent in individual common stocks as well as return be estimated. There is a need for careful appraisal of both market risk (beta) and nonmarket risk, including both extramarket covariance (the common factor group and industry effect) and specific risk (the unique, individual company effect). On an individual company basis, nonmarket risk averages about 70% of total risk. The question is how is this appraisal to be made.

---

[14]It is indisputable that specification of risk is an analytical function. However, because of the extensive use of statistical techniques in the analysis and estimation of particularly market risk and extramarket covariance, inclusion of appraisal and estimation of risk as a part of security analysis may be questioned by some.

A manager has three alternatives: (1) to have in-house analysts estimate risk in some form or manner, (2) to secure risk predictions from external sources, or (3) to combine the two. Nearly all management organizations are securing some type of risk estimates from external vendors. The manner in which these estimates are derived typically range from relatively simple to highly sophisticated statistical analyses of past relationships.

Some managers have their security analysts judgmentally review the betas from external sources and, if there are important reasons (principally significant near term changes resulting from a merger or other major factors) recommend modifications. Some managers require their analysts to appraise the probable accuracy of their forecasts of individual issues and in this manner estimate total risk (the sum of market and nonmarket risk). In these instances, estimation of total risk can be obtained either (1) directly from the analysts in the form of subjective judgments as to the degree of confidence that they have in each value estimate, for example, by using five or some other number of ratings, or (2) indirectly in the form of a probability distribution derived from an analyst's "best estimate" of value (or expected price change) and high and low estimates with assigned probabilities. If the analyst's efforts are centered on earnings and dividend forecasts and do not include valuation, one alternative is to judge total risk in terms of a quality rating for each company.

Valuation is the final step in the analysis and appraisal of individual common stocks. Across time, much thought has been given to methods for capitalizing expected earnings or dividends of a company to arrive at an estimated value or return on its common stock. These methods are in the form of valuation models, which are formalizations of the longer term relationships that are expected to exist between a set of corporate and economic factors and the value of the corporation's stock and thus the expected return from an investment in the stock. These models provide the linkage between principally the expected level and growth of earnings, growth of dividends, and risk and either (1) expected price and dividend yield (and thus total return) or (2) the return implicit in the current price.

A valuation model provides:

- A precise definition of the forecasts needed to value securities

- A framework for using the forecasts to arrive at explicit estimates of value or return

- An effective basis for operating in a systematic manner over time

- Assistance in evaluating analytical and predictive strengths and weaknesses of an investment organization.

Every investment organization employs one or more valuation models, although they are not always formalized. If variations are considered, there are a large number of models and much has been written about them. It is impractical to consider all of these models in this study. However, it is possible to group them roughly into two major categories: earnings models and dividend models. It is obviously impossible to value a common stock by examining solely earnings or solely dividends. However, it is necessary to capitalize one or the other in a specific valuation model.

- *Earnings models* have several different forms; a well-known one is the cross-sectional model. At the outset, it was stated that the value of a share of stock is a function of the level and growth of earnings, dividends, and risk. It could equally well be stated that the P/E ratio of a stock is a function of the growth in earnings, dividends, and risk. Cross-sectional models use regression analysis to measure the relationship at a point in time between one or more of these factors and P/E ratios of individual stocks. Alternatively, the relationship of P/E ratios of individual stocks to these factors and to the P/E ratio for the market may be appraised judgmentally across time.

- *Discounted cash flow models (DCF)* are based on the concept that the value of a share of stock is equal to the present value of the cash flows (cash dividends) that the stockholder expects to receive.[15] Most DCF models derive the present worth of future cash flows, either in terms of an estimated stream of dividends for an infinite time span or for some finite number of years plus an estimated terminal value. The DCF models can be solved for (1) an estimated value that can be compared with the current market price to determine relative attractiveness, (2) the rate of return that equates the future stream of benefits with present price and that can be compared with the rate of return considered by the investor to be appropriate, or (3) a normal P/E ratio, derived through dividing normalized earnings in the current year into the value estimate obtained from the DCF method, that can be compared with the P/E ratio at which the stock is currently selling.

---

[15]Also termed dividend discount models (DDM).

TIMING

As set forth in Chapter V, *market timing* entails changing the asset mix of a portfolio by major asset classes, such as stocks, bonds, and Treasury bills, to increase or decrease market risk (portfolio beta). Timing does not change the composition of the stock holdings or bond holdings. It is therefore *external* to those holdings.[16]

The important considerations for the corporate officer in exercising judgment on the timing function and judging a manager are the extent to which a manager uses market timing, the nature of the research supporting the timing decisions, and the probable accuracy with which the manager can predict mispricing in the security markets. It is generally held that, if employed aggressively, market timing decisions can swamp the impact of selection decisions on portfolio performance. Accordingly, this matter is of more than passing interest.

The extent to which a manager actually employs market timing can be readily determined through examination of shifts in the stock/fixed income ratio and other characteristics of representative portfolios over a span of time and through discussions with the manager. The nature of the research effort can in part be judged in terms of the methods cited earlier in this chapter. Market timing decisions can be based on market valuation methods (fundamental analysis) that provide risk-return estimates for the three principal security markets (stocks, bonds, and money market instruments) or on market price models that relate changes in stock market prices directly to changes in economic variables.

The manager's ability to predict stock price cycles and to exercise other judgments essential to successful market timing may be appraised in part from the record. However, it is emphasized that the more important ingredient in anticipating future performance is the manager's analytical and decision-making capability.

---

[16]Within limits, the market risk of a portfolio may also be adjusted by shifting the composition of the stock holdings from lower to higher beta issues or vice versa.

The findings of others provide the corporate officer with empirical evidence in assessing the difficulties of timing the market. In general terms, studies indicate that "beating the market" through timing is perhaps a more difficult and challenging undertaking than selection of individual issues. In part, this can be attributed to the fact that in selecting issues for a sizeable portfolio, a substantial number of judgments are exercised and this continues to be true as the portfolio is managed over the course of a cycle. In contrast, few market timing judgments are ordinarily exercised over a stock price cycle. This conclusion does not mean that it cannot be done but rather that its successful accomplishment requires considerable competence.[17]

Formula Plans

Primarily because of the difficulties of effective market timing, mechanistic approaches—known as formula plans—came into being. These plans had a limited span of prominence in the early postwar period.[18] Their subsequent fall from grace resulted principally from the fact that over approximately a 15-year span, the market, with only limited interruptions, moved to significantly higher levels. The stock price cycles from much of the 1950s through at least the mid-1960s were characterized by pronounced and extended periods of rise and by periods of brief and limited declines. These characteristics were significantly different from those that, with the exception of principally the 1921–33 span, prevailed over most of the period from 1871 to about 1950.

---

[17]William S. Gray, in "Index Funds and Market Timing: Harris Trust's Approach," *Trusts and Estates,* May 1976, stated that Harris Trust developed a commingled fund similar to an index of the S&P 500 to permit application of market timing decisions. By employing 110 stocks from the S&P 500, weighted according to market value and industry classification, the ex-post performance of the fund was compared to a naive portfolio with a fixed-asset mix of 75% stocks and 25% cash equivalents. (This asset mix was chosen because of a 75% average investment in common stocks and 25% in cash equivalents by the commingled fund.) The commingled fund's asset mix (common stock/cash equivalents) was changed according to the bank's historically documented cyclical timing decisions from 1966 to 1975. The result of this after-the-fact analysis showed that the commingled fund outperformed the naive portfolio in eight out of the ten years and by a cumulative difference of 16.7% (a compound annual performance differential of 1.6%).

[18]C. S. Cottle and W. T. Whitman, *Investment Timing: The Formula Approach,* McGraw Hill Book Company, New York, 1953. This book was written when formula plans had many adherents.

Although there was secular growth over the 80-year span, it was modest compared with that which existed from 1950 to 1966. Over the 1871–1950 span, price tended to plateau for a period and fluctuate about that level before moving to a moderately higher plateau. Mechanistic timing methods tend to operate most effectively in markets characterized by price fluctuations about plateaus. Accordingly, the demise of formula plans over the 1950–66 span is not surprising.

For a number of reasons, there now appears to be some reconsideration of the formula plan approach to timing. Some of the reasons advanced are:

- Over the last ten years, stock prices as judged by the S&P 500 have virtually fluctuated about a plateau.[19]

- Successful market timing is difficult to accomplish. Moreover, there appears to be some aversion by both plan sponsors and managers to placing such emphasis on timing.

- The basic element in quantified investment objectives for a pension fund is the normal stock/bond/Treasury bill proportions. There are usually constraints on the extent of departures from this normal asset mix. These asset-mix norms and constraints can be interpreted within a formula plan approach, because formula plans are based on the concept of established stock/bond ratios at market value with a rebalancing arrangement.

Reconsideration of formula plans by investors would now appear to be sufficient to warrant a review of their broad characteristics.

Formula plans constitute a mechanistic approach to market timing. There are two major types of plans: constant ratio and variable ratio. While the two major types of plans are distinct, they are both characterized by (1) incorporation of certain assumptions as to the future, (2) division of a fund into aggressive (common stock) and defensive (fixed income) portions, and (3) employment of rules whereby the stock/fixed income portions are changed.

Formula plans also have a common objective of seeking to increase the equity portion as prices decline and to decrease the portion as prices rise.

[19]A least squares regression of the logarithms of the monthly average closing prices of the S&P 500 from January 1968 through August 1979 produced a growth rate of +.01% for the entire time span. Accordingly, for this nearly 12-year period there was no predominant upward or downward trend in the S&P 500.

Fulfillment of this objective is based on the assumption that once stocks are sold (or purchased), the market will eventually reverse its current upward (or downward) movement.

Formula plans are ordinarily characterized by the trading rules specified for systematic purchase and sale of securities. There can be numerous rules that trigger adjustment of portfolio composition, but they can usually be grouped in two major categories according to their intent: to maintain a constant stock/fixed income ratio or to adjust the stock/fixed income ratio within prescribed limits.

Constant ratio plans are fully mechanistic since the objective is to maintain a predetermined stock/fixed income ratio. For example, in rising stock markets when the value of the stock portion rises above this predetermined ratio, stocks are sold and fixed income securities bought to bring the ratio back to its predetermined level. The reverse occurs in declining markets. The assumption behind the constant ratio plan is that a net gain will result from primarily selling stocks in rising markets and buying them in declining markets.

In contrast, variable ratio plans allow the portfolio's stock/fixed income ratio to fluctuate within predetermined ranges. This type of plan attempts to vary the aggressive or stock portion of the portfolio according to a set formula. Such a formula may be based on predictions using analyses of past stock prices, on an appraisal of past relationships of stock prices to one or more economic time series, or on the relationship of book value to EPS for specific stock indexes.

Options

The purpose of market timing is to "add value"; that is, to produce an additional return on a risk-adjusted basis by increasing risk (by proportionally increasing stock holdings) in bull markets and decreasing risk (by proportionally reducing stock holdings) in bear markets. The use of options also provides a basis for changing the risk exposure of the portfolio and seeking additional return. Accordingly, the role of options is included in this section on market timing.

To date, the most widespread use of option contracts in managing pension fund portfolios has been in writing covered calls. To illustrate, the portfolio manager writes (sells) a call at 50 on 100 shares of ABC in the fund for six months at a premium of $4\frac{7}{8}$ when ABC is selling at $48\frac{5}{8}$. If during the ensuing six months, ABC fluctuates in price between 45 and 50, the call will expire without value and the fund will have gained the full amount of the premium.

If ABC sells above 50, it will be called away and the fund cannot realize more than $54\frac{7}{8}$ on its investment, a limitation on gain, unless the call position is closed out by repurchase prior to exercise. If the price declines, the first $4\frac{7}{8}$ points are, of course, offset by the premium earned. Thus, an optioned stock position will have reduced exposure to variability in both directions. If the premiums are adequate (in the sense that the calls are fairly priced in relation to the volatility of unoptioned shares), the portfolio's total return will be supplemented by the options' time value as compensation for the reduction in the opportunity to attain large gains. The cushioning of declines in prices is the other contribution to stabilizing market values.

A portfolio of optioned stocks can therefore be expected to show significantly less variability in return than the same portfolio of stocks without call writing. A representative group of optioned stock portfolios under active management from April 1973 through the first quarter of 1979 showed a rate of total return well in excess of that for the S&P 500, but with a reduction of about 28% in volatility as measured by the standard deviation of return.[20]

Covered call writing is also appropriate for other purposes. If the portfolio manager is prepared to sell ABC on strength but is not anxious about making the sale, the writing of a call at 50 is appropriate with the hope that the stock will be called away. Greater eagerness to liquidate the position could be expressed by writing a call at 45, collecting the premium of $7\frac{1}{2}$ points with greater assurance that the stock will indeed be called. The realization of $52\frac{1}{2}$ (45 strike price plus the premium of $7\frac{1}{2}$) may be all that the manager expects.

Another occasion for selective covered call writing is when some or many

---

[20]The composite record of accounts managed by Analytical Investment Management Inc. of Irvine, California, for pension funds and other institutional investors. Security selection was not entailed, other than to attempt to index the underlying stocks to the S&P 500. Such results reflect, of course, the period's market environment, premium levels, and other factors.

stocks in the portfolio are believed to be fully valued. The alternative to the more drastic step of selling them is to sell the upside potential (an appreciation over the strike price) for what is considered a fair value. The conversion of possible gains into actual realization value is, of course, a conservative step in managing a stock portfolio.

Another loss-limiting device is the purchase of the stock and a put. Called a "protective put," this transaction might involve buying XYZ at $65\frac{7}{8}$ and a put at 65 for six months for $3\frac{3}{4}$. The total is now $69\frac{5}{8}$ (plus brokerage commissions) but exposure to loss is tightly limited because the stock can be put to the writer of the contract at any time during the six-month period. This protection against loss, without sacrifice of the opportunity to share in the upside potential, is another example of reducing the volatility without substantial sacrifice of return.[21]

The combination of a purchased call and liquid assets equal to the exercise price, designated a "fiduciary call," has not yet won acceptance as a prudent investment but its comparability to a convertible debenture is easily recognized. Limiting the possible loss to the amount of the call premium while acquiring the full potential return from ownership of the stock provides this combination with risk-reducing characteristics at a known price.

If a pension fund has both an assured positive cash flow and a clearly defined program for accumulating common stocks, an argument can be made for the fund to capitalize on this favorable situation by accepting premiums for writing "fiduciary puts." At the time of writing (selling) the put, the fund sets aside the cash equivalents for the purchase if the put is exercised.

For example, the fund could write a six-month put on XYZ at 65 and earn a premium of $3\frac{3}{4}$. If the buyer chose to exercise because the stock sold at 63, the writer would own it at $61\frac{1}{4}$ (65 minus the $3\frac{3}{4}$ premium). In the interval between writing and exercise, the cash equivalent would be earning the short term rate of interest.

The advantage of a listed market in any of these activities is the ability to change position in the event of new information or new objectives. The

---

[21]This concept has been well-defined by Robert C. Pozen, "The Purchase of Protective Puts by Financial Institutions," *Financial Analysts Journal,* July–August 1978.

readiness of liquid markets in option contracts to accommodate such changes has been amply demonstrated as investors have adopted this new tool to reduce variability of returns from equity portfolios.

Since the start of the listed market in options in April 1973 with the opening of the Chicago Board of Options Exchange, it has grown in size and liquidity. For the year ended June 30, 1979, the trading in options on five exchanges was the equivalent of about 80% of total trading volume on the New York Stock Exchange. Further expansion of the market and the raising of position limits are expected to enlarge the role of the market in options as a tool for managing risk in long term investment portfolios like pension funds. The experience of such investors has already paved the way for more comprehensive inclusion in the range of financial assets.

SELECTION

Security selection, like market timing, can most readily be explained in terms of common stocks. There are three reasons for this fact. First, stocks are not only more extreme in their risk-return characteristics than other asset classes but also the difference from issue to issue is greater. Second, because they have no maturity or contractual return, it has been necessary to develop passive market standards for stocks (such as the S&P 500) and these constitute more familiar frames of reference, in terms of issues and weights, than the standards for fixed income securities (the various bond indexes). Third, the amount of research on stocks has been much greater than that on fixed income securities. However, the principles set forth in the following discussion of stocks are also applicable to bonds and money market instruments.

At the outset, a manager will establish a "selection universe" of stocks. It will be that cross section or group of stocks that is considered appropriate in terms of the manager's investment style. For example, to create diversified portfolios, portfolio managers of an organization dedicated to a diversified style must be able to select issues from a universe representative of the market as a whole. In contrast, if the organization were dedicated to high growth portfolios, portfolio managers would need a selection universe concentrated in the growth sector of the market.

Stock selection must be made in terms of individual issues, because that is all that can be bought and sold. However, selection cannot be decided solely on a price basis—buying arbitrarily those stocks perceived to be most underpriced and selling those perceived to be most overpriced. In fact, for reasons of diversification, it may be desirable to buy some stocks that are not among the most underpriced. Careful consideration must also be given to the extent and nature of the risk in each issue and the expected impact on the risk-return characteristics of a portfolio resulting from its addition (or removal). To make this determination, it is necessary to consider not only *what* to buy (or sell) but also how much.

Stock selection must therefore take place within a total portfolio context. In this connection, the primary considerations are investment objectives established for the portfolio and the standard used in measuring performance. For example, if the S&P 500 is used as the standard, the weight of a given issue and its industry in the index may affect the amount of both held in the portfolio.

As the foregoing demonstrates, the selection function has three major aspects: (1) what issues are to be bought or sold—as determined by expected return and risk, (2) how much of each issue is to be bought or sold—as judged by the expected impact on the risk-return performance of the portfolio, and (3) comparison of the expected performance of the portfolio as judged in terms of both its investment objectives and the performance standard employed. In other words, stocks purchased and held should in the aggregate (giving full consideration to their comovement or covariance) create portfolios that are consistent with established objectives.

The selection function also embraces determination of industry and group weights. These decisions can be made on both a top-down and a bottom-up basis. The top-down conclusions are based on analyses of the relative attractiveness of the aggregate performance of homogeneous groups of companies (characterized by size as well as growth, stability, and cyclicality) or industries (drugs, chemicals, and oils).

The bottom-up approach is based on analysis of individual companies and provides both inputs to the group and industry decisions and a cross check on those decisions. If there are a number of attractive (or unattractive) issues in a given group or industry, a basis is provided for careful examination at the group or industry level. Contrariwise, if it is concluded that a particular group or industry is attractive and if few related companies can be found that are attractive, an effective cross check on the group or industry selection is provided.

SUMMARY

The discussion of fundamental analysis in Chapter VI rests on two premises: (1) that mispricing of securities exists in the marketplace and that fundamental analysis is essential to identification of mispriced issues and (2) that the effectiveness of timing and selection decisions depends on the accuracy of the predictions of fundamental analysis. For these reasons, it is important that the corporate executive understand the general nature of fundamental analysis and the key role it plays in the investment process. This knowledge is essential in appraising with reasonable competence the procedures and practices of a manager.

Investing can be defined as the discipline of comparative selection. To be comparative, analysis of individual companies, projection of earning and dividends, and selection of capitalization rates must all be part of a structured, consistent, and orderly process. The operations and earnings of all but a few companies depend on the overall business environment. Moreover, price movements of practically all stocks are affected by the sweeps of bull and bear markets. Thus, fundamental analysis involves a hierarchy of consistent forecasts for the economy and its major sectors, stock and bond markets, industries of investment consequence, and individual corporations and their securities.

The chapter also discusses the two major investment functions—timing and selection. Timing is examined in terms of market timing: changing the asset mix of a portfolio by major asset class, such as stocks, bonds, and Treasury bills. The nature of the judgments required in successful timing are discussed. Because timing encompasses formula plans and the use of options, these two subjects are briefly reviewed.

Security selection for construction and management of portfolios can be best explained in terms of common stocks. The principal steps in the selection process entail determining (1) the issues to be bought or sold, (2) how much of each issue to buy or sell, and (3) the resulting impact on the total portfolio.

CHAPTER

7 The Investment Process:
  Portfolio Construction
  and Management

THE NATURE OF PORTFOLIOS

From the standpoint of the pension plan sponsor, investment portfolios that constitute the pension fund (in a multimanager plan) are tangible results of investment objectives and strategies agreed on with the managers and the capabilities of the managers.[1]

From the standpoint of the managers, the portfolios are tangible results of (1) risk-return forecasts for security markets, groups of securities, and individual issues and (2) portfolio judgments exercised within the context of an established investment style. The aggressiveness of these judgments determines the amount of risk assumed in the portfolio. The amount of risk should, in turn, depend primarily on the portfolio's investment objectives, the manager's predictive accuracy, and the strength of the evidence as to present overpricing or underpricing.

---

[1]The dominant principles developed in this chapter are equally applicable to a single manager plan.

Strategic decisions usually agreed on by the sponsor and manager (and frequently included in objectives) determine the extent to which total risk in the portfolio can be increased beyond or reduced below that considered normal. As a result, in a period perceived by the manager as unusually risky in terms of marked common stock overpricing, the level of risk in the portfolio may be reduced significantly by reducing the equity portion and increasing the bond and/or Treasury bill portions (perhaps also by reducing the beta of the common stocks held). The reverse would be true in a period of perceived underpricing of common stocks.

Accordingly, in the course of a stock price cycle, timing and selection cause substantial changes in the composition of a portfolio. An understanding of the criteria that professional investment managers ordinarily apply in making changes in portfolio composition and risk is important to the plan sponsor when analyzing and interpreting portfolio results.

As noted above, both investment style and current valuation judgments (risk-return forecasts) are important determinants of the structure of a portfolio, given the constraints established by investment objectives. The relationship of portfolio structure to style is similar to that of product specification in industry with a company stating: "This is the general nature of the products that can be supplied." In investing, the products are portfolios. They can be diversified portfolios, high growth portfolios, portfolios characterized by substantial rotation among industries or sectors, and so on.

To the extent that the structure of a portfolio differs from that of the market (as a result of overweighting or underweighting sectors, industries, or individual issues) the portfolio consists of bets against the market. It is generally held that prevailing prices in the marketplace reflect consensus estimates of opportunities for return and uncertainties that accompany them. Otherwise, selling or buying pressures would force the price to different levels. Market divergent portfolio holdings can therefore be viewed as bets against consensus estimates. Only forecasts that are different from consensus forecasts and that are subsequently proved to be correct can produce an above average return on a risk-adjusted basis. Overweighting of particular sectors, industries, or companies in a portfolio relative to a market index (S&P 500) reflects the manager's conclusion that consensus forecasts of overweighted portions are too bearish and the securities are thus underpriced. In contrast, underweighting reflects the reverse conclusion and the securities are considered overpriced.

Given the manager's investment style, active portfolio management is largely a process of identifying and adjusting portfolio holdings to reflect the manager's conclusion that certain consensus forecasts are incorrect and that specific securities are overpriced and others are underpriced. The nature and size of the bets (selection of issues and extent of overweighting or under-weighting) should be controlled by the objectives and strategy governing the portfolio, the manager's forecasting capability, and the extent of apparent discrepancy between current price and estimated value.

With substantial forecasting ability and strong conviction as to the differential between price and value, composition of an actively managed portfolio can be considerably different from that of a market index (S&P 500) or some other passive standard. With lesser forecasting ability and conviction, composition should more closely approximate that of an index or passive standard.

THE PORTFOLIO CONSTRUCTION PROCESS

Pension funds almost always include portfolios of stocks, bonds, and money market instruments.[2] Money market instruments are generally treated as reserves and represent funds that can be invested in either stocks or bonds. The funds are held in high quality, short term debt instruments as an effective market timing device or as a means of managing better the cash flow of the total fund.

For the same reasons as those advanced in Chapter VI, attention in this chapter focuses primarily on the equity component of pension portfolios. However, it should be pointed out that underlying portfolio concepts are similar for stocks and bonds. In both instances, opportunity for additional return is accompanied by additional risk. Moreover, many of the same factors in the economic environment (such as inflation, business cycles, and economic uncertainty) affect potential and realized returns for bonds as well as stocks.

Because of the highly competitive nature of stock and bond markets, it is necessary to structure tightly the investment process for stocks and bonds. In this connection, particular attention must be given to predictive accuracy of the investment organization and to control of diversification in portfolios.

---

[2]In addition, some funds now include real estate holdings and other types of assets that have been relatively rare in the past. These specialized assets are not discussed in this study.

Portfolio Characteristics

An actively managed equity portfolio may be characterized in several ways. First, it consists of those stocks that, taken as a group (in a portfolio context), are considered by the manager to be more attractive and more appropriate for the sponsor than any alternative combinations of stocks from the universe under analysis. In other words, the manager has selected from the universe of stocks being analyzed those that currently appear to offer the most attractive risk-return tradeoff.

Second, the price and return experience of most equity portfolios of size is dominated by what happens to the stock market. Unless a portfolio is extremely undiversified, such as being confined to a single sector (i.e., emerging high growth companies), the risk-return pattern of the portfolio will be affected much more by risk-return characteristics of the market than by lack of diversification.

Third, as stated earlier, the composition of a portfolio is determined by forecasts that, on balance, are manifest through stock holdings that diverge from those in the market. For example, the portfolio may be overweighted in high growth companies, large companies, and those with strong financial positions relative to the same company characteristics in the total market, because it is considered that investors are currently undervaluing these stocks. The reverse logic would apply with respect to portfolio holdings that are underweighted.

The foregoing three characteristics of portfolios help one to understand major steps in the construction process. The steps are:

- Selection of issues and determination of weights (the proportion of the total portfolio to be invested in each issue, industry, and group or sector of the market)

- Diversification of holdings by number of issues, sectors, and industries (diversification can be appraised in terms of market weights, such as for the S&P 500, and in terms of the extent to which returns of industries or groups move together or covary)

- Evaluation of results of selection and diversification through determining the expected risk-return performance for the portfolio and comparing it with that expected for the market (or other selected standard).

This chapter is devoted principally to consideration of two of those three steps—(1) selection and weighting and (2) diversification. Chapters X and XI concentrate on measurement and diagnosis of achieved performance after the fact (ex-post) and expected performance before the fact (ex-ante). To provide perspective for the discussion of selection and weighting and diversification, the next two sections of Chapter VII examine (1) uncertainty or risk inherent in forecasts of returns and the tendency of investment returns to move together (covariance) and (2) sources of investment returns.

Risk, Return, and Covariance

In constructing portfolios, the manager deals with estimates and judgments of future conditions. The future cannot be anticipated with certainty; a substantial margin of error is always entailed. For this reason, uncertainty entailed in the results forecast from an investment in a specific security must also be estimated. This uncertainty is risk; it is the probability of the return on the investment being less than that expected. Thus, expected return and risk are essential analytical inputs in constructing and managing portfolios.

An additional important consideration in formation and management of portfolios is the extent to which the returns of the securities held are expected to move together because they are subject to common factors. To the extent that this comovement (or, in statistical terms, covariance) characterizes the returns, there is less diversification in the portfolio and thus more risk. In contrast, the more the movement of returns of securities held diverge because they are affected by different factors, the greater the diversification and thus the lower the risk in the portfolio. Fluctuations in the returns of one security are partially offset by different fluctuations in the returns of another security. Accordingly, covariance is an important concept in portfolio diversification and is discussed further in this chapter.[3]

---

[3]Covariance is a statistical measure of the extent to which the returns of two or more securities tend to move together. It combines the effects of correlation (correlation coefficient) among two or more variables with that of their individual variability (standard deviation).

Sources of Portfolio Return

For both stocks and bonds, the sources of portfolio return are current income, price appreciation, and return on reinvested income. Current income from high quality bonds is practically certain. Current income from common stocks is subject to a change in cash dividends but for stocks of investment quality dividends can usually be anticipated with a reasonable degree of certainty. In contrast, forecasts of the other two components of return—price change and the reinvestment rate—are subject to a considerable margin of error.

In making bond selection decisions, the portfolio manager focuses much more on the external investment environment than on internal corporate conditions. Since the coupon payment and the maturity (principal payment) are contractual, internal analysis of bonds is concerned primarily with appraising the possibility of a change in quality ratings or, in extreme circumstances, of default.

In those instances when investments are confined to high quality bond issues (typically, the top three ratings), the analytical effort and subsequent judgments by portfolio managers are centered largely on such external factors as the inflation rate, interest rates, yield curve, and spreads among issues of different quality. These factors are discussed in Chapters V and VI.

In contrast, in making stock selection decisions, the portfolio manager must give at least as much emphasis (and perhaps more) to internal corporate factors that affect return and risk as to the external economic and investment environment. Because dividends are not a contractual obligation and because the concept of maturity is irrelevant, such internal factors as a corporations's earning power and dividend-paying capacity must be examined and appraised with care. Chapter VI discusses at some length the analytical effort required in forecasting the level and growth of earnings and dividends for individual issues and choosing a capitalization rate to arrive at an estimated value.

The importance of internal corporate factors in selection of common stocks can be readily demonstrated. Common stocks have a much higher level of total risk than bonds, and the major portion of that total risk is independent of general market factors. For the average or typical stock, it is generally considered that about three-fourths of the total risk is attributable to specific company factors and distinct industry and market sector characteristics (the two types of nonmarket risk).[4] The remaining one-fourth of the risk is attributable to broad stock market factors.

SELECTION AND WEIGHTING

Risk-return characteristics of securities are the dominant considerations in forming portfolios. The key fact is that differential return is a function of differential risk. As a result, in constructing of portfolios, portfolio managers consider with varying degrees of emphasis the expected return and the estimated risk at security class, sector, industry, and issue levels. As discussed above, in selecting a bond portfolio, managers usually focus much more attention on expectation for the bond market and sectors of the market (in terms of maturity and quality) than on individual issues. The converse is true in selecting a stock portfolio.

Managers of stock portfolios are clearly aware of risk-return characteristics of stocks. Thus, they increasingly base selection decisions on risk-adjusted expectations. Knowing that expected outcomes for the sizeable list of individual stocks analyzed by an investment organization can cover a wide range, portfolio managers frequently first identify a list of candidate securities for purchase (or sale).

The next step is to decide on specific representation and weighting in the portfolio on an issue-by-issue basis. These decisions require careful consideration of the impact of security changes on the existing diversification and weighting of the portfolio.

One common approach is to use sector weights[5] in the total market as an initial guideline. For example, this could entail taking sector weights for the market as a reference and comparing with them present proporitons of the portfolio invested in growth versus cyclical stocks, large capitalization versus

---

[4]The relative proportions of market and nonmarket risk for individual issues can vary widely from this average.

[5]Issue weights are examined to determine company representation within a sector or industry.

small capitalization stocks, stocks of consumer oriented companies versus stocks of capital goods companies, and energy based stocks versus financial stocks.

Another step is to examine the composition of the portfolio from an industry standpoint—determine the percentage of the market index in drugs, chemicals, office and business equipment, and so on. The extent of the portfolio's industry diversification can be readily judged by comparing portfolio weights in each industry of consequence with those of a selected market standard (S&P 500).

In this connection, in active management of portfolios, managers will deliberately underweight or overweight specific market or economic sectors and industries. This under- or overweighting is consistent with their views of the relative attractiveness of individual stocks, industries, and sectors.

Some marginally attractive security holdings may be included in the portfolio. Experience and prudence require this diversifying tactic because of (1) the wide variability and uncertainty of expected returns of individual issues, and (2) the differing performance among securities over the course of a cycle.

Selection of issues and determination of appropriate weights have been improved by the findings of quantitative investment research. The contribution of this research to portfolio diversification and risk management is substantial. At the same time, it is emphasized that use of explicit numbers and a more sophisticated body of investment theory does not change the following basic aspects of the portfolio construction process:

- Security analysis provides estimates rather than assurances of future returns. The best of these estimates will be subject to a considerable margin of error; perfect foresight is impossible.

- Above average returns (after allowance for risks taken) require above average forecasting ability.

- The amount of risk assumed in a portfolio should be governed by a set of risk-return objectives that give consideration to both the risk aversion of the plan sponsor and the estimated forecasting ability of the manager.

- Except in portfolios concentrated in a single market sector or otherwise highly undiversified, actual risk-return performances of stock and bond markets will be by far the dominant factors in portfolio results.

DIVERSIFICATION AND PORTFOLIO RISK

Interrelationships of individual securities in a portfolio can create a risk-return pattern for the portfolio that is drastically different from a simple summation of risk-return patterns of each security making up the portfolio. Because the extent of the difference is determined largely by diversification of issues within the portfolio, it has been said that the primary investment function of a portfolio manager is diversification. Such a statement is obviously an oversimplification. In active portfolio management, it is also important for a manager to understand and respond to the different investment needs of various clients, make continuing judgments about the diverse and changing investment outlook, monitor the performance of the portfolio, and modify its composition as expectations change. Nevertheless, the above statement is indicative of the prominent role of diversification in management of portfolios.

William Sharpe, one of the principal figures in the development of modern portfolio theory, has stated the general problem of portfolio management particularly well by describing it as "making decisions involving interrelated uncertain outcomes."[6] It is generally agreed by practitioners as well as theoreticians that in investing, risk is uncertainty about future returns. (As expressed earlier, it is the likely magnitude of a shortfall in the actual return from the expected return.)

It is also generally agreed that uncertainty may be judged explicitly in terms of probabilities. The approach is illustrated in Chapter II (see Table II-1 and Chart II-1). To repeat briefly, assume that an analyst is asked to estimate the return on a specific stock. The analyst states that his or her best guess—most probable return—is 12% and that it is unlikely that the return will be less than 6% or more than 18%. Based on these estimates and the analyst's indication of the likelihood (probability) that each estimate will be

[6]W. F. Sharpe, *Portfolio Theory and Capital Markets,* McGraw-Hill Book Company, New York, 1970, p. 1. Used with the permission of McGraw-Hill Book Company.

the actual return, the risk (uncertainty) attached to the analyst's most probable estimate can be judged.

As noted in Chapter VI, investment decisions are based on a hierarchy of forecasts. Accordingly, return forecasts developed for individual stock issues depend on macroeconomic, stock market, and industry forecasts that determine the investment environment. These forecasts are interrelated. If future interest rates or economic conditions could be predicted with precision, the performance of individual issues and portfolios could be forecast with much more accuracy. However, because uncertainty exists at every level and because forecasts at a given level depend on those at the preceding level, the error factor tends to be cumulative rather than offsetting as one moves down the forecasting chain.

The forecasting problem is intensified by the fact that security markets are exceedingly competitive. A large number of competent organizations are developing risk-return forecasts, and each organization is seeking to excel. Since security prices are highly responsive to consensus views of this extensive body of forecasters and since a manager can outperform the market only by having some differential portfolio holdings (betting against the market), active management must incur additional risk in pursuit of additional return.

In view of the critical role of return and risk in portfolio construction, they are examined in the next sections.

Return Forecasts

Until a few years ago, a manager's performance was judged in terms of overall portfolio results, the "bottom line" method. This method does not explicitly deal with three factors important to a better grasp of a manager's actual and potential investment capability:

- Accuracy of the return forecasts when measured directly
- Amount of nonmarket risk takein in achieving the results
- Amount of market risk assumed.

The first measures the manager's ability to identify security mispricing. The second measures the extent to which the manager applies mispricing information in overweighting or underweighting securities within a portfolio. The third is a measure of implied market forecasting. For example, if, at the moment, market risk (the portfolio beta) is significantly greater than that for the market index (in excess of 1.0), the manager would appear to be expecting that stock prices will rise. Otherwise, he or she would not be holding an overweighted proportion of aggressive stocks that are expected to move proportionally more than the market. Conversely, if the market risk is significantly less (portfolio beta is well below 1.0), the expectation must be that stock prices will decline, because overweighted defensive stocks are expected to move less than the market.

A manager must know the forecasting ability of the investment organization.[7] The most effective method is to measure this ability directly. Otherwise, the manager has only a vague idea as to the amount of additional risk that can appropriately be assumed in pursuit of additional return. A generalized approach to measuring predictive accuracy undertakes to:

- Make explicit return forecasts for all securities that are analyzed and appraised by the investment organization

- Adjust these security forecasts for an estimated market risk component to arrive at risk-adjusted return forecasts

- Monitor subsequent actual performance periodically to determine how much better the risk-adjusted returns are than a chance distribution of returns and to develop knowledge of the effectiveness of the forecasting time horizon

- Apply the forecasts and measurement information in a risk-return context to determine how much market and nonmarket risk to assume in a portfolio with stipulated objectives.

Forecasting accuracy has been measured in a number of management organizations. If ability to forecast were perfect, the forecast returns and subsequent actual returns would be identical; the relationship as measured statistically by the correlation coefficient would be 1.0. If there were no relationship, the correlation coefficient would be zero. The results of measuring forecasts for large arrays of common stocks in a number of investment

[7]The plan sponsor should also have appraised this capability as fully as possible.

organizations typically approach 0.15 and usually range between 0.05 and 0.25.[8] Although this level of accuracy is sufficient for useful application in actively managed portfolios, the low correlation is indicative of risks entailed in common stock investing. The three types of risk (market, extramarket covariance, and specific) are discussed in preceding chapters but are examined more comprehensively here and in a portfolio context.

Market Risk

Market risk stems from underlying characteristics of the environment in which security markets operate. It is measured by the variability in annual returns of those markets. For example, as cited in Chapter II, over the 1926-78 span, the standard deviation of annual returns for stocks (based on the S&P 500) was 22.2% and for long term corporate bonds (based on Salomon Brothers High Grade Long Term Corporate Bond Index) was 5.6%. The average annual return for stocks during this period was 11.2% and for bonds was 4.1%.

The fluctuations of actual returns about these past average annual returns of 11.2% for stocks and 4.1% for bonds were substantial. In about two-thirds of the years, actual annual returns for stocks fell within a range of plus or minus 22.2% around the average of 11.2% or between 33.4% and −11.0%. For bonds, the range about the average return was 5.6% or between 9.7% and −1.5%. In about one-third of the years, the returns were outside these two ranges. These data make it clear that the return for each class of securities is subject to considerable uncertainty or risk. As one would expect, the return for stocks is much riskier than that for bonds, but it is also ordinarily higher.

A manager probably would not diversify a pension portfolio composed of domestic stocks and bonds much beyond the above two broad indexes. In a sense, the two indexes (or any other selected comprehensive indexes) can be taken as approaching the ultimate in stock and bond diversification. Thus,

---

[8]See K. Ambachtsheer, "Profit Potential in an 'Almost Efficient' Market," *Journal of Portfolio Management,* Fall 1974, and K. Ambachtsheer, "Where Are the Customer's Alpha's?" *Journal of Portfolio Management,* Fall 1977.

within the context of domestic portfolio diversification, the risks of these markets cannot be further reduced through diversification.

Most actively managed pension portfolios are less diversified than the indexes. For stocks, there will be overweighting or underweighting of market sectors, industries, or companies. For bonds, there will be overweighting or underweighting by quality, maturity, issue, or type of issue. As bets against the market, overweighting and underweighting bring additional risk. As set forth in Chapters V and VI, two components of risk unrelated to market risk are added — extramarket covariance and specific risk.

All issues are not equally sensitive to moves of the market as a whole. Moreover, the market sensitivity of single issues or even classes of issues with distinctive common characteristics often changes, as different fundamental risk attributes (e.g., financial leverage, cyclicality, or growth orientation versus dividend payout) change for the companies or become more or less important to investors as a group. For this reason and because there are generally differential holdings from those in the market index and usually a substantially smaller number of issues, a portfolio of selected issues rarely has the same market risk as a broad, capitalization weighted index.

The existence of a greater or lesser amount of responsiveness (sensitivity) to broad market price and return fluctuations of an actively managed portfolio (a beta either more or less than 1.0) than that of a market index can be thought of in two ways:

- As leverage: a beta in excess of 1.0 increases the effect on the portfolio of general price moves in the market; a beta less than 1.0 reduces the effect of general price moves.
- As an implied market forecast: the higher beta represents an attempt to achieve a higher return if the market rises; a low beta represents a buffer to the decline if the market falls.

The sensitivity of the return from individual securities and portfolios to market moves is usually related to market standard, most commonly the S&P 500. This element of return sensitivity is usually measured in terms of beta coefficient.

Beta can usually be regarded as a measure of the price sensitivity (volatility) of an individual stock or portfolio to the market. More precisely, it measures in percentage terms the extent to which, on average, the price of an issue or portfolio changes relative to a given percentage change in the price of a market index. For example, a portfolio made up of a list of securities with specific individual betas would have a beta reflecting the value weighted total. If the portfolio beta were 1.10, the portfolio's market sensitivity would be expected, on average, to be 10% greater than that of the market index. (By definition, the beta of the market index is set at 1.00.) Conversely, if the portfolio beta were 0.85, on average its price movements would be only 85% of those of the market standard.[9]

The extent to which market risk typically dominates any reasonably well-diversified portfolio can be readily demonstrated. Statistics set forth in Table VII-1 on three different equity portfolios and the S&P 500 are illustrative. The three are a large highly diversified and actively managed equity pension fund, an average for 30 equity pension fund portfolios, and a fund strongly oriented to small and medium sized growth companies.

On the basis of the data in Table VII-1, the following facts are to be noted:

- Market risk, as indicated by beta for the highly diversified fund, was nearly identical to the market standard (S&P 500), the average for 30 funds was slightly above that for the market and (as might be expected), the relatively undiversified emerging growth company fund beta was well above that for the market.

- The extent to which returns for individual portfolios would be the result of fluctuations in the market's return, as measured by the comovement (coefficient of determination or R^2), is significantly less for the growth fund than the other funds. Since R^2 can be taken as a general barometer of diversification, it is again to be expected that the growth fund would be less diversified relative to the market standard than the other funds.

- When the R^2 is less than 1.00, a residual portion of the return is caused by factors other than the market. The expected residual return is an average figure and the standard deviation indicates the likely extent of the residual return deviating from the expected value. Note that the standard deviation of the residual return rises as the R^2 declines. It is by far the highest for the emerging growth company fund.

- The percentage of total risk (total variance) attributable to the market ranges

---

[9]Beta represents an *average relationship*. For this reason and because of the other components of risk, there can be departures from the expected average in a given instance.

Table VII-1—COMPARATIVE MARKET AND NONMARKET RISK

S&P 500 and Selected Funds

Portfolio Risk Statistics	S&P 500 Market Standard	Highly Diversified Fund	Average 30 Funds	Emerging Growth Company Fund
Beta	1.00	.99	1.08	1.43
Coefficient of determination (R^2)*	1.00	0.997	0.945	0.797
Standard deviation of residual return†	0.00	1.12	4.85	13.78
Market risk				
Standard deviation#	20.9	20.8	22.6	29.9
Market variance**	436.8	432.6	510.8	894.0
Nonmarket risk				
Extramarket covariance	0.0	0.3	16.8	200.2
Specific risk	0.0	0.9	13.2	27.7
Nonmarket variance	0.0	1.2	30.0	227.9
Total risk	436.8	433.8	540.8	1121.9

*Coefficient of determination (R^2) measures in percentage terms the extent to which fluctuations in a portfolio's returns are attributable to fluctuation in market return (S&P 500). Thus, the closer that the percentage is to 1.00 the more closely the two returns move together. R^2 may be used as a measure of diversification because the more widely an equity portfolio is diversified, the more closely its return will approach that of the market.

†Standard deviation of residual return measures the extent of the likely deviation of a portfolio's residual return (actual return adjusted for market influence) from the expected mean of the independent return.

#Standard deviation measures the extent of the likely deviation of a portfolio's actual return from the expected mean or average return.

**Variance is standard deviation squared. It is used because standard deviations are not additive whereas variances are. In the table, the risk attributable to nonmarket factors needs to be added to that attributable to market factors to obtain a measure of total risk.

from 100% for the stock market (by definition it must be 100%) to 80% (894.0 divided by 1121.9) for the emerging growth company fund. (Note that even in such a deliberately undiversified fund, the risk factor is overwhelmingly dominated by market risk.)

Nonmarket risk

Active management changes the composition of stock and bond holdings in a portfolio so that the holdings do not replicate their respective market indexes. The almost inevitable result is assumption of some degree of nonmarket risk. As stated above, there are two types of nonmarket risk: extramarket covariance and specific risk. Extramarket covariance is risk resulting from the tendency of returns (after allowance for the market factor) of groups of stocks to move together (to covary) as a result of the effect of common factors. The security groupings are typically by homogeneous group or sector and by industry. Specific risk is that risk unique to an individual company.

Extramarket Covariance

Next to market risk, extramarket covariance is ordinarily the most important component of portfolio risk. It is exemplified in pronounced form by the emerging company growth fund described above. Some 18% of the fund's total risk (200.2 divided by 1121.9) is created by the manager's strong preference for companies smaller than the average of those in the marketplace and with distinctive growth characteristics. Stocks of companies with such distinctive attributes tend to move together in the marketplace. This pattern of comovement is the result of common group factors and has been termed extramarket covariance.

Long before portfolio risks were studied and estimated quantitatively, it was common practice to include in portfolios issues from a number of economically diverse industries. Exposure to a broad cross section of industries was considered prudent and concentration risky.

Subsequently, aided by availability of comprehensive statistics on components of broad market indexes, particularly the S&P 500, and by formation of specialized mutual funds, investment managers began to diversify and monitor portfolios with respect to diversification or concentration by stock groups or market sectors that cut across industry boundaries. At this stage, the most common standards were based on economic sectors; on earnings characteristics such as growth, cyclicality, or stability; and on general measures of "quality" (possibly carried over from bond ratings).

The ultimate to date in this progression toward use of the stock group or sector approach to diversification is to create an array of groups according to characteristics believed pertinent to valuation. The weights of each of these groups in a specific portfolio are compared with their respective weights in the market index (e.g., S&P 500). An example of this comprehensive group or sector analysis is shown in Table VII-2.

There are several advantages to creating security sectors in this manner. (The same concept can be used for bonds, for example, by clustering issues of different quality rating, maturity, call features, and earnings coverage.) The principal advantage is that it enables sponsors and managers to survey concentrations of assets in the fund relative to those of a market standard

Table VII-2—PORTFOLIO SECTOR ANALYSIS

	Percentage Weights		Percentage Point Difference
	Illustrative Portfolio*	S&P 500	
Growth sectors			
High growth	10.0%	15.0%	(5.0)%
Cyclical growth	25.0	23.0	2.0
Noncyclical growth	10.0	9.8	0.2
Cyclical	25.0	36.3	(11.3)
Noncyclical	30.0	16.9	13.1
Economic sectors			
Manufacturing and processing	5.1	8.9	(3.8)
Capital goods	14.0	19.2	(5.2)
Energy	22.7	18.2	4.5
General business	5.2	2.2	3.0
Transportation	0.5	1.7	(1.2)
Consumer—basic	15.6	12.3	3.3
Consumer—discretionary	11.0	15.4	(4.4)
Finance	8.5	5.8	2.7
Housing	0.4	2.8	(2.4)
Utilities	17.0	13.5	3.5
Market rist sectors			
1 (Lowest)	60.1	58.2	1.9
2	18.2	17.5	0.7
3	13.9	12.2	1.7
4	7.1	9.2	(2.1)
5 (Highest)	0.7	2.9	(2.2)
Size (market capitalization)			
Smallest quintile	0.4	1.8	(1.4)
4th quintile	4.8	5.2	(0.4)
3rd quintile	12.0	9.3	2.7
2nd quintile	18.1	15.2	2.9
Largest quintile	64.7	68.5	(3.8)

*Hypothetical portfolio compared with average weights of the S&P 500 during the quarter ending March 31, 1979.

according to attributes that are considered important to subsequent performance. It also is compatible with certain types of return forecasting and useful in judging the consistency of portfolio structure with the forecasts. For example, an organization that rotates investments from one sector to another and thus places considerable emphasis on forecasting the relative market performance of stocks in different economic or market sectors would certainly find sector figures useful.

Stock sector diversification, either in this form or in the more traditional industry categories, has one major deficiency. It does not provide explicit, quantitative information on the overall degree of diversification, because the covariance relationships among the issues, industries, and sectors remain unknown. For this reason, issues may be held with only a general and qualitative idea as to the level of diversification in a portfolio.

The problem of statistically measuring and classifying expected extramarket covariance in a stock portfolio in an efficient manner was first solved by Barr Rosenberg in the early 1970s. The approach is technical but straightforward. First, Rosenberg and his associates identified financial and economic risk characteristics that seem to account for the observed clustered performance of stock market sectors. They were able to identify seven broad "risk descriptor" categories:

- Market variability
- Earnings variability
- Low valuation or unsuccess
- Immaturity and smallness
- Growth orientation
- Financial risk
- Industry (SIC classifications).

Not surprisingly, companies were found to exhibit mixtures of these characteristics and to reflect them in various degrees, rather than the simple all or nothing pattern implied by earlier diversification clusters. The next step was to express them quantitatively to permit computer manipulation of the complex covariance relationships.

The approach taken was to use the frequency distribution of each factor in the total market index as the norm, calculating the average as the normal value and the full range of values above and below the mean as the expected distribution. For example, a company's stock might be characterized as about at the average level of the market in financial risk, significantly higher in growth orientation, and (if fairly large) substantially below the mean in smallness.[10] (A small company would obviously be above average in smallness.)

For a list of stocks in a portfolio, the positive and negative values of individual stocks around the market average for each risk descriptor tend to offset each other. In a fully diversified portfolio (such as an index fund), positive and negative values would sum to zero, meaning no bias for or against any particular form of extramarket covariance. In an undiversified portfolio, such as the fund oriented to small growth companies in Table VII-1, pronounced differences would exist. For instance, the fund would be heavily overweighted in terms of immaturity and smallness and growth orientation.

Specific Risk

The remaining portion of a portfolio's total risk, other than market risk and extramarket covariance, is specific risk. The amount of specific risk in a portfolio is determined by: (1) the unique characteristics of individual companies whose stocks are held, (2) an inadequate representation of important companies that are in the market index, and (3) number of securities in the portfolio. These points are discussed below.

The profit performance and status of every company is unique to some degree. Specific risk is attributable to unique factors that affect only a single company and are independent across companies. Risk can result from failure of a product, a lawsuit, an ineffective marketing strategy, a change in top management, or a host of other factors.

---

[10]Expressed in terms of standard deviations, the following numbers could be illustrative:

0.0 — Financial risk
1.5 — Growth orientation
0.6 — Immaturity and smallness.

Since the market index is the standard in judging diversification, the extent to which large and important companies are represented needs to be considered. For example, the 100 largest companies in the S&P 500 account for almost 70% of its total market value. If some of the largest of these with especially distinctive characteristics are missing or significantly underweighted in a portfolio, it may be difficult to duplicate their impact on the portfolio with other holdings. As a result, specific risk can be incurred by either underweighting or overweighting in a portfolio.

The final source of specific risk in a portfolio is a limited number of individual issues. In a diversified portfolio, as the number of issues is increased, the variability of portfolio return attributable to price fluctuations in individual issues unrelated to market movements declines rapidly. A well known study found that 95% of the "achievable reduction in standard deviation" (total risk) is obtained by holding 32 randomly selected stocks.[11] These figures are valid but they can give a misleading impression of the effect of diversification on portfolio risk. They do not reveal the fact that the risk remaining may be significant even though most of the risk in excess of that caused by the market has been eliminated. A more recent study has pointed out that, because of nonmarket risk, a substantially larger number of stocks than 32 is needed to avoid large deviations from market returns.[12]

Underdiversification (concentrating holdings in a limited number of issues) when based on forecasts of mispricing can create an opportunity for additional return. In fact, as explained later, it is one of the ways in which investment managers seek to outperform the market. However, concentrating holdings that create underdiversification also creates additional risk.

CRITERIA FOR PORTFOLIO CONSTRUCTION

Optimum Risk-Return Combinations

In constructing portfolios, there is a balancing of expected return with perceived risk in every investment decision. The foregoing discussion of risk

[11]L. Fisher and J. H. Lorie, "Some Studies of Variability of Returns on Investments in Common Stocks," *Journal of Business,* April 1970.

[12]J. G. McDonald, "Investment Objectives: Diversification, Risk and Exposure to Surprise," *Financial Analysts Journal,* March-April 1975.

and its components brought out the fact that diversification reduces variability of returns by investing in a number of different securities so that some of their price variations cancel out. Returns on individual bonds as well as stocks tend to move up and down together systematically with market indexes, making it impossible to eliminate risk entirely. However, diversification reduces nonmarket risk. Nonmarket risk components can be reduced as much as desired or tilted toward sector and company characteristics where the expected additional return more than compensates for the expected additional risk.

Securities in the marketplace offer a wide range of returns and risks. As a result, there are sets of portfolios appropriate for all kinds of investors, from the most conservative to the most aggressive. Given the range of possibilities, managers seek to construct portfolios that provide the plan sponsor with an optimum combination of expected return and estimated risk. Rather than trying to maximize return by investing in a single favorite security or favorite short list and thereby assuming the substantial risk entailed, managers seek to select from the alternatives available a combination of issues that provides an optimum risk-return tradeoff. A combination that provides the highest return for a prescribed level of risk is optimum. In the terminology of modern portfolio theory, such an optimum combination is an "efficient portfolio."

CHART VII-1—THE EFFICIENT FRONTIER OF ALL-EQUITY PORTFOLIOS

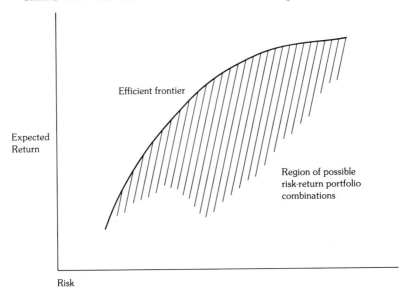

Efficient frontier

Expected
Return

Region of possible
risk-return portfolio
combinations

Risk

Investment managers seek to determine the highest level of expected return for a portfolio attainable at whatever risk level has been designated by an investor. A conservative investor will tolerate only limited risk and accept lower returns to attain it. An aggressive investor will tolerate much more risk in anticipation of much higher returns. For each level of risk, there must be a combination of securities that will provide the maximum return (an efficient portfolio). Since there is a risk spectrum, there is also a spectrum of efficient portfolios. In modern portfolio theory terms, this portfolio spectrum is known as the *efficient frontier.*

Chart VII-1 provides a graphic conceptualization of the efficient frontier for all-equity portfolios. As anticipated, the expected return increases as the risk increases.

Approaches to constructing efficient portfolios have received considerable attention from researchers over the last two decades.[13] As set forth earlier in this chapter, the key inputs to portfolio decisions are expected return and estimated risk and covariances of individual issues.

Although the technique or methodology is relatively straightforward, actual construction is difficult because it is fraught with uncertainty. Portfolio decisions must be based on judgments about the future. Advances in techniques and procedures have provided an important conceptual and analytical framework within which to undertake construction of efficient portfolios. However, much depends on the predictive accuracy of the management organization and the effectiveness with which predictions are used. The plan sponsor needs to appraise these all-important factors as fully as possible.

Selecting Securities in a Portfolio Context

The security valuation process provides estimates of future returns for individual issues and selected groupings of companies by industries or

---

[13]See H. M. Markowitz, *Portfolio Selection: Efficient Diversification of Investments,* the Yale University Press, New York, 1959; W. F. Sharpe, *Portfolio Theory and Capital Markets,* McGraw-Hill Book Co., New York, 1970, and K. V. Smith, *Portfolio Management,* Holt, Rinehart & Winston, Inc., New York, 1971.

otherwise. Using these estimates, evaluated common stock issues can be ranked according to expected return. Either directly, based usually on the analyst's judgment, or indirectly, by using external organizations, estimates of market risk can be assembled for the same securities. By adjusting return estimates for expected market risk, a ranking of issues by risk-adjusted return is possible.

The next step in the selection process is to identify underpriced and overpriced issues on the ranking list. Securities should be selected and combined into portfolios reflecting underpricing and overpricing judgments and having composite portfolio risk-return characteristics appropriate in terms of established investment objectives.

In constructing efficient portfolios, it is important that:

- The selection process be unbiased and symmetrical; just as capable of identifying an overpriced security as an underpriced one

- The list of securities be representative of the market as a whole or, at least, of the standard that will be used for judging relative risk and return and measuring performance

- The manager have some general or, preferably, explicit idea of his or her forecasting ability, because the justification for taking additional risk is the expectation of more than compensating additional return

- The ranking of securities by expected returns progresses from those that are clearly believed to be underpriced, through a gray area, to those that are clearly believed to be overpriced.

If a manager combines into portfolios only those securities considered underpriced, the diversification will probably be inadequate. Moreover, the manager is not taking advantage of the useful information in the form of fairly valued securities in the "gray area." These securities could be used to secure an average return and to reduce risk in the portfolio by increasing diversification.

If a more comprehensive approach is taken to selection of individual securities in a portfolio context, the manager may start with the full list and use initial weights identical to those of the same stocks, industries, or sectors as they exist in the market. Using these market weights as norms, the manager adjusts the proportions according to relative risk-return expecta-

tions, overweighting those perceived to offer the most attractive risk-return
tradeoff, underweighting or omitting those with the least favorable risk-return
expectations, and choosing some in proportions about equal to those in the
market standard where the value is neutral.[14] Using this approach, a higher
level of portfolio diversification will almost surely be achieved, thereby
reducing nonmarket risk. Equally important, all three categories of security
valuation ratings—overpriced, underpriced, and fairly priced—are used.

However, except at the individual security level, the manager has not dealt
explicitly with risk. Relationships among securities can only be inferred in a
general qualitative way based on their weighting relative to market norms. In
this connection, portfolio risk analysis systems, such as the one used in
calculating the data for Table VII-1, are available and can provide a manager
with the amounts and types of risk his or her manual portfolio construction
process has incurred. If desired, the security selections or weights can be
modified to adjust the risks. In doing so, the manager brings risk elements of
the portfolios under positive control.

A manager more familiar with modern portfolio theory and computer
applications might take a slightly different approach. Given a list of expected
returns and risks for securities and knowing a sponsor's portfolio objectives in
terms of risk and return, he or she would enter the data into a computer
terminal for processing by a portfolio optimization program. Because some
results are distorted unrealistically by extreme values and because there may
be other policy constraints on the positions indicated as desirable by such a
system, the manager would manually edit the output or specify constraints
before running the program a final time. Although this requires surrendering
the balancing of the three key variables (estimates of return, risk, and
covariance) to the computer, the remainder of the process is completely
under the manager's control. In contrast, if the manager wants to reserve
more control, such a system can be used for trial runs and modification of the
portfolio completed judgmentally.

INDEX FUNDS

An index fund is a fund constructed so that its risk and return patterns are
identical to or closely replicate those of a selected market index or other

---

[14]"Neutral" in the sense that the issue is considered neither overpriced nor underpriced.

standard. Most commonly a market index, particularly the S&P 500, is used but, depending on the fund's purpose, either a broader or narrower standard could be employed.

Two features of index funds are distinctive. First, there is little or no selection and absolutely no forecasting of return or risk. The fund holds every security in the index and in the same proportion as their respective weights in the index, or a sampling system is adopted that is so effective that risk and return patterns of the market are replicated. Second, if the fund is perfectly diversified with respect to the market index, only market risk remains.

Index funds are the product of two theories that grew out of investment research of the last two decades. First, there is the efficient market hypothesis (discussed in Chapter VI) that markets are so efficient in pricing securities that it is exceedingly difficult, if not impossible, to out-perform them. Second, there is a portfolio theory that suggests the desirability of eliminating all except the market component of risk through diversification and achieving the desired risk-return combination for each investor solely by combining index funds representing asset classes, particularly stocks and money market instruments.

A high degree of market efficiency has been demonstrated, but the concept of *perfect* market efficiency (strong form of the efficient market hypothesis) is being increasingly questioned by empirical evidence. Although the market is extremely competitive, the authors of this study do not concur in the conclusions of the strong form of the efficient market hypothesis. Similarly, the concept of meeting all investors' needs through a mixture of index funds representing asset classes, including borrowing at a low rate, seems more a theoretical ideal than a practical reality. Thus, factors other than theory probably better explain the use of index funds by pension plans in the United States.

Many professionally managed equity funds have been and are still so constructed that their portfolio betas (market risk) exceed 1.0 most of the time. Accordingly, in a sharply declining market, such as that in 1973–74, the leveraged sensitivity of such funds to a market decline caused their market values to decline more sharply, thereby depressing even the long term rate of return below that of the most commonly accepted market index, the S&P 500.

In many cases, the depth of the decline in market value of these funds in 1973-74 and their failure to recover in line with the market index during 1975-77 was exacerbated by another common characteristic that prevailed from about 1965—an overweighting of the growth stock sector of the market. Given these two powerful and unsuccessful biases of managed funds during the period, it is not surprising that it could be demonstrated that an unmanaged, passive index fund could have performed better than many actively managed funds and with lower management fees and transaction costs.

The unfavorable performance of many actively managed funds may have provided more initial impetus to index funds than the theories cited above. This conclusion does not negate the soundness of much of modern portfolio theory or limit the legitimate and imaginative applications that passive or index investing may have in the future.

The limitations of index investing are easy to outline. It gives up any potential value of informed forecasts different from and better than those of the consensus of investors, whose judgments are reflected in prevailing prices. It also limits, except within the boundaries of asset mix, the opportunity to tailor or customize a fund according to particular preferences of an investment client or plan sponsor. This latter point does not mean that index funds more imaginative than those based on strict replication of the S&P 500 or some other broad market index cannot be designed. (In fact, as indicated below, such is now beginning to occur.) However, problems of designing appropriate standards and controlling actual portfolios by standards other than those now available for a broad market index are substantial. There is a final important problem. Just as some investors turned to index funds when the S&P 500 outperformed many actively managed funds, there is the hazard that in the future they are likely to seek the pattern of investment currently providing the most favorable performance. Until the value of consistency and the merits of risk adjustment are fully understood, there will always be some who try to get into the latest game in town.

The two main advantages cited above for index funds are their consistent performance relative to the same market standard used in asset-mix simulations and corporate pension planning and their low cost. The certainty of performance, it should be emphasized, is only relative to that of the index. However, two other advantages of passive management may be more significant in the long run. The first is the efficient, low cost achievement of a high degree of diversification. The second is appropriateness of the nonselective investment response under conditions where there is no convincing or identifiable evidence of security mispricing.

Index funds are still in an early stage of development. Two new aspects that should be mentioned are use of a market index fund as a core portfolio in a large multimanager fund and development of new types of index funds.

Some plan sponsors have placed a portion of a large multimanager fund in a low cost, market-oriented index fund. The concept is to have a fully diversified core that will provide a return almost identical to the market. The noncore portion is then allocated among a selected group of active managers with less constraint on the investment holdings of the individual active managers.

The first index funds sought only to copy the S&P 500. They are still the prevalent type, with perhaps $8 billion to $9 billion invested by mid-1979. Two new types of stock index funds were recently introduced. The first type consists of international index funds, described in more detail in Chapter VIII. The second is essentially an S&P fund modified to achieve a higher proportion of its total return as dividend yield, rather than capital gain. The yield-biased index fund concept stems from studies indicating that preferential U.S. tax treatment of capital gains compared with dividends has tended to make growth slightly less attractive and dividend income slightly more attractive for tax-exempt investors, such as pension funds.

If tax-paying investors value $1.00 of capital gain slightly higher than $1.00 of dividend income to allow for the tax penalty and a sufficient number translate this into investment action, the impact of this action on the stock market could create an attractive opportunity for tax-exempt investors. There is supporting evidence for the concept but it is not free of controversy. Looking to the future, two factors should be mentioned. First, if enough tax-exempt investors bias their portfolios to emphasize yield, higher yielding securities could, on average, increase in price until the extra return opportunity would be priced away. Second, if the tax treatment of dividends is changed, as it was in West Germany a few years ago, the relative pricing of growth and dividends would also be affected.

Another development is the creation of bond index funds. They are less common and have attracted less investor interest than equity index funds. Bond index funds are discussed in Chapter V.

SUMMARY

This chapter stresses the fact that pension portfolios are the tangible results of (1) investment objectives and strategies established for the total pension fund and for individual managers and (2) capabilities of the managers. The strategic decisions usually agreed on by the sponsor and manager determine the extent to which total risk in the portfolio can be increased beyond or reduced below that considered normal. For example, in a period perceived by the manager as unusually risky in terms of marked common stock overpricing, the level of risk may be reduced significantly by reducing the equity portion and increasing the bond and/or Treasury bill portions. The reverse would be true in a period of perceived underpricing of stocks.

Insofar as the composition of a portfolio—in terms of its equity or bond holdings—differs from that of stock or bond markets, the portfolio contains bets against the market. Given a manager's investment style, active management is largely a process of identifying and adjusting portfolio holdings to reflect the manager's conclusions as to overpricing of individual securities and groups of securities in the marketplace.

The risk-return characteristics of securities are the dominant considerations in the formation of portfolios. The key fact is that a difference in return is a function of a difference in risk. As a result, portfolio managers carefully consider expected return and expected risk at the security class, sector, industry, and issue levels. They also give equal consideration to interrelationships of individual securities in a portfolio, because those relationships can create a risk-return pattern for the portfolio that is drastically different from a simple summation of risk-return patterns of each security.

The chapter concludes with an examination of index funds (passive funds). These funds are constructed so that their risk-return patterns are identical to or closely replicate those of a selected market index or other standard. Most index funds have sought to copy the S&P 500. However, index or passive funds are relatively new investment vehicles and further development can be expected in both their use and form. For example, in some large multimanager funds, an index fund has been used as a core portfolio. Also some new types of passive funds have been developed, such as international index funds and dividend tilt funds.

CHAPTER

8 International Common Stock Diversification

In recent years, there has been a growing interest in foreign securities and considerable research has been undertaken on attributes of foreign security holdings. Accordingly, this chapter provides corporate officers considering whether to diversify internationally the investment holdings of their pension funds with a review of key factors affecting the decision. To make the review meaningful, it is in sufficient depth to provide a basis for a preliminary judgment on the merits of foreign securities.

The key factors may be grouped under three major headings: (1) benefits, (2) deterrents, and (3) available forms of international diversification. The focus is on common stocks, because this class of assets most distinctively shows the different risk and return patterns from one country to another and, hence, the most effective diversifying characteristic.[1]

The first group of factors, the principal benefits of international diversification, stem largely from the extent to which returns on stocks in various countries move independently of one another. They also stem from the effects of these relatively independent patterns on risk-return characteristics of the total equity holdings of a fund when even a *small* international component is added to an otherwise purely domestic portfolio and on the

---

[1]The subject of funding local pension obligations with local investments in various countries is not included, because it is more often a legal requirement or matter of general policy than a discretionary investment decision.

differential absolute rates of return among countries. Differential returns among countries, as among domestic companies and industries, result from such familiar economic and financial factors as differences in growth rates in population and gross national product, patterns of investment and taxation, resources, profit attributes, and domestic business cycle influences. However, it must be recognized that independent patterns of return—the factor that most favors international diversification and smoothes portfolio returns— naturally causes returns on international portfolios to differ year by year from those of purely domestic funds or domestic market indexes.

The second group of factors—deterrents—encompasses primarily political and currency risks. Sovereign nations can, and from time to time do, handicap the free flow of investment funds across their borders, investment by foreigners, and private ownership of certain business enterprises. Varying rates of currency exchange also impact international investment results, both positively and negatively, introducing an extra and unfamiliar variable. There are also several lesser risks, including such economic or psychological handicaps as higher management and transaction costs in many cases, strangeness, and complexity.

The third group of factors, available management forms for an internationally diversified fund, focuses on the differences between active and passive management. Passive management means primarily the use of international index funds, while active management normally includes greater or lesser degrees of selection and shifting of investments among markets, currencies, and security issues or sectors within each market. The basic issue is how to structure a program using either or both of these styles of management so as to maximize the likelihood of achieving the desired investment objective— presumably maximum return for a given level of risk.

Both forms of management are available today. Although the passive or index fund approach is relatively new, it rests on a rather solid base of financial research and results to date have generally been in accord with expectations. Actively managed international portfolios are established investment vehicles for pension investing. The choice of particular active management styles can be based largely on the same considerations that apply in a domestic context. Realism, objectivity, and thorough understanding of the long term risk-return record of diversified foreign portfolios are important factors for a plan sponsor in weighing the merits of internationally diversified funds.

BENEFITS OF INTERNATIONAL DIVERSIFICATION

Diversification is the key to tailoring risk-return characteristics of a portfolio to investment objectives of a pension plan sponsor. As pointed out in Chapters V and VII, when the returns on different securities do not move in lock-step (the comovement or correlation is not high), the opportunity exists to reduce portfolio risk through combining a number of these different securities. This fact is well recognized among the principal asset classes in U.S. security markets—stocks, bonds, and money market instruments. These asset classes have risk and return patterns that differ significantly in both magnitude and cyclical phasing. As a result, their investment performance characteristics are not closely related (the correlation is relatively low). By combining the three asset classes, risk-return characteristics of a portfolio can be tailored to meet a pension fund's particular investment objectives.

Although patterns of risk and return for equities in different foreign markets are not so distinctively different as among, say, domestic equities and money market instruments, evidence indicates that systematic international diversification of portfolio investments plays an effective role in tailoring risk-return characteristics of a pension fund. Available evidence also suggests that addition of an international component to an otherwise purely domestic equity portfolio should result over a span of years in a higher return at a given level of portfolio risk or, alternatively, a lower level of risk for an expected level of return. In the following pages, the logic and evidence in support of international diversification are examined and consideration is given to deterrents to international investing.

Three types of evidence are presented here regarding benefits of international diversification of investment portfolios:

- The extent to which common stock returns in various countries move independently of one another

- Levels of return for simulations of internationally diversified portfolios based on market indexes

- Actual performance of international portfolios.

Independence of Common Stock Returns

As noted in Chapter V, individual stocks have three types of risk: market risk, which is associated with the course of the market as a whole; extramarket covariance, which is associated with the tendency of groups of stocks with common factors to have similar movements of returns (after allowing for the market factor); and specific risk, which is associated with risk factors unique or specific to individual companies.[2] (Extramarket covariance and specific risk combined constitute nonmarket risk.)

Most of these latter two types of risk can be diversified away in portfolios, but some small measure of extramarket covariance and specific risk typically remains. The greater the tendency of securities making up a portfolio to show independent patterns of risk and return, the more effective diversification becomes. The function of diversification is to protect against unanticipated fluctuations of return by incorporating in a portfolio securities with offsetting extramarket and specific risk characteristics.

In a single national market context, market risk remains because it is an inherent, inescapable feature of the asset class in its particular domestic market environment and a function of the nation's economic and financial system. Accordingly, it cannot be diversified away.

At this point, particular risk-return benefits of international diversification can enter the equation. Each foreign stock market has, to some degree, its own distinctive risk and return pattern; as a result, many market movements are not closely related to each other. These markets not only have their own distinctive national characteristics as to magnitude of fluctuations, trading conditions, investor composition, and responsiveness to domestic and international economic, financial, and political conditions, but also these economic

---

[2]Risk is discussed here in terms of common stocks because they are the focus of the chapter.

and other domestic conditions themselves will ordinarily differ from country to country.

Countries, like companies and industries, grow and prosper, experience the effects of economic cycles and changing supply and demand conditions, mature, decline, and undergo political and social change in different ways and on different time sequences. The explanations for these differences among nations lie in their diverging and sometimes unique resources and marketing positions, cultures, governments, patterns of savings, investment, taxation and regulation, education, productivity, and general adaptability to the changing world environment.

In each country, security markets reflect these national and international conditions through risk and return patterns appropriate to the investment climate, with higher returns generally accompanying greater rates of economic growth, change, and uncertainty. Moreover, the predominantly national orientation of investors and other conditions or attitudes are also factors in keeping foreign markets from becoming fully integrated. Despite any common world influences, most national markets show relatively high degrees of independent movement.

Therefore, there is an opportunity for meaningful diversification across countries and the importance of this fact is stressed. When stock investments reasonably representative of a national market are made in each of several national markets and combined in a single portfolio, risk is typically reduced below that for any single national market. This result is conceptually the same as that which results from diversifying across individual securities in the domestic market to reduce the nonmarket risks inherent in individual issues. A less risky total portfolio is created, because extreme swings in returns are moderated.

Since the combined return of the portfolio is the sum of individual returns of each market weighted by its proportion of the total assets in the entire portfolio, portfolio return is typically achieved at a reduced level of risk, compared with holding only one market.

The extent of the reduction in market risk depends on the extent to which returns of national markets move independently of one another. Markets in which returns are closely related, such as Canada and the United States (highly correlated markets), are less effective diversifiers. In contrast, markets with low correlation, that is, little tendency to move in the same direction at the same time, are effective diversifiers. This fact can be established by a simple example.

Imagine a highly exaggerated situation with two securities (A and B) that have identical return patterns but are one year out of phase with each other. Each returns nothing in one year, but a 20% return in the following year for an average annual return of 10% over a two-year span. If Security A earns a 20% return in odd-numbered years and B earns 20% in even-numbered years, the combination of A and B in a portfolio in equal weights will result in a level annual return of 10% for the portfolio. The negative correlation of the returns of A and B eliminates the variability of the portfolio's annual return. Although the mean of the annual returns remains constant at 10%, over a number of years the compound rate of return of the diversified portfolio is improved, as illustrated by the following figures:

| | Years | | | | | | Six-Year |
	1	2	3	4	5	6	Rate of Return
Security A	20%	0%	20%	0%	20%	0%	9.54% per year
Security B	0	20	0	20	0	20	9.54 per year
Portfolio	10	10	10	10	10	10	10.00 per year

This hypothetical example of two stocks with independent returns illustrates an important point. Effective diversification can reduce the variability or risk of a portfolio, leave the average annual return unaffected, and improve the longer term compound rate of return.

If returns of different national equity markets are to some extent independent of one another, the foregoing demonstrates conceptually in risk and return terms the primary reason for international diversification. But to what extent are market returns actually independent among countries? Fortunately, there is a substantial body of empirical evidence on this subject.

Numerous studies provide information on the degree to which returns on common stocks in countries have moved independently of one another, and thus provide a basis for appraising the extent to which risk can be reduced through international diversification. Most of the studies focus on relationships between broad market indexes; however, a few also examine relationships among returns on individual stocks. The general conclusion of these studies is that movements of different markets have been sufficiently distinct to allow substantial risk reduction beyond that attainable by portfolio diversification within a single national market.

As described in earlier chapters, the variability of annual returns, expressed as standard deviation around the mean annual return (or variance—standard deviation squared) is generally accepted as the most useful quantitative measure of risk. Currency exchange risk and political or "sovereign" risk are special topics in international investing and are treated separately later.

Using return variability as a proxy for risk, Table VIII-1 shows that during the 1973-77 period, which spanned the OPEC oil embargo and widespread economic disruption in the world, the United States and several major industrial countries showed generally similar levels of stock market risk. Only the United Kingdom, with a standard deviation of returns at 41.0% and France, at 26.4% were notably higher. Other studies, covering different and much longer periods, show generally similar patterns. The ranking of countries changes, but broad equity market indexes based on market capitaliza-

Table VIII-1—RISK MEASURES FOR FOREIGN MARKET PORTFOLIOS*

Country	Annualized Standard Deviation of Returns#	Correlation With U.S. Market†	Market Risk (Beta) from U.S. Perspective	Minimum Risk Premium from U.S. Perspective
France	26.4%	.50	.71	4.3%
Germany	20.4	.43	.47	2.8
Japan	20.1	.40	.43	2.6
The Netherlands	21.9	.61	.72	4.6
Switzerland	22.7	.63	.77	4.7
United Kingdom	41.0	.51	1.13	6.8
United States	18.5	1.00	1.00	6.0

*All figures estimated from data for the 1973-77 period.
#Measured in U.S. dollars.
†The S&P 500 is used to represent the U.S. market.
Source: D. R. Lessard, "An Update on Gains from International Diversification," unpublished, 1977. The basic approach is outlined in Lessard, D. R., "World, Country, and Industry Relationships in Equity Returns," *Financial Analysts Journal,* January-February 1976.

tion (shares outstanding times price) generally show approximately compara-ble levels of riskiness except at times or in places of unusual disruption, growth differential, and uncertainty. However, the correlation of each of the foreign markets listed in Table VIII-1 with the U.S. market (represented by the S&P 500) is modest.

The modest correlations of foreign markets with the U.S. market shown in Table VIII-1 are surprising in view of the fact that 1973–77 was a time of energy crisis, recession, and only partial recovery throughout most of the industrialized nations. In such a period, one could expect common fundamen-tal influences to dominate all or most security markets. However, the fact that the returns of individual foreign markets did not move closely with those of the U.S. market (S&P 500) made international diversification effective for a U.S. investor.

This phenomenon can be viewed in another way. The column labeled "Market Risk (Beta) from U.S. Perspective" indicates beta for the foreign market measured relative to the S&P 500 and thus indicates how adding a portfolio representing each foreign market would affect the risk level of a portfolio replicating the S&P 500 (beta of 1.00). Since in all cases, except the United Kingdom, the betas were less than 1.00, addition of the foreign market component would reduce the portfolio beta. The addition of a Japanese component would have had the greatest effect, because its beta (.43) is the lowest among these markets.

Although it was not closely correlated with the U.S. market in this unusual period, the U.K. market was somewhat more extreme in its reaction to economic and other forces, and its high market risk would have added to that of a U.S. portfolio, rather than moderated it. Other studies confirm that an aberration of this type is unusual; the effect of most international diversifica-tion programs on a domestic portfolio would be to reduce market risk. However, such aberrations in typical patterns of risk, just as in return, illustrate why it is important to invest in a number of foreign markets, rather than only one, to improve the probability of achieving expected benefits.

Table VIII-2 shows how the correlation of seven important foreign markets with the S&P 500 has varied in different periods during the past two decades. As a result of growing international economic interdependence and increased comparability in living standards, it is doubtful that the low correlations of the

Table VIII-2—CORRELATION OF MAJOR FOREIGN MARKETS WITH THE U.S. MARKET*
SELECTED PERIODS#

Country	1961–65	1964–68	1967–71	1970–74	1973–77†	July 1971–June 1973	July 1973–June 1975	July 1975–June 1977
Canada	.828	.830	.813	.836	.727	—	—	—
France	.364	.016	.081	.349	.499	-.240	.683	.392
Germany	.563	.120	.343	.349	.431	.161	.487	.500
Japan	.181	.070	.224	.301	.396	.364	.293	.727
The Netherlands	.695	.602	.570	.463	.609	.154	.671	.618
Switzerland	.559	.346	.532	.501	.629	.148	.689	.718
United Kingdom	.428	.187	.278	.483	.507	.312	.596	.256

*The S&P 500 is taken to represent the U.S. market, measured in U.S. dollars
#Based on monthly changes in value-weighted market indexes.
†Through June 1977, 54 observations.
Source: Computed by Rowe Price-Fleming International, Inc. from stock market data reported in *Capital International Perspective*, Capital International, S.A., Geneva, Switzerland.

last half of the 1960s will return. At the same time, it is difficult to expect that comprehensive international diversification will not continue to reduce portfolio risk substantially. Canada constitutes a possible exception. It has shown the closest conformance with U.S. market patterns. It also illustrates another important point. Solely in terms of diversification benefits, the greatest effect for each dollar invested abroad will come from the market whose returns have the lowest correlation with those of the U.S. market. Viewed from this standpoint, among these major countries, the Japanese market would have been the most effective diversifier; the Canadian market would have been the least effective.

Levels of Return

Investors are naturally more familiar with return statistics than with quantified measures of risk and diversification, which are recent developments in investment management. It would make little sense to consider a program of international diversification just to change portfolio risk patterns if returns in overseas markets were distinctly inferior or undependable relative to those in the United States. Neither has been the case. Table VIII-3 shows the annual return, year-by-year, and the compound rate of return for the U.S. and ten significant foreign markets for the 1969-78 decade. In no year did the U.S. stock market lead the list, and its compound return was next to the lowest (Australia). The data in Table VIII-3 have been adjusted for exchange rate movements relative to the U.S. dollar and are therefore affected by the weakness in the dollar after fixed exchange rates were abandoned in 1971.

Chart VIII-1 shows that the ten-year rates of return, without the dollar conversion effect, were generally related to rates of growth in real gross national product. The failure of dollar exchange weakness to explain dominant parts of the differences in total rates of return for a U.S. fund investing internationally is made clearer in Chart VIII-2. This chart separates experienced returns into three components: capital value change (appreciation or depreciation in market value), dividend income, and currency gain or loss. Only in Switzerland, West Germany, and The Netherlands was monetary strength versus the dollar more important than capital change and dividends, the other two return components.

Table VIII-3—TOTAL RETURNS OF MAJOR STOCK MARKETS*

	Market Capitalization ($ billion) 6/30/79	1969 %	1970 %	1971 %	1972 %	1973 %	1974 %	1975 %	1976 %	1977 %	1978 %	1969–1978 Compound % per year
United States (S&P 500)	900	− 8	+ 4	+14	+ 19	−15	−26	+ 37	+24	− 7	+ 7	+ 3.3
Japan	292	+34	−11	+52	+123	−20	−16	+ 19	+25	+15	+52	+21.6
United Kingdom	145	−12	− 6	+48	+ 3	−26	−48	+110**	−12	+56	+14	+ 4.8
Canada	86	+ 3	− 3	+16	+ 26	− 1	−26	+ 14	+ 9	− 2	+19	+ 4.5
Germany	74	+23	−23	+23	+ 18	− 5	+16	+ 28	+ 6	+24	+25	+12.3
France	50	+17	− 7	0	+ 23	+ 3	−22	+ 42	−20	+ 5	+68	+ 8.0
Australia	28	+18	−19	− 2	+ 20	−12	−32	+ 47	−10	+11	+20	+ 1.7
The Netherlands	24	− 4	− 7	+ 1	+ 28	− 5	−15	+ 46	+15	+15	+19	+ 7.9
Switzerland	42	+ 4	−13	+26	+ 28	− 4	−12	+ 40	+10	+28	+21	+11.4
Hong Kong	14	+38	+40	+74	+148	−38	−54	+106	+40	−11	+18	+21.8
Singapore	12	− 4	− 7	+84	+168	−32	−47	+ 62	+14	+ 6	+44	+16.2

*The returns have been adjusted for exchange rate movements relative to the U.S. dollar.
**Numbers inside rectangles indicate the best performance for that year.
Source: Rowe Price-Fleming International, Inc. based on data from Capital International S.A. Geneva, Switzerland, except 1969–72 Hang Seng Index, Hong Kong, Straits Times Industrial Index, Singapore.

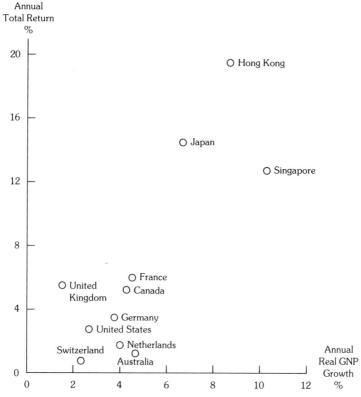

CHART VIII-1—TOTAL STOCK MARKET RETURN 1969-78
VERSUS
REAL GNP GROWTH 1969-78

(Compounded Annually)*

*Measured in terms of the domestic currency.
Source: Rowe Price-Fleming International, Inc.

Chart VIII-2 shows that the exchange rate has been an important factor in returns from some markets. This fact emphasizes further the desirability of investment programs that allow diversification among a number of overseas markets, rather than only one or two. If investors knew in advance which would be the strong markets and strong currencies, the prices of both stocks in those markets and the currencies would, of course, be rapidly increased by a surge in demand, just the same as would the price for next year's probable winners in the U.S. domestic market. Because future outcomes are uncertain, a diversifying approach is highly desirable.

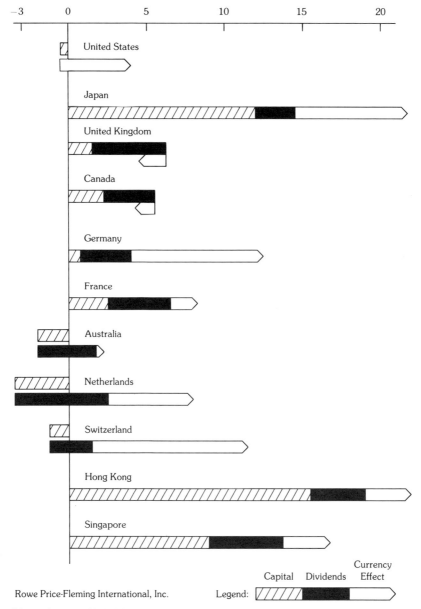

CHART VIII-2—TOTAL RETURN OF MAJOR STOCK MARKETS

1969–78 Compounded Annually*

-3   0   5   10   15   20

United States

Japan

United Kingdom

Canada

Germany

France

Australia

Netherlands

Switzerland

Hong Kong

Singapore

Currency
Capital   Dividends   Effect

Rowe Price-Fleming International, Inc.   Legend:

*Measured in terms of U.S. dollars.
Sources: based on data from Capital International S.A., Geneva, Switzerland and W.I. Carr (America) Limited,
    International Monetary Fund

Performance of International Portfolios

Actual performance is the most effective test of the possibilities of international investing. The following paragraphs provide two examples.

In an article published in the Fall 1975 issue of *The Journal of Portfolio Management,* Gary L. Bergstrom provided information and data on an international portfolio managed by Putnam Management Company.[3] The period covered was March 24, 1971, to June 30, 1975. Briefly, the investment policy was to (1) remain "as fully invested as possible," (2) "take maximum advantage of the diversification possibilities across world markets," and (3) maintain within each country selected "a diversified list of high quality companies."

For the span of more than four years, the results were:

Total international portfolio return	30.8%
S&P 500—total return	11.6
NYSE Composite—total return	8.4
Standard deviation of international portfolio	14.4*
Standard deviation of NYSE Composite	19.4*
Beta coefficient versus NYSE Composite	.40
R^2 versus NYSE	.35

*Annualized numbers based on 2.0% per week for international portfolio and 2.7% for NYSE Composite.

It is to be noted that the return was well above that for either U.S. series. The standard deviation was significantly less than that for the NYSE, and the beta was low. Also, it is to be seen from the R^2 that movements of the NYSE Index explain only about one-third of the performance of the international portfolio, whereas, the NYSE Index would ordinarily explain 85% to 95% of the performance of typical diversified U.S. equity portfolios. Accordingly, the correlation was low.

More recent experience is set forth in an address to the Financial Analysts Federation in February 1979 by Jon L. Hagler, Vice President and Treasurer of the Ford Foundation. Hagler stated that for the four and three-quarter

[3]G. L. Bergstrom, "A New Route To Higher Returns and Lower Risks," *The Journal of Portfolio Management,* Fall 1975.

years ending September 30, 1978, "the annualized rate of return of our total international portfolio, net of expenses, averaged 12.5%." Over the same period, the return on the S&P 500 was 5.2%. He then adds,

> Of substantial importance to us because we look to international investing primarily for its diversification—or risk reduction—characteristics, the variability of the returns on our program has been approximately one-half that of the Standard & Poor's 500, and only slightly higher than that of our domestic fixed-income portfolio.[4]

DETERRENTS TO INTERNATIONAL DIVERSIFICATION

Political Risks

For the most part, security markets in individual countries are dominated by national investors who cannot avoid local risks in those markets any more than in their business and personal affairs. Some political risks such as nationalization, antitrust actions, or punitive taxation may affect domestic and foreign shareholders alike. Others, such as restrictions on international capital flows or tax codes that favor resident investors over foreigners can have a differential impact.

Although all of these factors are forms of political risk, those arising from differential treatment of foreign investors are probably better termed "sovereign risks." They affect foreigners detrimentally and are ordinarily the direct result of the national government exercising its sovereign powers in conducting its affairs. Because of the dominance of domestic investors in national markets and the vulnerability of foreign investors to certain types of national governmental action, it may be argued that sovereign risks are not adequately reflected in the risk statistics of national markets. There has been little research on the subject, but several general observations are pertinent:

- To the extent that foreign investors are active in national markets, changes in sovereign risk may be quickly factored into prices and thus expected returns.

[4]Jon L. Hagler, "Address to the Financial Analysts Federation." February 5, 1979, pp. 9-10.

Prompt risk and return responsiveness to political risks is to be expected principally from the action of domestic investors.

- Among advanced industrial countries, with the exception of those at war with each other, foreign investors are usually treated at least neutrally relative to resident investors, rather than detrimentally.

Currency Risk

Currency risk may appear similarly formidable to a newcomer to international investing. Varying foreign exchange rates, which have little or no role in domestic investing, affect achieved security market returns when translated into the pension plan sponsor's reporting currency. As a result, actual changes in currency rates may offset, reduce, or augment experienced security returns in ways that are both unfamiliar and generally unexpected. Accordingly, attention must be given to the nature and significance of this characteristic risk element in international investing from the plan sponsor's point of view.

Currency risk may be defined as that element of variability in international investment returns that stems from exchange rate fluctuations relative to the investor's domestic currency. The currency element may be favorable while security market returns are unfavorable, or the reverse may be true, covering a full spectrum of combinations.

In a floating exchange rate environment such as the present, an examination of patterns of relative strength or weakness among currencies over successive past periods does not seem to provide useful information about future relative movements in exchange rates. In this sense, uncertainty about future rates prevails in much the same way that uncertain future returns represent risks in security.

To understand the nature of currency risk, it is necessary to consider briefly how exchange rates are determined and how they are related to both security markets and underlying economies. Exchange rates reflect supply and demand for different currencies, which in turn are affected by economic, political, and other conditions. The linkages of these fundamental forces to exchange rates are complex. The key financial elements are expected differences among nations in rates of inflation (purchasing power of the national currencies); differences in interest rates, which tend to adjust to changing inflation but often with leads or lags and with distortions; forward exchange rates with either discounts or premiums in currency future contracts; and expected changes in spot (current) exchange rates.

The goal is to solve for the change in spot rates. However, as in forecasting inflation and interest rates in a single country, predicting differential rates among countries is a formidable undertaking. Not only are financial linkages among these four elements inconsistent, but also the supply and demand for currency are distorted from time to time by political interference in exchange markets (creating the so-called "dirty float"), the psychological factors in some types of speculation, and the rather loose central bank control of credit expansion in private international banking.

If forecasting future exchange rates is difficult, how should an international investor responds to currency risks? There are several alternatives:

- Diversify investments among a number of foreign countries, which is the simplest and most obvious approach. Over long periods of time, currency gains in some countries should tend to offset losses in others much as returns on different stocks do in a diversified domestic portfolio. (If one could identify future winners with certainty, there would be no risk and no need for diversification.)

- Maintain perspective on the magnitude of currency risk relative to more familiar forms of investment risk and its relatively minor potential impact on total portfolio return in pension funds that are typically not invested more than 5% or 10% in foreign securities. Annual fluctuations in stock returns are ordinarily large, prevalent, and persistent relative to those in exchange rates (see Chart VIII-2).

Fund managers may choose to undertake two forms of direct and active response to perceived future changes in currency rates: (1) shifting some funds from areas of expected weakness to others of expected strength and (2) undertaking limited hedging by use of currency futures contracts. Regarding these two direct responses, shifting funds among markets is more commonly practiced than hedging. The currency outlook is one of the factors affecting return that is appraised by managers of active portfolios, but shifts of investments are made mainly in response to forecast changes in security markets, with currency change most often a secondary consideration. Hedging, because of its extra out-of-pocket costs, is generally limited to minor proportions of the international portfolio and special circumstances. It is more appropriate and more widely applicable in international trade.

Shifting funds from one country to another merits further discussion later, because of its large potential effect on market return beyond the currency exchange element. It is often considered akin to market timing in the domestic context but, because the rebalancing is usually among assets of the same class with approximately similar risk-return characteristics (rather than among U.S. stocks, bonds, and money market instruments), a closer analogy is the shifting of investments among stocks of different companies or industries. As in a number of other areas, the appropriate reference base for measuring active management effectiveness should be a passive standard—what the results in risk and return terms would be if no shifts had been made over the same extended period.

AVAILABLE FORMS OF INTERNATIONAL DIVERSIFICATION

Historically, large scale international portfolio investment has been primarily a European phenomenon. Particularly in the United Kingdom, Switzerland, and The Netherlands, widely diversified international investment has been common practice for more than a century. It reflects both investors' desires to broaden the opportunity for returns not available in their domestic markets and to diversify against distinctively local risks. Other countries, such as West Germany, France, and Belgium have also had active institutional participation. For several reasons, the United States has, until recently, lagged in international portfolio investment.

The large and highly diversified U.S. economy has provided investment opportunities that reduced the need for looking elsewhere. Furthermore, funded pension plans became prominent only in the period shortly after World War II, when domestic growth and economic strength were unquestioned. Corporations investing directly in overseas production facilities were the first to recognize the attractive size, growth rates, and profitability in other areas of the world, and a great expansion in direct international investment took place.

Institutional investment managers followed. An important product of the recent explosion of investment knowledge that has been achieved through advanced quantitative research in finance has been a greatly improved understanding of the effects of systematic international portfolio diversification.

Before turning to different approaches to management of internationally diversified portfolios, it is helpful to examine the dimensions of the foreign markets in which U.S. managers can invest.

Scope and Nature of Major Foreign Markets

In mid-1979, the market value of the stocks constituting the S&P 500 was $666 billion; that of the Wilshire 5000, the broadest index regularly available for U.S. stock markets, was $966 billion. Without question this country has the largest equity market in the world. Table VIII-4 provides perspective on

Table VIII-4—FOREIGN STOCK MARKETS AS OF JUNE 30, 1979

	Market Capitalization billions of U.S. dollars	Market Value as Percentage of S&P 500 Market Value[1]	Ten Largest Companies' Percentage of Market[2]
Japan	$292	44%	15%
United Kingdom	144	22	28
Canada	86	13	23
Germany	74	11	41
France	50	8	24
Switzerland	42	6	64
Australia	28	4	27
The Netherlands	24	4	75
Hong Kong	14	2	48
Belgium	13		59
Singapore	12		
South African golds	11	12	
Other	43		
	$833		

[1]Percentage of S&P 500's market value, based on $666 billion.
[2]The percentage in each stock market represented by the companies with the ten largest market capitalizations (United States 20%).
Source: Rowe Price-Fleming International, Inc.

the size of different markets relative to that of the S&P 500, the typical U.S. standard.

The market value of stocks listed on nearly all foreign exchanges totaled $833 billion in U.S. dollars or 125% of the market value of the S&P 500 and 86% of the Wilshire 5000. The combined market value of stocks on the six largest foreign markets exceeded that for the S&P 500. Using the cited $666 billion value for the S&P 500 as the standard, the Japanese market was about 44% as large in market value, the United Kingdom was 22%, West Germany was only 11% (attributable to the large number of private and bank controlled companies, among other factors), and Switzerland was 6%. However, the practicality of large scale investment cannot be judged solely on the basis of the relative market value of the listed securities; liquidity and other factors must also be considered.

Japan and The Netherlands are examples of the importance of a well-established market and liquidity. Japan, with a total market capitalization approaching half that of the S&P 500, is a country with active securities trading and many business practices similar to those in the United States. The Netherlands, with a total market capitalization only 4% as large as that of the S&P 500, is also well-established and respected for its stock markets. In fact, the Amsterdam Exchange is the oldest in the world.

In most of the markets listed, patient, knowledgeable, long term investors can build or liquidate positions for portfolios without serious trading problems or frustrations. However, except for such countries as the United Kingdom, Japan, Canada, and The Netherlands, rapid and significant changes cannot usually be made without substantial effects on prices. Trading strategies are therefore particularly important.

In stock markets characterized by limited size, less active trading of securities, and differences in trading practices or regulations, large scale, rapid portfolio change may be either prohibitively expensive or impossible. Patience, experience, an index fund approach (giving up both the potential benefits and continuing trading requirements of active management), or deliberate restriction of the program to the most liquid securities and markets are all alternatives. If the last option is chosen, the proportion of the total national market value accounted for by the ten largest companies in each market (as shown in Table VIII-4) can be a helpful guideline. For comparison, the ten largest companies in the S&P 500 account for about 20% of its value. Concentration is especially great in The Netherlands (75%), Switzerland (64%), and Belgium (59%). It is remarkably low in Japan (15%), being less than that in the United States (20%) and any other country.

Although the gross figures conceal many nuances and complexities, market liquidity can also be measured usefully by turnover. Turnover is the total trading volume expressed in number of shares, divided by the average number of shares listed during the same period. Charts VIII-3 and VIII-4, respectively, show world market capitalizations and share turnover for 1966, 1975, and 1978. In both Japan and Western Europe, market liquidity as measured by turnover has been improving, which should gradually reduce some of the handicaps to portfolio change described above.

CHART VIII-3—PERCENTAGE BREAKDOWN OF WORLD STOCK MARKET CAPITALIZATION

1966, 1975, and 1978

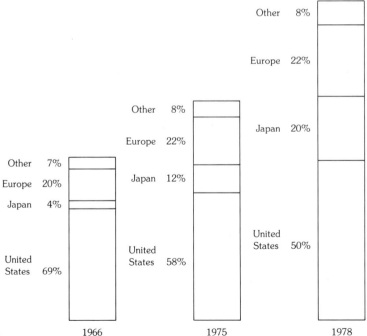

Source: Estimated from data published in *Capital International Perspective*.

CHART VIII-4—PERCENTAGE BREAKDOWN OF WORLD SHARE TURNOVER
1966, 1975, and 1978

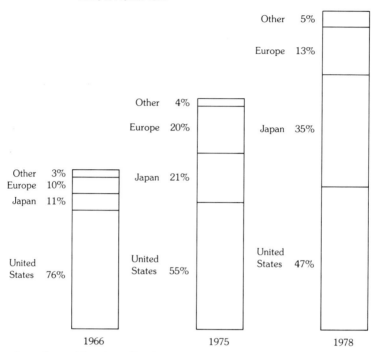

Source: Estimated from data published in *Capital International Perspective.*

Active and Passive Management

Few corporations attempt to invest directly in foreign equity markets. Rather, they employ external managers and seek international diversification either through establishment of separate accounts large enough to spread investments across a reasonable number of countries and issues or through participation in a commingled fund. International funds have traditionally been actively managed with managers changing issues and shifting investment emphasis in response to perceived changes in risk and return opportunities. More recently, commingled passive funds, which are broadly similar in concept, structure, and rebalancing rules to domestic index funds, have become available. Because few corporations engage directly in international investment management and because investment considerations are similar for both separate and commingled funds, the emphasis of this section is on external management of commingled funds.

Active Management

Investing in foreign securities is distinguished from domestic practice in several respects. Some of the differences, such as languages, accounting and financial reporting practices, and market regulation, are much more the problem of external managers than of their corporate pension clients. Others, such as composition of the fund and management practices that affect its risk and return characteristics, impinge directly on the plan sponsor's investment objectives. These latter aspects are of primary concern to the sponsor in selecting a manager and making other decisions in regard to international diversification.

Key decisions by an external manager in regard to an actively managed international portfolio of importance to the corporate pension or finance officer include:

- The nature and number of countries invested in and the manner in which available funds are apportioned among them
- The extent to which national market timing is practiced by shifting funds from one country to another
- The degree of diversification sought within each country
- The nature of response to perceived currency risks.

Investments generally tend to be concentrated by active managers in countries and stocks that are relatively large, familiar, and considered attractive in fundamental terms. However, active international managers sometimes specify neutral or normal market positions that may be based on relative market capitalizations and expected comovement (correlation) with the U.S. market.

Diversification and the role of different countries may be brought into perspective by thinking of the portion of the portfolio invested in each country as we are accustomed to thinking of company or industry positions in a domestic portfolio. For example, if total foreign holdings in a pension portfolio were to aggregate as much as 10%, on a proportional world market-weighted basis (excluding the United States) Japanese stocks would amount to 3.5% of the total (35% of 10%), U.K. issues 1.7%, and German issues 0.9%. For maximum risk diversification, the object is to combine assets of different attractiveness and risk, so that selections represent as much as possible offsetting patterns of return as world and national economic and security market conditions change.

There are additional benefits from thinking about the investment holdings in individual foreign markets within a "single security" context. In a broadly diversified international portfolio representing, say, 10% of a pension fund, the weights of each country may under normal conditions be similar to those of prominent stocks in a U.S. portfolio. Statistical measures of risk are thus easy to compare for foreign market indexes and familiar U.S. companies, providing a comfort factor for those accustomed to fluctuations in company stock prices but apprehensive about those in foreign components of the portfolio.

Shifting funds among foreign markets is commonly referred to as market timing, but it has different risk and return connotations from the same phrase when used to describe domestic shifts between stocks and money market instruments. The risk and return patterns for stocks in different markets are more alike than those of different asset classes. However, because stock returns among nations can vary significantly over the short run, the change in realized return may be large. As a result, the spread between the return of a typical actively managed portfolio and a "passive" benchmark may be substantial. If a series of shifts of this type are successful, they are perhaps the most important decisions that the portfolio manager can make. Whether successful or not, aggressive shifting of funds among countries can swamp the effects of good or poor selection of issues in a reasonably well-diversified portfolio component within single markets.

Active international investment managers have not tended to seek the same high degree of diversification within single foreign markets, that in recent years has been characteristic of U.S. pension equity funds in domestic markets. As a result, it is less common for their investments in individual countries to track domestic indexes closely. A first impression is that this is a riskier investment strategy, but diversification among countries appears to have a considerable offsetting effect.

Currency risk management is discussed earlier in this chapter. Generally, diversified investments among several countries moderate the effect more reliably and consistently than any other single step that a pension plan sponsor can take. Selective, small scale hedging is also used. In addition, anticipated changes in exchange rates are at least a secondary or tertiary consideration in the decision as to how to deploy or shift funds among different markets.

Passive Management

Within the past few years, U.S. investment managers (for example, Batterymarch Financial Management and State Street Bank and Trust Company) have designed and are operating international passive funds designed to replicate the risk and return characteristics of market indexes in one or a selected set of foreign countries. A number of other managers are also considering introducing such vehicles. Essentially, specified representative samples of stocks in each market are bought and held, and typically little or no effort is made to earn extra returns or to modify risk-return patterns by active security selection or timing.

Market efficiency, cost savings, and more predictable results relative to those of specified market indexes have become key elements in the rationale for index investing in the United States. In view of the higher costs and greater complexity of selection and timing decisions in operating in a number of foreign markets, the same rationale appears to apply with at least equal force in international investing.

If these facts are true—that foreign security markets are relatively efficient and that reasonably well-diversified portfolios are representative samples of those markets—it should be a fairly straightforward procedure to capture most of the available returns in a given market by investing passively in it through an index fund. A well-diversified portfolio is affected overwhelmingly by the risk and return pattern of the market it is invested in. In typically well-diversified equity portfolios more of the total variability in annual return is attributable to general market forces, and only 10% or so to nonmarket factors.

Through an international index fund, a pension plan sponsor can be assured of performance close to some composite of foreign markets covered and at somewhat lower costs. There is, of course, a price for this certainty of relative performance and high diversification. In terms of opportunity cost, the sponsor participating in a passive international fund gives up all possibility of outperforming individual markets in which the fund invests in return for the assurance that he or she will not underperform. Moreover, distribution of investments among countries may be in proportion to their market capitalizations. As a result, the weighting of different markets relative to perceived attractiveness, inclusion or exclusion of particular countries, and overweighting of markets with the lowest correlation with the U.S. market may be sacrificed in an international indexing approach.

The main initial goals of passive international investing have been to capture the large proportion of potential return that is associated with market moves alone and to minimize costs and the unpleasant surprise of underperformance. In addition, several hybrid forms of the approach have been introduced or are under development. For example, one permits dropping or adding particular countries or over- or underweighting markets desired by the sponsor. This can require an initial country selection but thereafter the fund operates passively.

A second modification is closer to active management but differs in that no individual issue selection is done within single markets. The active element consists of forecasting overall return, risk, and correlation characteristics for each of the national market indexes periodically and using a computer program to optimize the mix to maximize expected return at a given level of expected risk. Funds may then be shifted among various markets accordingly. This variation of the passive international approach is almost identical to that used domestically in some asset mix strategies, entailing no selection of individual issues but using indexes as proxies for classes of securities.

Fundamentally, fund sponsors may be interested in considering actual historic performance records of active as well as passive international managers. Generally, there have been fewer comprehensive studies of the performance of international managers than has been the case with U.S. managers.

It should be pointed out that neither passive nor active approaches should be viewed as intrinsically superior; indeed, they may be complementary in many respects. Each has strengths and weaknesses. The choice, based on present knowledge, depends on balancing these tangible strengths and weaknesses with the psychological elements of confidence and comfort playing an additional role.

SUMMARY

The principal factors to be considered by the corporate executive in deciding whether to diversify internationally investment holdings of a pension fund may be grouped under three major headings: benefits, deterrents, and available forms of international diversification.

The benefits are centered on the extent to which risk-return patterns of stocks in each national market are independent of those in every other national market and particularly those of the U.S. market. Evidence compiled for past periods ranging from five to fifteen years indicates that comovement of returns of most foreign markets with those of the U.S. market (as represented by the S&P 500) was limited (only modest covariance existed). For this reason and because the returns have for the most part been higher, the potential has existed for decreasing the risk and improving the return of a purely domestic portfolio through international diversification.

Actual performance is the most effective test of the possibilities of international investing, and two examples are provided. In each instance, the returns realized were in excess of those for the S&P 500 and the variability was less. Two instances of success obviously do not provide conclusive evidence but they are illustrative of what can be done. However, there are deterrents to foreign investing—primarily political and currency risks—that need to be recognized and considered. Sovereign nations can restrict the free flow of investment funds across their borders and otherwise constrain foreign investing. Fluctuations in rates of currency exchange can either positively or negatively affect investment results, and thus introduce an extra and perhaps unfamiliar consideration. There are also several lesser risks.

Few corporations attempt to invest directly in foreign equity markets. Instead, they use external managers and secure adequate diversification either through establishment of a separate account large enough to spread the investments over a reasonable number of countries and issues or through participation in a comingled fund.

CHAPTER

9 Selection of External Managers

The proportion of U.S. corporations that manage either all or some of their pension funds internally is limited. For this reason, the overwhelming majority of plan sponsors reading this material are expected to be concerned with external management of pension fund assets rather than with internal management. This chapter is therefore devoted entirely to the selection of external managers. (Some of the criteria for manager selection, however, are relevant to structuring an internal management function.)

There are substantial differences in the size, nature, investment style, and performance records of managers. For this reason, careful thought needs to be given to the manager selection process. The nature of the manager selection process will depend on a number of factors. These include whether the corporation has the assistance of a consulting organization that devotes itself primarily to manager searches and the extent to which the corporation has knowledge and experience in this regard. A comprehensive selection process would primarily include questionnaires, interviews, and performance and portfolio analyses.

Questionnaires are frequently used as initial screening devices and provide broad background information on potential managers that may not otherwise be available. Interviews on their "home grounds" with the investment organizations that remain after the initial screening provide an opportunity to explore investment style, analytical and portfolio concepts and procedures, and managerial capabilities at various levels of the investment process. If effectively handled, these interviews should make it possible for the sponsor to arrive at overall jugments as to how well individual managers appear to be running their businesses. Portfolio analyses will provide information important in judging performance records of managers and will statistically identify their risk-return characteristics. Some pension plan sponsors, either through their corporation's computer processing division or through consultants, run portfolio return simulations to assist in formulating performance expectations for individual managers.

Chapter IX has three tasks: (1) to examine principal factors to be considered in determining whether to have a single or multiple manager arrangement, (2) to discuss different classifications of managers, and (3) to suggest criteria for selection of external managers.

SINGLE INVESTMENT MANAGER

In practice, there is no established definition of a "single manager" fund. Accordingly, some interpretation is needed at the outset. For example, in some instances a portion of the assets may be invested in such forms as insurance contracts or real estate and kept separate from the main body of the fund, which consists of stocks and fixed income securities. Real estate holdings and insurance contracts represent distinctive investment vehicles requiring specific investment talents or types of organizations, but stocks and bonds constitute about 80% of separately funded pension assets. Therefore, if the stock and fixed income portions of a fund are managed in their entirety by one investment organization, we suggest that the funds be classified as a single manager fund even if different portions of the total fund are managed in different divisions of the organization.

Asset size may leave the plan sponsor with no practical alternative to a single manager arrangement. However, since many funds are growing at rates that result in a doubling of asset size within five years, the multimanager alternative is increasingly becoming a practical alternative. In those instances where the plan sponsor is considering whether such an alternative exists, the corporate executive needs to weigh the advantages and disadvantages of the alternative courses of action. The principal factors to be considered are size, performance, and convenience.

Size

A pension plan's assets may be judged too small to divide and still obtain the investment attention of particular managers. This factor can be a valid concern in the case of relatively small funds. However, it is possible to split even modest sized funds if the assets are placed in an investment organization's "pooled" or commingled fund (or funds) and managed as part of that total. Many investment firms have the facility to combine assets of small pension plans in a single fund. Through aggregating assets in this manner, a level of management attention and expertise is obtainable that would not be feasible if individual pension funds were managed separately. Whether a sponsor considers participation in such a pooled fund desirable will depend in part on the comparability of the pooled fund's investment objectives and performance with those of the sponsor. Investment companies offer participation in a wide range of asset pools designed to meet specific investment objectives.

FRS surveys of large as well as small corporate pension funds and discussions with investment managers do not reveal any generally accepted asset-size standard for splitting funds. This is not surprising because such a decision entails a number of considerations specific to an individual fund (such as future growth of the fund, investment style and size of the existing manager or managers, and satisfaction with a manager). However, from time to time, some general amounts are mentioned in the press or elsewhere. For example, a total asset amount recently cited for shifting from single to multiple management was $50 million.[1] However, smaller funds have been split and larger funds have not. Meetings with corporate pension officers of 40 funds in the $5 million to $80 million range (median size $30 million) revealed that most of the funds have more than one manager. In some instances, however, the division was confined to separate stock and bond managers.

---

[1] See *Institutional Investor,* November 1977, pp. 65-66, 72, 144. This article informally estimated the maximum amount that any one manager can effectively manage is $50 million to $60 million and the minimum amount that will still gain the desired level of attention from an investment management organization is $10 million to $20 million.

Performance

If an existing investment manager satisfies the plan sponsor's expectations and there is no reason to believe that the management will become unsatisfactory, there may be no need to change the single manager arrangement. Superior results would perhaps be deterred by adding managers.

Some corporations with modest sized funds have had excellent relations with a single manager over an extended period. There are decided advantages in this kind of a relationship, including the probably lower level of management fees incurred. At the same time, there are potential disadvantages that at least suggest the desirability of regularly reviewing a single manager arrangement. (The merits of regular review also apply to multimanager arrangements.)

A single manager arrangement means placing total reliance on the skills and capabilities of a single investment organization. If the organization is substantially wrong in its investment judgments, the total portfolio suffers and there may be nothing to offset the impact on the market value of the fund except additional employer contributions. It is less likely that all of the managers will be wrong simultaneously in a multiple manager situation.

Continuation of a satisfactory single manager arrangement assumes continuity in the investment organization; i.e., continuity of investment style and key personnel related to the sponsor's fund. For example, if the fund has been managed by a single key person in either a small or a large organization and that person leaves, there may be some discontinuity in the management of the fund. The same could obviously occur under a multimanager arrangement but the impact on the total fund would be less.

A single manager who has performed well by actively managing a relatively small fund may encounter difficulties when attempting to provide active management for a fund that has grown substantially in size. This often depends on the style of management that has been employed. For example, an aggressive growth manager who has performed admirably at the small fund level may find that his or her research capabilities are inadequate to identify enough aggressive growth issues to satisfy diversification requirements of a larger fund. The size of the fund relative to the amount of assets under management and personnel depth is a factor that most corporate officers consider in selecting a manager. In fact, some have a rule that the market value of the fund cannot exceed some predetermined percentage of total assets under management.

Convenience

A single manager relationship may prove to be particularly convenient, especially if the manager also handles government filings and plan disbursements. A small fund in the hands of a single manager may be of sufficient size to receive a level of attention that would not be warranted if it were divided between two or more managers. Furthermore, monitoring of performance and periodic meetings are thereby confined to a single manager. In this and other ways, the time that a corporate officer devotes to following the investment management of the pension fund may be kept at a minimum and still be effective. In the final analysis, however, convenience should be given the least weight as a selection criterion.

MULTIPLE MANAGERS

Under a multimanager arrangement, a pension fund is divided into two or more parts and each part is managed by a different investment firm.

As discussed in Chapter V, there are four principal categories of investment styles. They are distinctive in terms of both concepts and risk-return characteristics. Accordingly, it is necessary to decide the type or types of managers to be employed. Several alternatives exist but most plan sponsors select managers with different investment styles particularly with reference to management of common stocks. For example, equity managers might include diversified, undiversified (e.g., growth stock or income stock managers), and rotator managers.

Irrespective of the final decision in regard to the mix of managers to be employed, the plan sponsor must consider (1) risk-return and other distinctive characteristics of the different styles, (2) how will individual managers fit into specific styles, and (3) given the objectives of the total fund, the most effective combination of managers.

A number of factors require consideration in deciding on a multimanager arrangement. In addition to asset size of the fund, the principal factors to be considered include reduced dependence on any one manager, diversification among investment styles, specialized investment skills, increased corporate involvement in the investment process, and time requirements.

Reduced Dependence on Any One Manager

Multiple management obviously reduces the extent to which the plan sponsor is dependent on a single investment organization. If discontinuities in management, unsatisfactory performance, or other critical factors develop, it is less likely that they will be experienced by several managers simultaneously. As a result, certain risks associated with a single manager arrangement are reduced.

Diversification Among Investment Styles

Additional portfolio diversification is frequently mentioned as an advantage of multiple management. If managers have significantly different styles, they will typically hold significantly different portfolios. Accordingly, diversification in the total fund will be increased and risk reduced. However, the extent to which this will be true depends substantially on investment styles of existing individual managers. To illustrate, assume a fund with a single manager who manages portfolios that in terms of equities are well diversified by company, industry, and market sector and in terms of fixed issues are well diversified principally by maturity (a diversified manager). Under the circumstances, addition of another manager (unless he or she is another diversified manager) would probably reduce diversification in the total portfolio and thus increase risk.

In contrast, if the existing manager confines portfolio investments to a specific sector of the market, such as high growth or income stocks (an undiversified manager), addition of managers will probably increase diversification of the portfolio and probably reduce risk. Accordingly, in regard to the diversification factor, the corporate pension officer will need to give careful consideration to the existing manager's style, the extent to which the portfolio is currently diversified, and the styles of potential managers.

On the other hand, the process of increasing diversification of a fund can be carried to the point that it may almost eliminate any possibility of earning an excess return from active management. The combined portfolio, indeed, can turn out to be a market portfolio that will underperform the market because of transaction costs and payment of fees for active management.

Specific Investment Styles

The benefits to be gained from combining a mix of managers each of whom adheres to a specific style is one of the most frequently cited reasons for employing multiple managers. However, investment styles are not consistently defined. For example, some managers identify their capabilities and specialties by asset classes (e.g., stocks, bonds, options, and real estate). Others identify themselves by sectors within classes of assets (e.g., high growth, income, low P/E ratio, and small and emerging company stocks). Still others may identify themselves by their ability as "market timers" or in terms of their emphasis on individual issue selection.

The case for the use of managers each of whom is a dedicated adherent of a specific style is usually based on the view that the skill level of managers who concentrate their talents on valid approaches to investing will exceed the level of those who do not. However, dedicated adherence to a specific style does not guarantee the ability to excel; thus, selection of managers cannot rest on the single consideration of style. Whether adherence to a specific style makes it possible for a given organization to excel may be judged in part from its performance record. Although adherence does not automatically ensure superior results, shifting from one style to another may well produce inferior performance, especially during the transition.

Corporate Involvement in the Investment Process

A multiple manager structure inevitably increases involvement of the plan sponsor in the decision-making process. The extent of this involvement will depend principally on the number and nature of the managers added. To illustrate, assume that a single manager fund employs an additional manager. Further, assume that the new manager is comparable in style and other respects to the existing manager, who manages well-diversified and balanced portfolios. Under these assumptions, the increased involvement of the plan sponsor can be minimal. Only two principal decisions are needed: (1) initial allocation of existing funds between the two managers and (2) subsequent allocation of cash flows. A simplistic decision rule (but not necessarily the best) would be to allocate all cash flow to the new manager until the portfolio's size equaled that of the first manager and to allocate subsequent cash flows equally.

In contrast, assume, as before, one existing manager (who manages well-diversified and balanced portfolios), but instead the addition of two managers, both of whom are "specialists." One is a fixed-income securities manager and the other a high growth common stock manager. The plan sponsor is now confronted with several questions that do not lend themselves to simplistic answers and decision rules.

First, how is the asset mix of the total fund to be maintained? At present, one investment organization manages the entire fund; thus control of the asset mix rests exclusively with that organization. However, if part of the bonds are given to the fixed income manager and part of the stocks to an equity manager, clearly no single manager can control the overall asset mix. The plan sponsor must now accept a role in the allocation process and also assume much of the responsibility for timing asset shifts.

Second, how are the risk and return characteristics of the total portfolio to be controlled?. The high growth equity manager who has been added can be expected to have a significantly different risk-return posture compared with that of the present manager with well-diversified equity holdings. Accordingly, a decision is necessary as to whether specific portfolio objectives tailored to this manager's style are to be developed. Furthermore, the timing and the proportion of the total fund to be transferred to the high growth manager must be decided.

Third, how are the performances of the three managers to be measured and evaluated? The managers are all different and thus need to be judged against different standards. But what standards? For example, should the performance of the high growth equity specialist be measured against a market index designed to represent the total market such as the S&P 500? Or against an index representative of a cross section of high growth stocks?

Time Requirements

A multimanager arrangement requires more corporate executive time than does a single manager arrangement. There are additional meetings to attend, more reports to read, more performance data to review and analyze, and more decisions to be made. Accordingly, in addition to increased involvement in the decision process that results from a multimanager arrangement, the corporate pension officer must consider the increase in time required. However, surveys by FRS and others indicate that, as the market value of a corporation's pension assets grows, there is a definite tendency to move from a single manager to a multiple manager arrangement. Moreover, the cost of time and attention required is productively applied if the composite results can thereby be improved.

CLASSIFICATION OF MANAGERS

Investment organizations may be classified in a number of different ways. Some classifications are so well-known that they need no discussion; for example, classification by type of organization such as insurance companies, trust institutions, and investment counsel firms and by class of assets managed, such as stocks, bonds, real estate, and so forth.

Investment organizations are also classified by their investment style or approach to the management of funds. These alternative styles are considered at some length in Chapter V.

In addition, such organizations can be classified by the breadth of services provided in addition to the investment function. For a pension fund, these supplementary services might include safekeeping assets, record-keeping and rendering appropriate accounting statements, filing government reports, and making disbursements to plan beneficiaries. One vehicle for performing such services when multiple managers are employed is the master trust arrangement, which is discussed below.

Investment organizations differ widely in the extent to which they perform services that go beyond the investment function. Broadly based trust institutions, insurance companies, large investment counseling firms, and some small investment organizations specializing in management of employee benefit plans offer most or all of the above-mentioned services. Others may go no further than the record-keeping function; still others render investment advice only. Fortunately, services that extend beyond the investment function can usually be obtained separately.

MASTER TRUST ARRANGEMENT

This study is confined to the investment function; therefore, it does not examine these supplementary services except the master trust arrangement. Master trust arrangement services are discussed here because they constitute a bridge between other supplementary services and the investment function.

Arrangements made with institutions to perform trust services can vary according to the type of trust agreement. A master trustee will generally provide such basic services as centralized trust accounting reports, covering transactions and holdings for individual portfolios and on a combined basis by specific pension funds, plan accounting that details inflows and outflows and meets ERISA reporting requirements, performance reports and diagnostic analyses including risk measurement and portfolio analysis, and fund disbursements to pensioners.

Many institutions are actively competing to provide master trust services to pension sponsors. As a result, different and innovative services are continuously being developed to attract new clients.[2] These services are principally

---

[2]See E. Matthin, "The Battle for Mastery of Master Trusts," *Institutional Investor,* February 1977.

built around a substantial computer capability. For example, one particularly important service is cash management. In this regard, one institution's brochure points out that it has a fully computerized cash management system that "invests to zero."[3] In other words, under this system there is no idle cash in a fund.

Other special or unique services tied to the master trust arrangement may include market inventory funds, which is a risk controlled equity fund that among other things seeks to limit transaction costs; index funds; short term investment funds; and special reports.

Among the principal factors advanced in support of the master trust arrangement by those providing these services are that it improves the plan sponsor's control of a total fund and individual managers, provides uniform pricing and accounting and standardized communication for reports and benefit payments, and reduces the number of people and procedures required. Most of the same services can be obtained from a master custodian for foundations and endowment funds with multiple management.

SELECTION CRITERIA

Although criteria that should be useful in selecting external investment managers are discussed here from the standpoint of a pension plan sponsor, they will be equally applicable in selecting managers for profit-sharing or savings plans or for foundation, university, or other tax-free funds. The discussion covers seven criteria:

- Reputation
- Size and professional staff
- Style
- Performance record
- Risk-return profile
- Decision-making process
- Objective-setting process.

[3]See *Master Trust Services*, Bankers Trust Company, Trust Department.

Reputation

An investment organization's reputation is ordinarily a logical starting point for evaluating prospective external managers. A good reputation is typically an indication of client satisfaction. It is a valuable guide when based on the organization's ability to fulfill the investment expectations of the fund sponsor according to a prescribed manner. Accordingly, some checking with present clients is an essential preliminary step.

Size and Professional Staff

Size may be approached from several standpoints but, for purposes of this study, it refers to the amount of money under management, and the number of professionals employed.

In using money under management as a selection criterion, the key consideration is the dollar amount of pension, profit-sharing, and other tax-free assets being managed by the prospective investment organization. Limited relevance can be attached to amounts managed in accounts for individuals or personal trusts or held under custodianship, or amounts in funds for which no investment service is rendered.

To assist in bringing the size of an organization into perspective, it would be helpful to know the amount of new pension business developed over at least the last three years and to contrast this figure with the amount of any pension business lost over the same span. In regard to pension assets, another dimension of interest would be the number of accounts under active management.

In the case of small and, perhaps, moderate sized organizations, the financial position and ownership of the firm will be additional relevant considerations because they will indicate the capacity to recruit, motivate, and retain good people in the highly competitive search for talent.

Professional staff includes security analysts, portfolio managers, economists, and operations research (management science) personnel. It also includes professionals in direct supervisory capacities.

In addition to the number of personnel in each area, it is important to determine experience levels, length of employment with the organization, and educational background, including the number of Chartered Financial Analysts.[4]

Determination of the foregoing does not guarantee that abilities identified are being effectively used. To the extent practical, an attempt should be made to appraise the organizational and decision structure. Among other things, the ability of a capable employee to do his or her job well depends on overall management of the total organization and support services provided. If management discourages innovative thought, bogs the organization down in time-consuming rules and procedures, or does not provide needed support services, neither individual ability nor staff size may be able to overcome these impediments to effective performance.

A measure of some importance is turnover in professional staff. A relatively high rate of turnover suggests that something is wrong in the organization, at least from the employee's viewpoint. A high turnover rate among professionals can be a warning signal; it suggests the possibility of discontinuities in the investment operation.

The widely accepted rule against hiring a manager without a personal visit to the investment organization derives its validity from the importance of the atmosphere, working arrangements, communication channels, and potential for interchange of ideas in this highly personal type of service business.

Finally, there is the useful concept of trying to identify where an investment organization stands in its life cycle, particularly with reference to professional staff. Stages range from relatively new organizations not yet experienced and tested under fire; to vigorously growing and innovative firms; to those approaching maturity and facing problems of complacency and reliance on past performance; to mature organizations in the transition phase with problems of second-generation management succession and "changing of the guard."

---

[4] The Institute of Chartered Financial Analysts confers on those financial analysts who have met a certain length of experience and testing requirements the title Chartered Financial Analyst. To qualify, one must be practicing in the fields of portfolio management and security analysis and be involved in overall investment decision-making.

Style

At this point, the purposes of investigating style are to understand the manner in which the prospective investment manager plans to produce the expected return and to judge the amount of risk that a manager will assume. The investigation will also reveal the clarity and coherence of the manager's own perception of the style employed.

The primary significance of style lies in its implications for the risk-return profile of an investment organization. As suggested in Chapter V, styles are not consistently defined and thus they do not have neatly quantified risk-return characteristics. Moreover, styles can be implemented within a broad spectrum of aggressiveness. Consequently, unless examined thoroughly, identification of an organization's style provides only a limited indication of probable results from management of the account. Nevertheless, some broad generalizations are possible.

Performance Record

The performance record is considered by many to be the major criterion for selecting external investment managers. This section defines performance concepts, discusses standards of comparison, and states the significance of a performance record as a criterion for selecting investment managers.

Performance is typically measured in terms of the total rate of return; that is, both income received and changes in the market value of assets over a specified time period. The two relevant methods of measuring absolute returns are internal or dollar-weighted and time-weighted.

The internal rate of return measures the average rate of return of all funds invested in a portfolio over a specified time span. It is identical to the interest rate at which the beginning portfolio and all subsequent net cash flows must be invested to arrive at the end-of-period value of the portfolio. Both the timing and magnitude of contributions and withdrawals bear heavily on the result. Since all of the portfolios of a multimanager fund may not have cash flows of like magnitude at the same time and since portfolio managers generally have no control over these flows, the internal rate of return is not a satisfactory measure in comparing performance among managers. Instead, it is used in comparing the perfomance of a fund with its actuarial assumptions and overall objectives.

The time-weighted rate of return is a more appropriate measure of a manager's investment capability. In essence, it is the rate at which a dollar invested at the beginning of a period would have compounded during that period, irrespective of interim cash flows. Since there are no distortions resulting from cash inflows or outflows, it is a useful measure in comparing performance results among managers.

Identifying and measuring the risks taken in the portfolio constitute the second key aspect of performance measurement. Risk-adjusted returns are important because they make possible comparisons among managers in terms of the risk levels at which they operate. As set forth in Chapter X there are several different approaches to calculating risk-adjusted returns.

Comparison, principally with the results of others or, alternatively, with a market standard, is one of the key reasons for performance measurement. If comparisons are to be effective, the results must be risk adjusted. Various standards of comparison may be used. One common standard is to compare a manager's performance (in terms of relevant pension portfolios) with that of other managers operating at the same risk level. Another common standard is to determine the manager's ability to produce a positive alpha (a rate of return greater than that attributable to a market index alternative after adjustment for difference in market risk).

The appropriate length for the performance evaluation period is subject to debate. No time horizon will meet all requirements under all circumstances. Sponsors customarily ask prospective investment managers to provide a three- or five-year performance record. Monthly performance data are ordinarily preferable if the time horizon is a three-year period, whereas quarterly data are generally requested for a five-year span. In general, the objective is to secure data that cover a complete market cycle, i.e., from peak to trough to peak or from trough to peak to trough.

Account performance data provide direct evidence about how managers performed in the past. However, such historic data are, at best, only inferential in regard to the future. Among other things, pronounced cyclical and secular changes can occur in the security markets. Furthermore, the character of an investment organization can change as a result of changes in investment style, strategy, or key personnel. For these and other reasons, evaluation of prospective fund managers must extend beyond historical return information, helpful though it may be. It is necessary to take account of such factors as the position of the organization in its life cycle, personnel changes, ownership and motivation, and scale of activity. Consequently, the extent to which such computations of the past are meaningful measures of future investment management capability will, in practice, depend on a number of factors.

Risk-Return Profile

A risk-return profile is an array of measurements based on quantitative methods and concepts stemming from modern portfolio theory and the capital asset pricing model. It is designed to reveal the risk characteristics of portfolios and to provide information for identifying sources of portfolio returns among both accounts and investment managers. Risk-return profiles focus primarily on the level and character of risks assumed by managers in portfolios to generate above average returns.

At present, most risk-return profiles center on analyzing the common stock component of portfolios. Total portfolio characteristics are frequently determined by treating the bond component as a homogeneous asset group. Techniques are being developed, however, so that the bond component will eventually be analyzed in equal depth with the stock component.

The ability to identify substantive differences in risk aversion and risk control among various investment managers is especially important where multiple management is already in existence or is contemplated. It is also important before selection of a manager for any portion of a fund or before addition of a manager. In these instances, the plan sponsor must make a choice. The desire usually will be to find a manager who meets certain predetermined risk-return specifications or to add a manager who has a significantly different style (and thus usually different risk-return characteristics) from those already employed. Little can be determined from absolute performance figures, and even less from verbal definitions of style, as to the extent to which prospective managers actually differ from one another with respect to risk aversion and risk control. This can be accomplished only by calculating a risk-return profile that details these differences between prospective and existing managers. It is also relevant to determine the extent to which a manager differentiates portfolio characteristics to make them conform to diverse client investment objectives.

Decision-Making Process

Evaluating an investment organization's decision-making process is an important criterion in selecting external fund managers because it helps in judging whether past performance data are relevant for the future. The decision-making process encompasses the totality of the factors and functions that result in investment action.[5] As a result, it includes not only decision steps, but also the manager's investment strategy; methods, concepts, and techniques used to analyze securities and manage portfolios; and the organizational structure.

In essence, investment strategy determines within the parameters of an organization's chosen investment style the aggressiveness with which the organization will act on its judgments as to the relative attractiveness of individual issues, industries, and security markets. Investment strategy includes such basic considerations as the permissible range of risk levels for accounts, the desirable stock/bond ratio range for representative pension accounts, and a range for cash reserves based on the outlook for security markets. Strategy may also include diversification guidelines, quality selection criteria for stocks, and bonds, and definitions of prohibited transactions.

The research function includes economic analysis and stock and bond market analysis as well as security analysis. Irrespective of their in-house

[5]An evaulation of this kind is not easy. It requires a considerable amount of specialized knowledge, and consultants are increasingly used by plan sponsors to examine and evaluate the decision-making process. If the plan sponsor does not have the requisite skills internally and it is impractical to secure the information through an external organization, the evaluation may need to be restricted to identifying the investment institution's decision centers and making intuitive determinations about the effectiveness of the overall organizational structure and abilities of the people employed.

capabilities, all investment organizations draw some research from external sources. Thus, an important consideration is the firm's internal research capacity.

To be effective, internal research must be developed (and external research digested) within the structure of a conceptually sound valuation model. Moreover, a consistent set of asset selection criteria sufficiently complete to permit comparative selections from a universe of alternative investment possibilities is essential in constructing portfolios from research inputs. Determining whether these requirements are met entails examination of the conceptual framework within which investment analysis takes place and review of the analytical methods and techniques employed.

The broad decisions that form portfolio management encompass asset selection, diversification, and timing. These may be controlled to a greater or lesser extent by the organization's investment policy. Portfolio management decisions, however, are circumscribed by account objectives. Consequently, evaluation of the portfolio management phase of the decision-making process begins by identifying the conceptual framework within which account objectives are set, the method by which they are determined, and the terms (quantitative or qualitative or both) in which they are expressed.

Aside from those relating to communications with plan sponsors, the remaining decisions at the portfolio manager level include assessing the risk-return estimates for classes of assets (e.g., stocks and bonds), evaluating risk-return estimates for individual issues, and making other decisions considered necessary to achieve account objectives.

There are several primary concerns in evaluating the investment process as it relates to constructing and managing portfolios. In addition to the amount and quality of the information available to the portfolio manager, there are the conceptual framework within which the portfolio manager considers such matters as selection, diversification, and timing and the methods and techniques used to optimize the risk-return tradeoff relative to account objectives.

All organizations operate within an administrative structure, which impacts on the decision-making process. At one extreme are those organizations that control all major investment decisions at the top through an investment policy committee. At the other extreme are those organizations that leave virtually all matters of selection, diversification, and timing to the discretion of the individual portfolio manager.

During the 1960s the move was away from committees and top-down structures and toward the "free-form" or total individual portfolio manager discretion. This approach became known as the "star system." In recent years, opinion has substantially reversed and the structured approach to investment administration has returned with greater emphasis on a horizontal structure or group decision-making.

It is not necessary to argue the merits of one or the other of these approaches. Most organizations appear to lie somewhere between the extremes. It should be pointed out, however, that the decision centers are decidedly different for the two extremes. In the structured approach, major decisions relating to levels of portfolio diversification and market timing usually reside with committees and senior investment personnel. In the "free form" approach, those same decisions reside mostly with individual portfolio managers who may or may not be senior investment personnel. Only by identifying the decision centers is it possible to know the weight to assign to the skills and abilities of individual portfolio managers and security analysts.

Objective-Setting Process

Portfolio objectives control investment action; therefore, it is highly desirable for a set of objectives to be established for each manager in a multimanager fund. If individual managers all have the same investment style and reasonably comparable risk-return profiles, the sponsor may consider that the same set of investment objectives is appropriate for each manager. However, when styles and risk-return profiles are different (as is ordinarily the situation), some modifications of the basic set of objectives may be appropriate.

The extent of modifications would depend on the risk-return characteristics of the portfolios constructed by the prospective manager. It would also depend on what the sponsor expected from the specific manager. The modifications may be formulated solely by the plan sponsor, with the participation of an external consultant, or with the assistance of the individual manager. In any case, there needs to be considerable discussion between the sponsor and manager to assure mutual understanding of, and agreement on, the objectives. It is therefore important that the fund sponsor be informed as to the manager's general approach to setting objectives and to the methods and techniques used.

The objective-setting process is examined in depth in Chapters II, III, and IV. Those chapters emphasize that substantial effort is being devoted to developing both the procedures and research inputs necessary to formulation of explicit quantified objectives. Although investment objectives for many funds are still set forth in general and qualitative terms, the move toward quantification is pronounced. Unquantified objectives, no matter how useful or necessary or unavoidable in other contexts, are poor guides to investment action. They lack the explicitness on which investment expectations should be founded and against which investment results should be measured.

In view of the increasing importance of quantified risk-return and other objectives in management of pension portfolios, advances that have been made in setting objectives, and techniques now available for developing quantified objectives, evaluation of an investment organization's objective-setting process merits inclusion among selection criteria. This evaluation will also provide insights into the manner in which the organization monitors the conformance of portfolios to objectives.

SUMMARY

Selection of an investment manager or managers is a particularly important step for the plan sponsor. The corporation with a small but rapidly growing fund must at some point consider the merits of shifting from a single to a multimanager arrangement. The logical starting point for a chapter on the selection of external managers is, therefore, an examination of factors to be weighed in determining the number of managers to be selected.

The nature of the services desired by the plan sponsor, in addition to the investment management of the pension assets, is the next determination to be made. Investment organizations differ widely in the extent to which they provide safekeeping of assets, record keeping and rendering accounting statements, making disbursements to plan beneficiaries, and other services that go beyond the investment function. Accordingly, the chapter emphasizes that investment organizations may be classified in a number of different ways.

When the foregoing determinations have been made, the plan sponsor is ready to concentrate on investment characteristics and capabilities of managers. The nature of the selection process will vary in terms of the knowledge and experience of the plan sponsor and whether the assistance of a consulting organization is employed. However, in general the process will include the use of a questionnaire for initial screening purposes; interviews with investment firms being considered to explore investment styles, analytical and portfolio concepts and procedures, and managerial capabilities; and analyses of performance records and portfolio composition. Seven important manager selection criteria are: reputation, size, style, performance record, risk-return profile, decision-making process, and objective-setting procedures.

CHAPTER

10 Measuring Performance

Measuring and diagnosing performance, the final link in the investment process, provides information that can be used to evaluate and appraise managers, rethink investment objectives, alter portfolio strategy, and even influence the relationship with external managers. An ineffective or inappropriate measurement and diagnostic system weakens the entire process of managing a fund. An effective system will provide maximum assistance to corporate executives in exercising informed judgment and reaching effective decisions. A clear understanding of the uses and limitations of different measurement and diagnostic techniques is the key to assembling an optimum system.

The first section of this chapter discusses the purposes of performance measurement and general criteria for an effective measurement system. Many of the newer methods of measuring and diagnosing performance are based on knowledge gained from the findings of modern portfolio theory. The section begins with a short discussion of the connection between theory and practice in performance measurement.

The second section discusses key aspects of a measurement system. It identifies the choices to be made in methods for measuring returns and risks and setting standards of comparison and relevant time periods. The emphasis in this section is on the practical and usable, rather than on the theoretical.

The third section discusses representative measurement services and identifies the principal differences that characterize each service.

Throughout this chapter, the emphasis is on "bottom-line" performance; that is, measuring final results of the investment process as shown by the return earned and thus changes in total value of a portfolio including income. Chapter XI deals with diagnosing performance; that is, analyzing a portfolio (increasingly on a security-by-security basis) to determine the principal reasons for final results.

PURPOSES OF PORTFOLIO PERFORMANCE MEASUREMENT

The primary purpose of performance measurement is to obtain information on which to base decisions in regard to investment objectives, portfolio strategy, and manager selection. Fiduciary prudence requires measurement of results to track accomplishments of the fund. Another purpose of measurement is to improve communications with managers by creating a standard format for discussions, and other purposes in specific situations. The ideal measurement system would be defined by all purposes it needed to serve including those unique to an individual user.

Clear understanding of the uses and limitations of different techniques of performance measurement is the key to selecting an appropriate system. The effectiveness with which a corporate officer can choose among systems also depends on the care exercised in setting investment objectives. When definitive objectives are established and explicit portfolio strategy is formulated (as described in Chapters II and IV), the choice of a measurement system becomes much easier.

In choosing a system, a user should look for measurement techniques that can be thoroughly understood and easily explained to others, such as a board of directors. It is difficult for anyone, whether pension executive, trustee, or manager, to have confidence in a "black box" system that cannot be understood. The techniques should measure all factors appropriate to a specific situation. This may require use of more than one measurement system, such as one for equities and another for bonds. Results of the system should be available on a timely basis to permit prompt analysis by a corporate officer or pension executive, reporting to the directors, and discussions with managers. All of this should occur while the data are current. Furthermore, the user must feel comfortable with the quantity and form of the system's output.

Effective performance measurement requires four steps:

- Definition: Establishment of investment objectives and, to the extent practical, clearly formulated portfolio strategy.

- Input: Availability of reliable and timely data. Incorrect and tardy data will render the most sophisticated system ineffective.

- Processing: Use of appropriate statistical methods to produce relevant measurements. The complex interaction of objectives, strategies, and manager's tactics cannot be understood if inappropriate statistical methods are used. A meaningful summary will make possible analysis of the investment process at the necessary depth.

- Output: Analysis of the process and results presented in a useful format. Presentation should relate realized performance to objectives and preestablished standards. Enough material should be available to understand and analyze the process. Exhibits should be designed to highlight weaknesses in the investment process and to suggest possible improvements.

Careful integration of these four steps can create a measurement system that closes the pension investment process loop, feeding back important information for improvements in objective setting, strategy formulation, manager selection, and, frequently, management of assets.

Four important caveats must be kept in mind in choosing a performance measurement system. The first is the danger that a hastily chosen system, poorly related to real needs, can rapidly degenerate into a mechanistic, pointless exercise. If a system is chosen primarily to document a trail of fiduciary prudence, it will probably be useless except in defending a suit. Equally unsatisfactory, however, are overly complex or hopelessly slow systems that provide neither understanding nor value. After struggling with such a situation over a period of time, it is easy to become disillusioned with the entire measurement process.

The second caveat is that the system should fit the investment objectives and not the reverse. Setting objectives and formulating strategy for a pension fund are important tasks, unique to each situation. In contrast, many performance measurement vendors have ready-made solutions to measurement problems. The hazard is that the solution prejudges the analysis, affecting or replacing objectives.

Failing to measure a relevant factor or repeatedly measuring and discussing an irrelevant factor can seriously weaken the entire process. This fact leads to the third caveat: measuring the process may alter it. When human beings compete in a remunerative activity such as investment management, they can be expected to respond to the method of "keeping score." For example, if in a multimanager situation it is recognized that a manager with a low performance ranking relative to other managers is likely to be fired by the sponsor regardless of the achieved absolute return, there may be a tendency for the manager to "play it safe" and stay near the middle of the rankings to keep the sponsor as a client. However, this disincentive to risk-taking may not be appropriate to the specific situation.

Because the reward system between investment manager and pension client is often unclear, many opportunities arise for misunderstandings and inappropriate investment action. Not only should the method of measurement be carefully and directly related to long term objectives of the fund, but also as much care should be given to selecting a measurement system or systems as to setting the objectives. When the two tasks are appropriately accomplished, revisions in either objectives or the measurement system will usually be infrequent.

Fourth, to save time and cost, it is important that overmeasurement be avoided. There is an amount of measurement and data appropriate for each specific situation. Overmeasurement, which usually appears in the form of collecting and processing unimportant data, can be detected by asking what decisions will be affected by the results. If the measurement has no decision value, it should be dropped. Overmeasurement can be harmful as well as wasteful. As mentioned above, managers will respond to feedback from the measurement system. Overmeasurement can waste time, confuse communications, and result in less than optimal behavior.

KEY ASPECTS OF PORTFOLIO PERFORMANCE MEASUREMENT SYSTEMS

The five key questions in regard to performance measurement are:

- How should returns be measured?

- How should risks be identified?

- How should returns be adjusted for risk?

- How should standards of comparison be chosen?

- How should relevant time periods be identified?

These five questions—returns, risks, adjustments, standards, and time periods—are discussed in turn in this section.

Methods of Measuring Returns

The two relevant methods of measuring returns are internal or dollar-weighted and time-weighted.

Internal Method

The internal rate of return is affected by cash flows in and out of a fund. It is the rate that will discount the year-end (or end of period) value of the portfolio back to the value of the beginning of period portfolio plus interim contributions. It is logically identical to the interest rate at which the beginning portfolio and all net cash flows must be invested to arrive at the ending value of the portfolio.

The internal rate of return must be calculated by approximation. An equation is set up to include the beginning value, cash flows and ending value. The only unknown is the internal rate. To find it, one approximates an answer, solves the equation, and reapproximates and resolves until the appropriate ending value is derived.

The internal rate of return is used primarily to compare the progress of the fund to its actuarial assumption and overall objectives. The actuarial rate is, itself, an internal rate concerned only with returns being earned on the relevant pool of assets without regard to sources of the returns. Some cash flow patterns can produce multiple solutions to the internal rate of return calculation. This fact raises serious questions about the value of using internal returns for performance measurement. The example below illustrates the method of calculating the internal rate of return.

Example. Suppose the fund allocated $50 million to a new manager on January 1 and then allocated another $45 million on July 1. If the market dropped 10% during the first six months, the initial $50 million might fall to $45 million by midyear. The second allocation then comes in, raising the portfolio value to $90 million. If the market rose 20% during the second half of the year, the portfolio might also rise 20% to $108 million. The internal rate of return is dollar-weighted, thus performance during the second half of the year would be much more heavily weighted than that during the first half of the year.

The equation to solve for this internal rate is:

$$\$108 = (\$50 \times (1 + r)^1) + (\$45 \times (1 + r)^{1/2}).$$

A reasonable first approximation might be $+10\%$ for the year. Substituting .10 for r leads to an ending value of about $102.2 million. Because this is too low, the interest rate must be increased to raise the ending value.

Suppose $+20\%$ is used for a second approximation. Substituting .20 for r leads to an ending value of about $109.3—too high. By dropping r to $+18.2\%$, one can arrive at an ending value of $108.0; therefore, the internal rate of return is 18.2%.

Time-Weighted Method

In 1968, the Bank Administration Institute (BAI) published a study[1] urging adoption of a newer method of calculating returns—the time-weighted method. In the usual case, the timing of contributions and withdrawals is not under the control of the investment manager. The BAI suggested that a more appropriate measure of the investment manager's skill, as distinct from total portfolio results, would be to calculate the rate at which a dollar invested at the beginning of a period would have compounded during that period,

[1]See Measuring the Investment Performance of Pension Funds for the Purpose of Inter-Fund Comparison, published by Bank Administration Institute, Park Ridge, Illinois, 1968.

regardless of interim cash flows. The practical implementation of this approach requires setting up a certain number of "units" or "shares" with a calculated net asset value per unit. The concept is identical to that used in mutual fund accounting.

To handle a contribution or withdrawal during the year, units are "bought" or "sold" at the then-prevailing net asset value per unit. At year-end, the ending portfolio value divided by the outstanding units gives an ending net asset value per unit that can be compared directly with the beginning value or any interim calculation. The example below sets forth the method of calculating the time-weighted rate of return.

Example. To find the time-weighted return using the numbers in the internal method example, suppose the fund begins with $50 million and 50 million units, each worth $1.00. By midyear the fund has declined 10% to $45 million. With 50 million units still outstanding, the net asset value per unit is:

$45 million ÷ 50 million units = 90¢ per unit.

This is, of course, a decline of 10% per unit. When the second allocation of $45 million comes in on July 1, it will buy more than 45 million units:

$45 million ÷ 90¢ per unit = 50 million units.

The fund now has 100 million units outstanding valued at 90¢ each, for a total fund value of $90 million.

During the second half of the year, the fund rises 20% to $108 million. With the same 100 million units outstanding, the net asset value per unit is:

$108 million ÷ 100 million units = $1.08 per unit.

The time weighted rate of return for the year is $1.08 divided by the beginning value of $1.00 or +8.0%. This 8% return is the result of the manager first losing 10% of the money ($1.00 goes down to 90¢) and then making 20% in the second half (90¢ goes to $1.08). It contrasts with the 18.2% internal rate of return calculated in the first example.

Comparison of Internal and Time-Weighted Methods

The potentially dramatic effect of cash flows on the internal rate of return can be seen by considering a case in which the fund had a $20 million withdrawal rather than a midyear contribution. With the initial portfolio down from $50 million to $45 million by midyear, a $20 million withdrawal would leave only $25 million. The 20% increase in the second half of the year would increase this figure to $30 million. The equation for the internal rate of return would be:

$$\$30 = (\$50 \times (1 + r)^1) - (\$20 \times (1 + r)^{1/2}).$$

The first approximation should be 0%, which is correct. Thus, the same manager using the same stocks can show a wide variation in the internal rate of return, depending on the timing of cash flows. Meaningful comparisons of managers are almost impossible using internal returns.

The time-weighted rate of return in this present example is calculated by retiring rather than issuing units; it remains at 8.0%.[2] This method is an appealing way to separate management skills from cash flow decisions and is usually the best choice for performance measurement of managers. The internal rate can be used effectively to compare overall progress with actuarial assumptions.

Methods of Identifying Risk

In Chapter V, Determining Strategy, three kinds of risk were defined — market, extramarket covariance, and specific. Identifying and measuring the risks undertaken in the portfolio is the second key aspect of performance measurement.

Portfolio risks are commonly measured in one or more of three ways:

- Total variability in absolute terms

- Total variability in relative terms

- Market-related variability.

Although there are less common risk measures, such as estimates of portfolio marketability and weighted quality ratings, variability of returns is usually used as a proxy for risk. While there is not total agreement in this area, the terms "variability" and "risk" are used interchangeably in the following discussion.

_____

[2]8% is the geometric mean, calculated from the general formula: $(1 + r_1)(1 + r_2) = (1 + r)^2$.

Absolute Risk

Absolute risk refers to the range of actual realized investment results that has occurred or is likely to occur during specific time periods. This total variability is normally measured in one of two ways. The most accepted method is to calculate the standard deviation of periodic returns (such as monthly or quarterly) as a proxy for absolute risk. A less frequently encountered measure is the semi-interquartile range. This is calculated by ranking the periodic returns, normally high to low, and dividing the number of returns into quartiles. The range between the top of the second quartile and the bottom of the third quartile (actually, the 25th and 75th percentiles) is the semi-interquartile range. This measure is less affected by a few extraordinarily large periodic returns than is the standard deviation. It was used in the BAI study and appears in its COMVEST measurement system.

Relative Risk

Relative risk refers to the range of realized investment results of a portfolio relative to the range of results of the market or a comparison-standard portfolio. Total variability in relative terms is calculated by dividing portfolio variability (the standard deviation of portfolio returns) by market variability (the standard deviation of market returns). An index, usually the S&P 500, is used as a proxy for the market. Variability is calculated exactly as for the portfolio with the same statistical method (standard deviation or semi-interquartile range) over the same period using the same measurement points.

Market-Related Variability

Market-related variability refers both to the range of realized returns of a portfolio relative to the market over a period and to the degree to which movement of portfolio and market returns coincided during the period. Market-related variability (market risk) has become the most important method of measuring relative risk. The difference between total variability in relative terms and market-related variability is important. Over a period of three years, for example, two portfolios could have the same variability as the market. Each would have a total variability relative to the market of 1.0 (the standard deviations of the monthly returns would be identical). However, the individual monthly returns of one portfolio in terms of monthly amplitude and timing might be significantly different from those of the market. In fact, the portfolio might have gone up in months when the market went down. The market-related variability might be low because of the low comovement of the two returns even though total variability in relative terms (on the basis of standard deviation of returns) is identical. The other portfolio might have fluctuated closely with the market, indicating a higher market-related risk than in the first portfolio.

To calculate market-related variability or market risk, the relationship of fluctuations in portfolio returns to fluctuations in market returns needs to be calculated. This relationship is usually calculated through least squares regression and, as noted earlier, is stated in terms of beta.[3] Different methods of structuring the data and analysis can give different estimates of beta.

Most performance measurement services use an approach based on excess returns (actual period returns minus the risk-free rate), nevertheless, variations are still common. Because theory and practice are so closely linked in

---

[3]Least squares regression is a statistical technique used to find a single line that best fits or summarizes a group of data points. Thus, the calculation determines the most representative average relationship over the selected period. This relationship indicates how much on average the portfolio return fluctuates with a given fluctuation in the market return. One of several approaches may be used:

- Periodic (such as quarterly) portfolio returns are regressed on periodic market returns. This is the oldest method and is still used in some measurement systems.

- Risk-free rates of returns (as represented by Treasury bills) for each period are subtracted from each portfolio return and market return, then excess portfolio returns are regressed on excess market returns.

- All returns are converted to logarithms rather than using reported arithmetic returns. Least squares regression has better results for statistical testing with logarithms because the distribution of logarithmic changes is closer to a normal bell-shaped distribution than the distribution of arithmetic changes when using long differencing intervals.

- Instead of using regular periods, returns are calculated over market swings. While this technique generally improves the reliability of the systematic risk calculation, it is most practical if daily valuations are available.

this area, technical advances in performance measurement closely follow technical advances in models of capital asset returns.[4]

Methods of Adjusting for Risk

An important aspect of performance measurement is comparison with the results of others and frequently with a so-called naive alternative. For comparisons to be meaningful, it is essential that results be risk-adjusted. However, before examining techniques for risk adjustment, it is helpful to consider briefly the practical use of risk-adjusted comparisons. The following comments on standards of comparisons are therefore in summary form. The choices of standards of comparisons are discussed in detail in the next section of this chapter.

One common comparative standard of effective investment management is an ability to produce a positive alpha, which is a rate of return greater than that attributable to the market index alternative after adjustment for differences in market risk. A positive alpha can be produced by an ability to buy underpriced and avoid overpriced securities (selection skills) or by an ability to anticipate general market moves (timing skills).

Another common comparative standard of effective management is the ability to outperform other managers operating at the same risk level or, alternatively, to achieve similar performance at less risk. Understanding portfolio performance measurement as related to these two standards is an important prerequisite to assembling an effective measurement system.

A useful addition to the preceding standards is the "naive alternative." In many parts of the investment process, it is possible to find a reasonable course of action that could be taken by someone without making forecasts. For example, some measurement systems "freeze" the portfolio as it exists at

---

[4]The capital asset pricing model has had broad but never unanimous acceptance; until recently, most areas of disagreement were highly technical. Recently the model has come under broad attack and it is possible that a new theory of capital asset returns will develop over the next several years. For further information, see R. Roll, "Ambiguity When Performance Is Measured by the Security Market Line," *Journal of Finance,* September 1978; and S. A. Ross, "Arbitrage Theory of Asset Pricing," *Journal of Economic Theory,* December 1976.

a particular point in time and compare subsequent values of the managed portfolio with subsequent values of the frozen portfolio. Another and perhaps more frequent example of the naive alternative is to use a market or index portfolio as a yardstick; that is, a portfolio consisting solely of a stock market index (S&P 500) or, if necessary, in combination usually with Treasury bills to create the same level of risk as that of the real portfolio being measured.

This methodology fits two of the three requirements of a naive alternative. First, it is relevant because an index fund (S&P 500) can be substituted for the equity portion of most managed portfolios. Second, it is practical because a market-weighted index can be replicated with a real portfolio. Third, it can be made fair; in this case fairness requires deducting any necessary (usually small) transaction costs from index results. Using the S&P 500 as an example, additions and deletions are made on Wednesday at the closing prices. These prices will not necessarily prevail for an actual index fund until the next day's trading. Because such changes are normally few (typically around ten a year) and primarily occur for the smallest companies, the net effect on a calculated rate of return is minor and can be safely ignored. However, the wholesale revision to the index that occurred effective July 1, 1976, highlighted this problem.

Regression Analysis: Beta, Alpha, and Correlation

Risk adjustment begins with choice of a historic period, usually three to five years at a minimum, and choice of the differencing interval or period between measurements. Some services use a monthly differencing interval, and others use quarterly data. Five years of quarterly data provides 20 data points, which is usually considered the minimum number in calculating meaningful least squares regressions. Three years of monthly data provides 36 points, and the resulting calculations may be more accurate and certainly more timely.

Once the historic period and the differencing interval are selected, returns on the portfolio and ordinarily on a market index are collected. Current state-of-the-art measurement systems typically subtract the risk-free rate from actual returns to derive excess returns. Excess returns are plotted on a graph for each period, and a line is fitted using least squares regression. This line shows the average relationship between fluctuations in the portfolio and in the market.

In Chart X-1, each dot represents the relationship of performance of a portfolio and the market index for a single quarter. The 20 dots, representing five years of quarterly data, are plotted and the regression line fitted.

In Chart X-2, the dots are eliminated because calculation of the line provides the three important pieces of information needed for the period: beta, alpha, and correlation coefficient.

Beta is the beta coefficient of the portfolio, measured as the slope of the regression line. It measures the average market-related risk of the portfolio over the five year period. A portfolio exactly as risky as the market will have a beta coefficient of 1.0; that is, for each additional unit of market return the portfolio will, on average, have one additional unit of return. (A one-to-one relationship exists between the market return, typically that of the S&P 500, and the portfolio return.) A portfolio that is riskier than the market will have a regression line with a steeper slope and thus a beta coefficient greater than 1.0 (a change of one unit in the market return will produce a change in excess of one unit in the portfolio return). Conversely, a portfolio that is less risky will have a regression line with a shallower slope and thus a beta coefficient less than 1.0.

Chart X-1—RELATIONSHIP OF PORTFOLIO RETURNS TO MARKET RETURNS

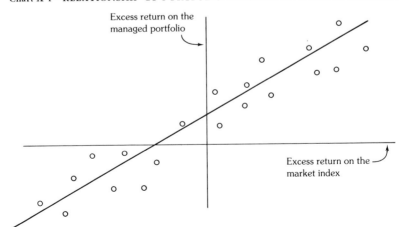

Chart X-2—CORRELATION OF PORTFOLIO RETURNS TO MARKET RETURNS

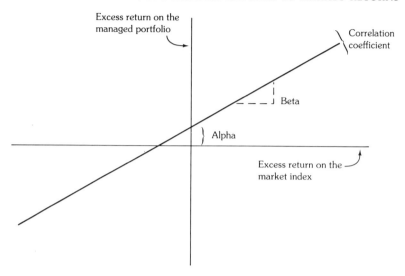

Alpha is the alpha coefficient, measured by the intercept of the regression line with the vertical axis. If the intercept is above the hortizontal axis, the alpha is positive; if below it the alpha is negative. As plotted in Chart X-2, the portfolio has a positive alpha. This positive alpha is the average excess return (in excess of the risk-free rate) earned when the market excess return is zero, but alphas are earned not only in zero return markets. Because the regression line summarizes actual data, alpha is the same at any point along the line. In other words, the portfolio's return will on average exceed that for the market by the same differential amount irrespective of the market's return.

Correlation is the correlation coefficient, sometimes called r, measured in terms of the dispersion of the data points about the line. This is the closeness of fit between fluctuations in excess returns of the actual portfolio and in excess returns of the market portfolio and is a measure of portfolio diversification. A perfectly diversified portfolio such as an index fund, will have a correlation coefficient of 1.0; it will be identical to a market portfolio (e.g., S&P 500). A typical, actively managed diversified institutional equity portfolio will move in the same direction as the market most of the time and have a correlation coefficient of about .85 to .95. An undiversified (highly concentrated) portfolio will have a much lower correlation coefficient and a much more erratic relationship to the market.

Comparison with Results of Others

To this point, risk adjustment has been used in measuring the performance of a single portfolio primarily in terms of the portfolio's alpha relative to that of a market index. However, the process of calculating an alpha has also provided an estimate of market risk (through the beta coefficient) and diversification (through the coefficient of correlation). The use of these three types of information in comparing the portfolio results of one manager with those of other managers is demonstrated in the following paragraphs.

At the outset, each portfolio is risk-adjusted using identical time periods, differencing intervals, and statistical methods. Returns are time-weighted to remove the influence of cash flows on the various portfolios.

Market Risk. The first comparison is in terms of return and market risk (beta). A graph is drawn comparing the rate of return achieved with the amount of market risk undertaken (Chart X-3). The return on the risk-free asset, usually 90-day Treasury bills when using quarterly differencing intervals, is plotted at a 0.0 (zero) beta. The return on the market portfolio as represented by an index (S&P 500) is plotted at a beta of 1.0. A straight line extends from the Treasury bill return to the market return and on to higher levels of beta. A naive portfolio with a beta less than 1.0 will lie on the line to the left of the market plot. This portfolio can be constructed by mixing

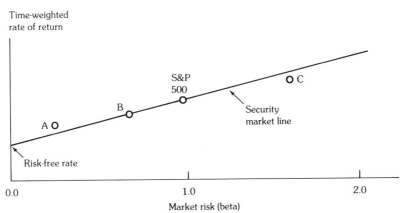

Chart X-3—PERFORMANCE COMPARISON ADJUSTED FOR MARKET RISK

appropriate amounts of the market portfolio (S&P 500) and the risk-free asset (representing lending by the investor at the risk-free rate).

Higher risk naive portfolios lie to the right of the market plot. These portfolios can be constructed by appropriately leveraging the market portfolio (theoretically representing borrowing at the risk-free rate). The entire line, called the "security market line," represents returns available during this period for naive portfolios at different risk levels.[5]

Chart X-3 shows a security market line with the results of three managed portfolios (A, B, and C) plotted. Note that the time-weighted rates of return for portfolios A, B, and C and the S&P 500 are plotted against market risk (beta). The alpha coefficient will equal the vertical distance from the plotted portfolio rate of return point to the security market line. (As set forth above, by definition the S&P 500 has a beta of 1.0 and its return is on the line.)

The effect of risk adjustment on the rankings of these three portfolios is dramatic:

- Portfolio A had the lowest market risk of the three portfolios, substantially lower than that for the S&P 500, and earned a positive alpha. Portfolio A's return lies above the security market line; accordingly, it earned a positive alpha. In other words, the return exceeded that for a market portfolio (or naive portfolio) consisting of that proportion of Treasury bills and stocks (S&P 500) that had a market risk identical to that of Portfolio A.

- Portfolio B had a lower beta than that for the S&P 500 or Portfolio C but a higher beta than Portfolio A. It had a zero alpha because the return exactly matched the market alternative with the same risk.

- Portfolio C had the highest time-weighted return. It also had higher than market risk (higher beta) and earned a return less than the market alternative. Therefore, it had a negative alpha.

Clearly, in terms of absolute return, Portfolio C did the best, portfolio B ranked second, and Portfolio A ranked last.

---

[5]An alternative to the security market line is the "empirical market line." This is a line fitted by least squares regression to the actual returns earned at different levels of risk during a specific period. The risk-return data may be drawn from actual results of many portfolios or calculated from hypothetical portfolios set at different risk levels at the beginning of the period.

In terms of return adjusted for market risk, Portfolio A ranked first, Portfolio B ranked second, and Portfolio C ranked last. The rankings are exactly reversed from those on an absolute basis.

At this point, modern risk-adjusted performance appears to conflict with common sense. If Portfolio C earned the highest return and Portfolio A earned the lowest return, the question is whether it matters if A outperformed C on a risk-adjusted basis.

The answer lies in the risk-return implications of the two portfolios. In this regard, three points are to be made. First, it is difficult consistently to select underpriced securities and produce a positive alpha. If the positive alpha for Portfolio A is representative, the management of A is doing an above average job of security selection. If the negative alpha is representative for Portfolio C, the reverse is true for its management.

Second, it is well-recognized that across a span of time and on average, returns in the security markets will be approximately proportional to the risk assumed. The market risk assumed in Portfolio C was substantially more than that in Portfolio A; that is, the likelihood of *not* receiving C's higher return was much greater than in the case of A's return.

Moreover, because Portfolio C had a negative alpha, its additional return over A was not proportional to its additional risk. If the negative alpha of Portfolio C persists, the plan sponsor will not be paid for all of the risk assumed. Portfolio C will gain less than a naive alternative with the same risk level and the dollar amount of the shortfall will be equal to the negative alpha times the value of the assets under management. It is possible that the return on Portfolio C before risk adjustment will exceed that for the S&P 500, but even under these circumstances, the plan sponsor with Portfolio C would be better off to move to a naive portfolio at the same risk level.

Third, differences in the risk-adjusted returns emphasize the importance of plan sponsors establishing their tolerance for risk in quantitative terms. If Portfolio A represents a mature pension fund with heavy disbursements, constraining risk as severely as indicated may be highly desirable. However, if the fund has no current disbursements and a long time horizon, a less restrictive approach might well be appropriate. Such a posture would be particularly desirable if the plan sponsor were convinced that the manager of

Portfolio A could continue to generate positive alphas at higher levels of market risk. In fact, under such circumstances, the fund would be unnecessarily foregoing additional income.

Total Risk. The preceding discussion of modern risk adjustment techniques for measuring performance relates to market risk as calculated statistically through regression analysis and stated as beta. An alternative is to measure performance in terms of the ability to achieve returns with a minimum of total variability or with less variability than other portfolios with the same returns.[6]

Total variability (total risk) in an equity portfolio includes not only market risk but also nonmarket risk resulting from less than perfect diversification in the portfolio compared with a market index (S&P 500). As a result, two portfolios with the *same* betas (market risk) can have different *total* risks if one is well diversified and the other is poorly diversified.

One result of this situation would be that the poorly diversified portfolio would have a much lower correlation coefficient with the market index than the well diversified portfolio. The dispersion of the returns of the poorly diversified one about the regression line would be much greater than that of its counterpart. If the two portfolios had the same returns as well as betas, risk averse investors would clearly prefer the one with the lower total risk. There would be more assurance of getting the average results indicated by the regression line in the portfolio with the lower risk.[7]

Chart X-4 is similar to Chart X-3 except that the horizontal axis is changed from market risk to total risk. The total variability of the risk-free asset is still zero. The total variability of the stock market (S&P 500) remains 1.0, by definition. The total variability of each portfolio relative to that of the market can be calculated by dividing the standard deviation of portfolio returns by the standard deviation of market returns.

---

[6]Another alternative is to measure the excess return per unit of variability; see W. F. Sharpe, *Investments,* Prentice-Hall, Inc., Englewood Cliffs, New Jersey, 1978, pp. 552–53.

[7]There is a mathematical relationship between the two factors: the ratio of total variability of the portfolio relative to that of the market always equals the market risk (beta) divided by the correlation coefficient. For example, assume two portfolios each with a beta identical to the market (1.0) but well diversified Portfolio A has a correlation coefficient of .80 whereas poorly diversified Portfolio B has a correlation coefficient of .40. Portfolio A's total risk is $1.0/.80 = 1.25$ whereas Portfolio B's is $1.0/.40 = 2.5$ or double that of A.

Chart X-4—PERFORMANCE COMPARISON ADJUSTED FOR TOTAL RISK

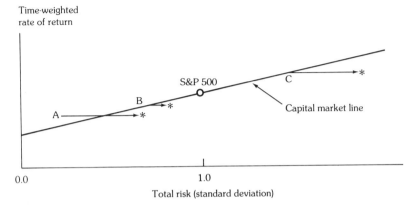

As can be seen from Chart X-4, the capital market line does not change because it is anchored on the risk-free asset and the market portfolio (S&P 500). (Note that the expression "capital market line" is used to designate the risk-return relationship when risk is measured in terms of standard deviation.) Returns for the three portfolios (A, B, and C) remain the same. Only the relative risk positions change, causing the portfolio plots to move horizontally to the right. In each instance, the amount of the move is in proportion to the amount of additional risk resulting from less than perfect correlation to market fluctuations.

Portfolio C's return, which produced a negative alpha when adjusted for market risk alone, looks much worse on a total relative risk basis because that portfolio is so poorly diversified. Portfolio B's neutral alpha becomes only slightly negative. Portfolio A, which has low market risk, is also poorly diversified and moves substantially to the right. The vertical distance from each asterisk to the capital market line measures the relative performance of each portfolio. On this basis, Portfolio B ranks first, Portfolio A falls to second place, and Portfolio C remains the worst.

The appropriate method for developing risk-adjusted returns depends on the objective of the portfolio under review. To assure thorough comparison and analysis, returns must be adjusted for both market risk and total risk. If the manager is charged with running a well-diversified portfolio, the emphasis should be on total risk. If the manager is one of several in a multimanager situation and each manager is expected to specialize in a particular strategy

Chart X-5—TESTING FOR MARKET TIMING

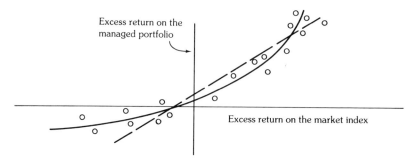

or style, the emphasis in performance measurement of individual managers should be on market risk. However, performance of the aggregate portfolio should also be analyzed on a total risk basis for insight into diversification of the total portfolio and as a check on overall control of the multimanager system.

Market Timing

A final topic in measurement of risk is detecting, measuring, and adjusting for the effects of market timing. Someone successful in market timing would be heavily invested in aggressive securities in up markets and defensive securities, possibly including cash, in down markets. Chart X-5 shows a possible pattern of the 20 quarterly data points for a successful market timer.

A straight line can be fitted to these data in the normal manner. The statistics will show a strongly positive alpha but a relatively low correlation coefficient. However, a curved line can be fitted to the same data (using multiple regression to produce a quadratic rather than a linear equation). Because the curved line has a steeper slope during up markets and a shallower slope during down markets, it will fit the data better. If significant curvature in the appropriate direction is found, it suggests an ability to predict stock market cycles.[8]

---

[8]The mechanics of testing for market timing ability are relatively simple. The normal linear regression includes the portfolio performance as the dependent variable and the market performance as the independent variable. Use of the quadratic equation requires one additional independent variable—the square of the market performance. If this second variable is statistically significant, the curved line fits the data better than the straight line.

The straight-line alpha includes performance resulting from both security selection and market timing. The curved line will show a lower alpha attributable to security selection plus significant curvature attributable to market timing.

In actual practice, consistently significant market timing is relatively rare. The quadratic equation will usually detect some insignificant curvature, which may or may not be in the correct direction. When a manager attempts to time the market but does not succeed consistently, the regression line stays straight but the correlation coefficient falls because periodic returns deviate more widely. This increased portfolio variability plus accompanying transaction costs causes the compound return on the portfolio to fall.

Referring back to the earlier comparison of portfolios adjusted for market risk, it is possible that the manager of Portfolio C might want credit for positioning the portfolio for an up market and achieving a better than market return, even though the manager's alpha was negative. However, it can be seen from Chart X-5 that when a successful market timer is measured using a straight-line regression, the alpha tends to be high. The only way a successful market timer can have a negative alpha is if security selection is so bad that it completely overcomes market timing success, which is not likely.

Choice of Standards of Comparison

The fourth key aspect of performance measurement is choosing relevant standards of comparison. The choice of a standard is closely linked with other key aspects because it must be compatible with the method of adjusting for risk and ultimate objectives of the fund. An example of the major effect the comparison standard can have on the investment process is the progression of the S&P 500 Index from a convenient standard in the 1960s to an investment product in the 1970s.

Historically, there have been three primary standards and modern portfolio theory has made a significant contribution to each. The standards are:

- Actuarial interest rate assumptions and specific portfolio return objectives (e.g., yield, realized capital gains, total returns)

- Results of other pools of assets

- Market index results.

Comparison with Actuarial Interest Rates and Return Objectives

To calculate the current pension expense, actuaries must use an estimate of a long term rate of return that will be earned by the pension assets; this rate is the so-called interest rate assumption. It is often taken as a minimum investment return requirement, and the actual return objective is based on levels of return forecast for principally markets for stocks, bonds, and money market instruments over the next five or ten years or longer.

Irrespective of the manner in which it is generated, the return objective for a pension fund constitutes an internal (dollar-weighted) rate of return for the total portfolio rather than a time-weighted rate. Accordingly, if each manager is measured only on a time-weighted basis, it is possible to lose track of the dramatic effect that the timing of cash flows can have on the internal rate of return of the aggregate portfolio.

By measuring the difference between time-weighted returns of individual managers and the internal rate of return of the fund, some insight can be gained into the amount and direction of the influence of cash flows. In 1976 and, to a lesser extent, in 1975, much of the year's performance occurred in January before most new contributions were allocated to managers. Although the full impact of the January gain would be included in time-weighted returns, in the internal (dollar weighted) return calculation the January gain would be diluted by subsequent investment of additional funds.

In those somewhat unusual instances when either the actuarial assumption or the investment return objective is the only standard and the manager is free to choose a risk level and asset mix to meet the objective, the absolute standard may be the correct one for comparisons. For example, if the actuarial rate assumption is 6% and the investment return objective is 8%, a manager may be able to meet either requirement by investing entirely in high grade bonds. During subsequent bull markets, the portfolio can ordinarily be expected to rank low relative to other pools of assets that include equities or to stock market indexes. However, the objective is met with little or no risk of shortfall. Accordingly, if the investment objective is solely an absolute rate of return, bottom-line performance measurement should concentrate on calculating performance relative to that standard. Nevertheless, even in these instances it will be helpful if risk-adjusted numbers are calculated for such purposes as reevaluating objectives or making future comparisons with results of other potential managers.

Comparison with Other Pools of Assets

Comparison with results of other asset pools is the traditional standard; this comparison has a natural appeal in a competitive world. Theoretical research has raised many caveats about the approach. Comparisons formerly were reported using internal returns without risk adjustment. Theory contributed the time-weighted return to neutralize the effects of differing cash flows and thereby improved the usefulness of comparisons. However, most research suggests that without risk adjustment, limited usable information is gained from simple comparisons. Risk-adjustment comparisons with other pools of assets were discussed earlier in this chapter under market and total risk.

Services providing nonrisk-adjusted comparisons usually show the time-weighted rate of return for the measured portfolio ranked within a large group of other portfolios over several time periods. Modern portfolio theory suggests that portfolios with different risk-return objectives will be managed differently and have different risk postures. The amount of risk inherent in the portfolios of the comparison universe is not ordinarily presented; accordingly, the relevance of a particular ranking may not be readily clear. Many funds also have restrictions on holdings of specific companies or industries and specific requirements in terms of diversification, yields, quality, P/E ratios, and so forth. If the dimensions of these constraints are sufficiently large, comparisons with broad universes of portfolios may yield little usable information.

In an effort to imporve comparability, some services segment the portfolio universe by size, type of manager, or stated objective to provide more comparable subsets. Other services use only bank commingled funds and mutual funds, which are assumed to be free of specific restraints and have similar risk profiles after adjusting for stated objectives. The purpose of segmentation is to equalize risk without going through the statistics of risk adjustment, but it is unlikely to achieve a similar level of accuracy. The user will need to appraise the degree of precision in this type of risk segmentation and thus its usefulness in specific circumstances. It should be noted, however, that segmentation after statistical risk adjustment can be useful to check for nonmarket-related differences between groups of funds with different sizes and objectives.

If nonrisk-adjusted comparisons are used, there must be a clear under-standing between client and manager regarding which subsets and time periods are meaningful for a specific portfolio. It is easy to generate a large number of comparisons by altering subsets and time periods, but if each comparison is not chosen to fit a specific situation the performance measurement report will be characterized more by overwhelming detail than by effective measurement.

Comparison with Market Results

Market index results have been used as a standard for many years. The two main issues in this area are:

- Which index should be used
- Whether the comparisons should be risk-adjusted.

As mentioned in Chapter I, the composition and statistical calculation of stock indexes can be substantially different. As a result, performance can vary dramatically among them for significant lengths of time. Some indexes are calculated by arithmetically averaging share prices, some by weighting price changes by prices of stocks, and some by weighting price changes by the market value of outstanding shares. Changes in the index from one period to another are sometimes calculated arithmetically, sometimes geometrically, and sometimes as an average of the two. An index chosen as a comparison standard should be constructed and calculated to be compatible with objectives and requirements of the portfolio.

An index weighted by the market value of the outstanding shares (capital-ization weighted) is usually chosen for performance measurement because it has a theoretically desirable property—all shares could actually be held by all investors at the given prices. Standard & Poor's indexes and the New York, American, and NASDAQ indexes are all capitalization-weighted. The Dow Jones, Value Line, and Indicator Digest indexes are not capitalization-weighted. The Wilshire 5000 Stock Index, published weekly in *Barron's*, is a comprehensive capitalization-weighted index.

The most frequently chosen index is the S&P 500. It is large enough to be reasonably comprehensive and correlates well with most other capitalization weighted indexes. Since the major revision in this index in 1976, it more closely reflects the typical institutional investment universe. However, the more broadly based indexes may be preferred.

When a manager is operating in only a portion of the U.S. universe of stocks, as would be true for a manager of small stocks, low P/E stocks, or income stocks, a broad market index would not ordinarily be relevant. The same is obviously true for foreign common stocks. Communications are simplified if objectives, performance measurement, and beta coefficients of individual securities are expressed in terms of the same naive alternative. The best index will be the one that most closely approximates the relevant naive portfolio.[9]

Managers should only be measured on decisions that are within their discretion. If the naive alternative includes bonds or cash, but the manager has been instructed to invest fully in equities, comparisons will be flawed. If the portfolio includes restricted or unsaleable assets, they should be excluded from performance measurement unless purchased by the manager, as in the purchase of privately placed debt. If the manager has been instructed to avoid investment in a significant portion of the market index, e.g., oil stocks, the index performance should be recalculated excluding that sector. The method of recalculation will depend on the type of index used. The necessary data can be obtained from the publisher of the index or from data banks of securities prices and dividends. Standard and Poor's Corporation publishes the performance of various industry subgroups of the S&P 500 on a weekly basis. Using these price data and S&P's quarterly report on relative weightings of each stock and subgroup in the index makes it possible to exclude specific stocks, industries, and sectors.

[9]Measurement of the performance of homogeneous stock groups is growing in importance.

Choice of Relevant Time Period

The final key aspect of a measurement system is choosing a relevant time period for performance analysis and an appropriate differencing interval (the subperiods for which interim portfolio valuations are collected).

There is a considerable amount of "random noise" in short term measurements that tends to disappear in longer differencing intervals. For this reason, it is not ordinarily practical to use intervals as short as days or weeks; the error ranges and period-to-period fluctuations are too high.

Statistical validity will also improve if more intervals are used. For example, quarterly data for ten years are more useful than those for five years. However, as the overall length of the period covered is increased, the timeliness of the data may decline. This problem arises because results of the regression analysis are actually estimates of average values of measured factors (such as alpha and beta) during the period. These estimates can be thought of as most applicable to the midpoint of the total period. Thus, using five years of data gives one an estimate of the factors two and one-half years ago. Ten years of data gives one a more accurate estimate of the factors, but as of five years ago. The loss of timeliness tends to overcome the improved accuracy. Weighting techniques are available that give more importance to the most recent data in an effort to improve the timeliness/accuracy tradeoff.

Because at least 20 (preferably 30) data points are needed for useful least squares regression, most performance measurement systems use quarterly data for five years or monthly data for three years as the most practical compromise between timeliness and statistical accuracy. Alternatively, the differencing interval can be defined as a small market swing (usually in the 2% to 5% range) rather than a fixed time period. Risk adjustment based on market swings is probably more precise than risk adjustment based on fixed intervals, but there are practical problems entailed in obtaining portfolio valuations on the specific days that mark each interim peak and trough. Also, during some years, the market experiences many interim swings while during others there may be a general trend up or down with few reversals. This can make it difficult to understand changes in factor estimates and error ranges produced by market-swing risk adjustment.

If three to five years of data constitute the lower bound of the relevant time period, the question remains as to what is the upper bound. It is certainly possible that a manager with a fundamental ability to produce a positive alpha could show a negative alpha over any one-, three-, or five-year period. Random chance or a single pervasive error could cause this to happen. Many managers suggest a couple of market cycles or a ten-year period as a reasonable minimum to allow their underlying skills to be fully evidenced. This allows time for the market process to test the manager's skills for consistency in different economic environments.

In practical terms, the question as to how long below average performance can be tolerated is probably answered by internal management and other considerations rather than statistical analysis. Informed, objective, and fair judgment by the corporate executive can contribute more than statistical analysis over a three- or five-year period. Poor performance resulting from high personnel turnover, an investment approach departing from the client's original understanding, or repeated errors in specific predictions would make a manager subject to dismissal on judgmental grounds long before firm statistical grounds became available. Statistical weakness is a serious drawback to bottom-line measurement and has been an important motivation for developing the diagnostic systems discussed in the next chapter.

The Employee Retirement Income Security Act of 1974 appears to require three-year reviews of experienced gains and losses and appropriate adjustment of contributions. An ideal measurement system would provide feedback early enough in the three-year period to alter the process sufficiently to affect the three-year results. This is beyond the state of the art of bottom-line performance measurement today.

A final caveat on the choice of time periods is the danger of placing too much reliance on any one-, three-, or five-year period. Shifting the beginning or ending date a few quarters either way can often make a dramatic difference in performance statistics. For marketing purposes, money managers may be tempted to use the time period that casts their results in the most favorable light. The corporate financial officer should obtain comparative results for several periods, perhaps using a moving average of three or five years, to ensure a less biased measurement of the manager's performance.

BOTTOM-LINE PORTFOLIO PERFORMANCE MEASUREMENT SERVICES

Bottom-line performance measurement services concentrate on the total portfolio or major asset portions, such as the equity portion. They emphasize measurement and analysis of aggregate fluctuations rather than changes in individual holdings. They have each made choices and compromises in the key aspects of measuring returns and risks and choosing standards and time periods. If these choices are well understood by the corporate executive, a significant amount of information can be obtained from bottom-line measurement.

COMVEST

The COMVEST program is available only to banks, which use it to provide performance measurement services for their clients. The principles of the system have been used in other measurement services that are available to nonbank managers and perhaps most widely by Telstat Systems of New York. The entire emphasis is on risk-adjusted measurement of a specific portfolio rather than comparison of the portfolio with other pools of assets. It is possible for a bank or measurement service to assemble a universe of portfolios, analyze them all with the COMVEST system, and present comparisons similar to those in the discussion of risk adjustment earlier in this chapter.

Returns are calculated both internally (dollar-weighted) and on a time-weighted basis. The BAI developed a method of estimating the portfolio value on the date of each contribution or withdrawal that did not correspond to a regular valuation date.[10] The method uses regression analysis and was the best of several alternatives tested, providing an average error of less than 20 basis points.

Risk is calculated as the mean absolute deviation of quarterly returns, which is simply the average of absolute differences between actual quarterly returns and mean quarterly returns.

[10]See footnote 1 for reference.

The system can handle any relevant index; however, the S&P 500 is normally used. The measurement period can be any length up to ten years, using quarterly data.

Nonrisk-Adjusted Results

Services that use nonrisk-adjusted results usually maintain a data bank of market indexes plus up to several hundred funds on a monthly or quarterly basis. The primary emphasis is on interfund comparisons in which performances of all or a large subset of funds are ranked and displayed in summary terms such as quartiles or deciles. The fund being measured will usually be plotted on the display. Returns may be calculated on both an internal and a time-weighted basis, but comparative displays will typically show time-weighted results. Ranks may be calculated for many time periods such as individual quarters or years, cumulative performance since market highs and lows, performance for multiple year periods, or performance during quarters bracketing market highs and lows.

The *Institutional Funds Evaluation Service* of A. G. Becker, Incorporated is the largest example of this type of service.[11] Additional data are provided on smaller sets of funds, selected by type of asset or manager and by stated objective. Risk measures are calculated, but the emphasis is clearly on interfund comparisons.

Pensions & Investments magazine has begun a performance measurement service called PIPER, an acronym for Pension & Investments Performance Evaluation Review. This tracks a large universe of bank commingled funds and accounts managed by insurance companies. Similar services are offered by Computer Directions Advisers of Silver Springs, Maryland, and Evaluation Associates of Westport, Connecticut. These services usually present ranked performance results with the names of the best and worst managers over various time periods, sorted by broad investment objectives. They have the advantages of economy, identifying managers by name, and providing some

---

[11]Some other examples of this type of service, with differing emphasis on risk-adjusted comparisons, are those offered by Frank Russell Co., Tacoma, Washington and Callan Associates, Inc., San Francisco, California.

segmentation of results. Typically, they do not provide risk-adjusted comparisons.

Risk-Adjusted Results

Services that use risk-adjusted results also maintain a data bank of funds for comparison, but their primary emphasis is on risk adjustment of the client's portfolio and risk-adjusted comparisons. The key exhibits frequently look like Charts X-2 and X-3. (Some measurement services are offered by Merrill Lynch, Pierce, Fenner & Smith, New York, and Wilshire Associates, Santa Monica, California.)

Portfolio betas and alphas are calculated for various time periods. Returns are related to portfolio mix, selection effect, and timing ability—often on a quarter-by-quarter basis. The risk-return profile of a client account can be related to profiles of other funds and to the security market line.

Some services use achieved results by the universe of funds to derive an empirical market line; this is a regression line summarizing the actual risk-return experience of the universe for a particular period. The client can observe the position of the fund in comparison with others and investigate the cause of results. Some facets of risk-adjusted measurement are found in many other systems, including some of the diagnostic systems discussed in the next chapter.

SUMMARY

An effective performance measurement system provides information used to evaluate and appraise managers, rethink investment objectives, and alter portfolio strategy. Establishing an effective system requires four steps: defining objectives and strategy, obtaining reliable and timely data, using appropriate statistical methods to produce relevant measurements, and providing output information in a useful format. The key questions to address are measurement of return and risk and selection of standards of comparison and relevant time periods.

Internal or dollar-weighted returns can be used to compare the progress of the fund with actuarial or overall objectives. Time-weighted returns usually are more appropriate to measure the performance of individual managers. Returns should also be measured on a risk-adjusted basis. One risk adjustment procedure provides estimates of the alpha, beta, and correlation coefficient of the portfolio relative to a market index. These factors can be compared with the same factors produced by other portfolios. Comparisons can be made adjusted for market risk, which is usually appropriate in the multimanager situation, or for total risk, which is usually appropriate for the total portfolio or in the single diversified manager situation.

The question of the relevant time period for useful measurement requires a choice between shorter periods, using only more recent data but having less statistical precision, and longer periods, providing a higher degree of statistical accuracy with the possible penalty of less relevancy. The most practical compromise between timeliness and statistical accuracy appears to be five years of quarterly data or three years of monthly data. However, even the five-year period is too short to develop precise statistical measures of risk-adjusted results. This weakness is a serious drawback to bottom-line measurement and has been an important motivation for developing the diagnostic systems discussed in the next chapter.

CHAPTER

11 Diagnostic Analysis

Diagnostic analysis differs from bottom-line performance measurement in that it analyzes portfolio composition beginning with individual security positions. Bottom-line measurement can be performed using only fluctuations in values of the total portfolio or major asset categories, such as common stock holdings. Modern risk adjustment can extract a significant amount of information from aggregate data (such as alpha, beta, and coefficient of correlation) that helps to analyze the sources of results. However, as pension executives have implemented risk-adjusted measures, they have not been satisfied with the magnitude of the error ranges associated with these broad descriptive statistics. Partially for this reason, such decisions as choosing a new manager or reallocating cash flows have continued to be based primarily on subjective factors. As a result, pension executives have come to need more detailed and timely information.

At the same time, investment managers have become increasingly concerned with delivering more consistent and improved results to clients. Accordingly, many managers have implemented partial diagnostic systems that concentrate on a limited part of the investment process, such as security analysis or trading. In some cases, these pioneering efforts have run ahead of supporting theory and techniques; consequently, partial systems have been tried that measure the wrong things or use inappropriate statistical methods.

When accurate diagnostic data are available, the present or potential client can ask to review them for deeper insights into the manager's analytical and portfolio management strengths and decision-making process. When risk-adjusted bottom-line measurement shows a positive but not statistically significant alpha, the diagnostic data may show value being added at different points in the process and raise both the understanding and the comfort level of the client.

Risk-adjusted performance measurement divides portfolio risk into market risk (beta) and nonmarket risk. Diagnostic analysis goes further into the nonmarket risk portion than bottom-line performance measurement. There are two sources of nonmarket risk:

- The risk associated with large groups of securities that tend to fluctuate together after removing the influence of the general market, such as growth, income, energy, bank, or electric utility stocks

- Specific risk for each individual security.

The group or industry type of risk (extramarket covariance) represents the major source of nonmarket risk in a portfolio. It can be important in certain situations. For example, a pension portfolio might have considerable exposure to this type of risk because of substantial holdings of interest sensitive companies or high growth companies or some other major grouping of companies. Not only is the group or industry risk high in such a portfolio but if the corporation's earnings are sensitive to the same economic variables as the group, an undesirable situation might occur in which pension results are weakest when the funding corporation's earnings are weakest.

Risk attributable to the operating and management situation of individual companies (specific risk) is unique to each company and therefore independent across companies. Accordingly, specific risk tends to cancel out in a well-diversified portfolio. When one company's stock is doing surprisingly well, another may be doing surprisingly poorly. However, some minimum amount of specific risk remains unless an index fund is formed. As a result, one area for future research in diagnostic measurement is finding better methods of identifying these risks and understanding their effects more fully.

PURPOSES OF DIAGNOSTIC ANALYSIS

Diagnostic analysis assists the corporate executive in three principal ways:

- Understanding the logic behind and the results of portfolio composition
- Relating portfolio activity to a manager's investment style
- Measuring and controlling a fund with several managers.

Understanding the composition of a portfolio gives the executive insight into the sources of performance and allows detailed discussion with the manager about the intermediate term portfolio strategy (and, if desired, short term tactics). If a manager can list the assumptions, explain the strategy, and produce a portfolio that is diagnosed as compatible with that strategy, the plan sponsor can have more confidence in the validity of statistical results. Thus, diagnostic analysis should improve the unavoidable subjective judgments of both the sponsor and the manager.

Diagnostic analysis can also assist in relating portfolio actions to a manager's style. This relationship can be important in several ways. First, if a particular segment of the market, such as large market capitalization growth stocks, has been doing especially well it can affect the alpha calculation in bottom-line, risk-adjusted measurement for a manager operating primarily in these stocks. As set forth in an earlier chapter, the stock market is not a monolith. Widely disparate price and return results can exist among major sectors of the market over extended periods. Accordingly, care should be exercised in diagnosing and appraising the performance of a manager who concentrates his or her activities exclusively in a specific sector or sectors of the market (such as high growth stocks, income stocks, or energy stocks). Otherwise, results of diagnosis may affect the manager's appraisal and selection process in an inappropriate way.

Second, a manager selected because of a particular style may begin to depart from that style as a result of market experience, changes in basic concepts, personnel turnover, or inadequate investment controls. Initially, this departure could be difficult to detect without diagnostic analysis of individual securities.

Third, if a manager makes an explicit change in style that materially changes the portfolio's composition, diagnostic analysis should reveal this fact. As a result, the corporate executive will have the basis for clearer understanding of any future improvement or shortfall in portfolio performance caused by style change.

The other principal way in which diagnostic analysis can assist the plan sponsor is in measuring and controlling a multimanager portfolio in the aggregate. For example, assume a multimanager situation in which all or most of the individual managers are specialists concentrating their efforts in different sectors of the market. It is possible that bottom-line, risk-adjusted performance measurement may detect that the aggregate portfolio is poorly diversified. However, these measured results may well be difficult to relate to results for individual managers and thus difficult to relate to specific objectives set for each manager. Moreover, the amount of nonmarket risk in such undiversified portfolios may be so high that error ranges of the statistics are too wide to be of much practical value.

Diagnostic measurement and analysis can be designed to test individual security positions for comparability with individual manager objectives and aggregate portfolio objectives. Managers are comfortable knowing they will not have to account for performance shortfalls inherent in the prescribed objectives, and plan sponsors are more comfortable with diagnostic evidence that the assignment is being fulfilled. Some diagnostic systems try to extract as much information as possible from security holdings and transactions without defining all key factors in advance. Unexpected biases or problem areas may be revealed that neither the manager nor the sponsor would have thought of in advance.

A good example of effective use of diagnostic analysis in selecting a new manager was part of the Massachusetts Institute of Technology's (MIT) program in 1978. After reducing the number of manager candidates to a moderate number, an analysis was made of every stock and bond trade for several years. By looking at turnover, the performance of buys versus sells, and other key factors, MIT was able to learn more about the manager's investment process than some of the managers actually knew.[1]

---

[1]Rohrer, Julie, "Using MPT to Find a Manager," *Institutional Investor,* November 1978.

REPRESENTATIVE DIAGNOSTIC ANALYSIS SERVICES

Diagnostic services share a common goal of providing information about a portfolio through analysis of its composition beginning at the individual security level. Nevertheless, they can differ dramatically in the concepts and techniques used to achieve that goal. At one end of the spectrum are diagnostic services that fundamentally display data on the range of P/E ratios, yields, types of companies by industries, sales volume, and so forth. Each of these is often compared with the range for the same factor in the S&P 500 or in a universe selected by the service. At the other end are services principally based on substantial research on various aspects of risk.

Four services representative of the spectrum of approaches are discussed below. Of the four, the first two have been available for several years whereas the second two measurement services incorporating risk adjustment are available from a number of trust institutions.

Watnik & Co., New York

The Performance Analysis System traces each dollar invested in the portfolio as it progresses through sequential purchase and sale transactions. Analyses are performed to assist in appraising the manager's selection, weighting, timing skills, risk/reward decision outcomes and the persistence of positive or negative performance. Careful track is kept of the subsequent performance of securities sold compared with those purchased.

The system is based on quarterly decisions sets: holds, buys and sells. Decisions are first measured and grouped by the number of quarters for which they have been in effect. This permits detection of patterns of performance. For example, a manager who consistently buys too early might show a pattern of underperformance for two or three quarters following the average decision and then a period of overperformance. Results are measured relative to the S&P 500 and to a naive alternative portfolio constructed of the 20 largest stocks on the New York Stock Exchange.

Decisions are then regrouped into the quarters in which they occurred to detect periods of superior or inferior decisions. All results are adjusted both for total variability and market-related variability, and rates of returns are cash-flow adjusted. All types of measurement are performed separately on buy, hold, and sell decisions. This allows the pension executive to discuss sources of performance without addressing individual security positions. However, managers do make formal quarterly forecasts, by security and by portfolio of future returns on equity and payout. These forecasts can be checked for bias, variability, and accuracy, and the returns actually earned on the portfolio can be compared against the manager's portfolio forecasts.

A. G. Becker Incorporated, Chicago

The Portfolio Analysis Review Service takes a significantly different approach. Each position in the portfolio is treated as a minicorporation. Sales, earnings, and dividends of the minicorporation are taken as a percentage of the sales, earnings, and dividends of the actual corporation. The data for these minicorporations are then aggregated. The underlying philosophy is to treat the portfolio as a holding company with numerous minority-ownership positions that are consolidated for financial statement purposes. Becker maintains a large data bank of other portfolios analyzed by the same techniques. Each diagnostic report displays the universe of portfolios in rank order and positions the client portfolio within the universe.

The first section presents an "Equity Portfolio Profile," comparing the position of the client portfolio with the universe in terms of P/E ratio, debt/equity ratio, and the various financial and stock market ratios. Beta, alpha, and R^2 are included. The second section presents "Individual Stock Analyses" for the specific portfolio. Graphs show the relationship of the P/E ratio to earnings growth and beta. The third section covers "Equity Portfolio Characteristics" compared with those of other portfolios; earnings growth rates and portfolio diversification are included.

Subsequent sections analyze such characteristics as P/E ratio, yield, capitalization, return on net worth, and liquidity. An appendix provides a list of individual issues in the portfolio with industry codes, price, earnings per share, number of outstanding shares, and so forth.

BARRA, Berkeley, California

The two newer services are based on theoretical research into extra-market covariance and prediction of a security's market risk (beta) using fundamental accounting data in addition to the history of past prices.

A group of diagnostic services are available from BARRA (formerly Barr Rosenberg & Associates). *The Fundamental Risk Measurement Service* includes a portfolio analysis system, PORCH, that describes the current position of a portfolio and effects of various potential revisions. The service also includes a portfolio optimization system that selects the best portfolio for a plan sponsor's objectives from a manager's predefined list of possibilities, subject to any restrictions or guidelines established by the sponsor or manager, such as size of position or liquidity. The service has been expanded to include a bond system.

BARRA also offers the *Conditional Forecasting Service,* which includes a performance measurement system that diagnoses sources of risk and return on a monthly basis. The final service is the *Consulting/Aid Service,* normally available only through subscribing bank master trustees and independent consultants, which includes the MULMAN system for analysis and control of the multimanager environment.

Although the array of services, systems, and options is broad, certain general principles and theories underlie them all.

Fundamental risk measurement is based on the hypothesis that future risk can be predicted better using balance sheet and income statement data, industry classifications, and other fundamental information in addition to analyzing historic price changes. A series of papers by Rosenberg[2] supports this hypothesis. After checking a large number of possible factors, six groups

---

[2]See B. Rosenberg, "Extra-Market Components of Covariance in Security Markets," *Journal of Financial and Quantitative Analysis,* March 1974. B. Rosenberg and V. Marathe, "The Prediction of Investment Risk: Systematic and Residual Risk," *Proceedings of the Seminar on the Analysis of Security Prices,* University of Chicago, November 1975. B. Rosenberg and V. Marathe, "Common Factors in Security Returns: Microeconomic Determinants and Macroeconomic Correlates," *Working Paper No. 44,* Research Program in Finance, Graduate School of Business, University of California, Berkeley, 1976.

of factors were found useful in predicting systematic risk:

- Market variability

- Earnings variability

- Low market valuation and a history of unsuccess

- Immaturity and smallness

- Growth orientation

- Financial risk.

The higher a company ranked on each of these measures such as, high on the immaturity and smallness scale, the more risky it was. Market variability includes the historic beta and some other factors such as share turnover and typical stock price range. Thus, fundamental risk measurement seeks to improve the estimate of future risk by including and adding to the analysis of historical price changes.

In addition to improving the prediction of future systematic risk (beta), the fundamental factors permit calculation of extramarket covariance, which arises from common factors of residual return. For example, an economic event might have a marketwide (systematic) effect, another event might have an effect on all growth stocks (extramarket covariance), and a third event might have an additional effect on a specific growth stock (specific risk). By identifying areas of extramarket covariance, the diagnostic system can provide deeper insight into the comparative performance of portfolios.

The performance measurement system reports the sources of monthly return in the following format:

Sources of Return	Percentage Return	
A. Risk-free		0.42%
B. Systematic excess return at		
normal beta policy	−1.91%	
due to beta policy	0.13	
Total		−1.78

Sources of Return	Percentage Return	
C. Residual return: common factors		
at normal position	0.00	
risk index policy	−0.17	
industry policy	0.23	
Subtotal		0.06
D. Residual return: specific factors		
at normal position	0.00	
active policy	0.15	
Subtotal		0.15
E. Total residual return		0.21
G. Total return		−1.15
Total excess return of normal policy		1.91
Total return resulting from active management		0.34

In the example above, the risk-free rate of return for the month was 0.42%. Given the change in the market for the month and given the normal beta level, systematic returns would have been −1.91% for the month. However, the manager deviated from the normal beta policy in an appropriate way and provided a positive increment of 0.13%. This partly offset the expected negative systematic return producing an actual systematic excess return of −1.78% for the month.

Returns resulting from common factors, or extramarket covariance, would be 0.0 at the normal level of complete diversification. By deviating from the index weighting and positions, the manager produced a −0.17% return related to the six risk index factors and a positive 0.23% return related to industry deviations. These returns net to a positive 0.06% return resulting from extramarket factors.

Returns resulting from specific factors are also 0.0 at the normal level of complete diversification. The manager's active policy provided a 0.15% improvement in this area. Adding the extramarket and specific returns together gives a total of 0.21% for residual return. Adding residual return to systematic return and the risk-free return equals the total monthly return for the portfolio of −1.15%. Adding the returns resulting from normal policy together gives the total excess return of normal policy of -1.91%. Adding the returns resulting from beta policy, risk index and industry policy, and active policy together gives the total return resulting from active management of 0.34%.

In addition, the estimated beta and standard deviation are calculated. The system then reports the contribution to return, standard deviation, and risk exposure, first for the six factor groups listed above and then for each industry group and individual security.

Similar concepts are used in the MULMAN program for diagnosing multimanager situations. In addition to diagnosing the holdings of each manager, the aggregate portfolio can be analyzed to gain insight into the way that managers' decisions interact with each other and affect portfolio risk. Some pension executives using diagnostic analysis have found that they are using multiple managers to reduce risk rather than to improve the risk-return tradeoff; there are more economic ways to reduce risk than paying several active management fees. The program measures:

- Systematic and specific risk and extramarket covariance

- The "information ratio," which relates alphas required to risks undertaken

- The degree to which managers operate independently, using a matrix of diversity and security exposure for each manager against each other manager and a market index.

Wilshire Associates, Santa Monica, California

The other representative service based on recent theoretical research is the *Portfolio Review and Investment System Measurement* (PRISM) system. Wilshire Associates is the same company that provides the risk-adjusted performance measurement service using an empirical market line, discussed in the previous chapter. The PRISM service is based on fundamental risk measurement theory and is available to both investment managers and corporate pension executives. The service provides six diagnostic reports on the equity portfolio.

The Portfolio Volatility and Diversification report analyzes the weightings and fundamental data by stock and industry, shows each stock's contribution to quarterly standard error, and provides summary information on the portfolio yield, diversification, and beta.

The Optimization report selects the best portfolio given the manager's investment predictions and the plan sponsor's diversification and risk guidelines and tradeoffs and calculates the turnover required to move from the existing portfolio to the optimal portfolio.

The Transaction Analysis report analyzes the turnover required on a step-by-step basis using the most effective path. Cumulative effects on expected return and risk are listed wth cumulative turnover, permitting insight into the effect of moving only partially toward the optimal portfolio.

The Comparative Volatility and Diversification report represents a side-by-side analysis of existing and proposed portfolios in terms of sources of systematic and nonmarket risk.

The Portfolio Risk Composition report details fundamental risk for each security and industry by the six groups of factors used to predict systematic risk.

The Market Timing and Security Selection report analyzes the performance of the existing portfolio during any time period, by security and industry, in terms of market timing and industry and security selection. Performance is compared with both that of the S&P 500, before and after risk adjustment, and that of the naive alternative of holding the beginning of the period portfolio without any subsequent transactions.

All diagnostic systems, whether based on traditional or new approaches, are valuable to the pension executive who wants to see beyond the portfolio aggregates into the individual decisions that determine risks taken and returns earned. A system that is overly complex, time-consuming, or irrelevant to the executive's needs and resources should not be adopted. As with bottom-line performance measurement, confused communications and wasted energies will be the result. The executive wishing to progress to this more intensive level of analysis should be aware that because of the required level of detail, all diagnostic systems take a substantial amount of time to understand and use effectively.

OTHER APPLICATIONS OF PERFORMANCE MEASUREMENT AND DIAGNOSTIC ANALYSIS

Detecting "Closet Indexing"

The diagnostic systems discussed are being used by some pension executives to detect a phenomenon labeled "closet indexing." This is an unfortunate term, because it carries an intimation that something is being done secretly and because it means different things to different people. It appears to cover at least three situations. The first is an individual money manager who deliberately structures a portfolio to track closely with the index. The second situation is an individual money manager who takes the weight of an industry or company in the S&P Index as a normal position, and adds or subtracts on the basis of fundamental factors but does not stray too far from index weights. For example, this manager might hold a 4% position in IBM stock at a minimum, 6% normally, and 8% as a maximum positive position. The third situation is a group of managers in a multi-manager environment with each running a significantly different active portfolio but with the resulting aggregate pension portfolio approximating an index fund.

The first situation is typically impractical. To track closely with the index, a manager must own at least 200 securities, and even these would have to be chosen by sophisticated computer analysis to replicate index performance. If a manager simply buys the index from the heaviest weighted stock down, nearly 350 stocks are needed to come close to an index fund. The idea that an active manager can assemble an individual pension portfolio of normal size that will replicate the market's performance in most instances is not tenable.

The second situation describes an investment approach that many managers believe is an intelligent way to seek superior performance. It is compatible with recent theoretical research into the active/passive management approach and should be judged on a case-by-case basis using risk-return standards rather than rejected out of hand as closet indexing.

The third is a situation that actually does exist in many multi-manager portfolios. The aggregated portfolio of all individual managers is almost certainly closer to the construction of an index than any single manager's portion. It probably will still not be close enough to qualify as an index fund, but it may be too close to leave room for enough superior performance to cover incremental management fees. Thus, a better term than "closet indexing" is "accidental indexing," and the concept is applicable at the aggregate level of a multimanager portfolio, if anywhere.

Performance Measurement of Other Assets

Little has been done to address the particular problem entailed in measuring the performance of options. Existing systems, such as the one available from Merrill Lynch, Pierce, Fenner & Smith, New York, calculate past performance with and without options to show the differential return attributable to the options program. More work is needed in analyzing the effect of options on risk as well as return and on forecasting the effect of various options strategies on expected risk-return profiles.

Convertible bonds, with characteristics of both fixed-income investments and long term options, are usually treated like equities for risk adjustment. This is less than satisfactory because of the different nature of the asset; linear correlations to the S&P 500 are frequently poor for convertibles. Because convertibles are a small part of the total market, specific techniques for performance measurement have not been widely implemented.

Real estate performance measurement is another area that is in its infancy. The lack of frequent, widely accepted valuations for real estate of institutional interest is a major roadblock. Some preliminary work has been done on creating an index of real estate values, but more theoretical and empirical work is needed before practical performance measurement comparable to that available for common stocks can be implemented.

KEY REMAINING ISSUES

There are many unsettled issues in performance measurement, and the corporate officer will find it helpful to spend some time following new theoretical developments and measurement services created to implement them.

One major remaining issue is the appropriate attitude of a plan sponsor toward risk. If the pension fund is only one of many assets held by the beneficiary, it can be argued that there is no need to make the fund efficient in terms of total risk but only in terms of market risk. The beneficiary can treat the fund as an equity asset and diversify other holdings into real estate, tangibles, and so forth. Empirical studies both of what plan sponsors' attitudes are toward risk and studies of what they should be are needed.

Another continuing issue is the need for more powerful statistical techniques. The level of superior performance most investment managers are seeking will have a significant effect on the rate of return of the fund, but it is difficult to measure with precision over reasonable time periods using current statistical techniques. It is also difficult to identify effective and ineffective managers at a high level of statistical confidence, so the pension executive must continue to use subjective judgments. More powerful statistical methods, more detailed analyses of nonmarket risk, and more accurate specification of security and capital market lines will be continuing goals of research.

DIRECTION OF FUTURE DEVELOPMENTS

Plan sponsors increasingly are interested in calculating risk-adjusted results and understanding sources of risk in the portfolio. Bottom-line performance measurement services will respond to this interest by placing more emphasis on risk adjustment and improving the reliability of the analysis through more frequent valuations and use of more powerful statistical methods.

More and more managers will be willing to commit the time and study required for effective use of a diagnostic system. The use of these systems will spread throughout the corporate sector, supplementing or replacing older methods.

The diagnostic systems currently available concentrate on the securities purchased and sold. To anticipate and control the events currently measured, investment managers will need even more intensive specialized diagnostic systems for such activities as security analysis and trading. These systems will have to be close to "real time" to permit managers to correct problems before they severely impact measured results. Some pension executives, in turn, will request the output of these specialized systems to provide a still deeper level of insight and analysis. Considerable theoretical research needs to be done in the area of specialized systems.

Finally, advanced performance measurement services will provide comprehensive systems that link specialized analyses, overall diagnostics, and bottom-line measurement with portfolio objectives. These systems will permit greater insight, clearer communication, and more precise improvements in the investment process. These are the continuing goals of effective performance measurement.

SUMMARY

Diagnostic analysis deals with portfolio composition beginning with individual security positions. It developed because pension executives have not been satisfied with the magnitude of error ranges associated with broad descriptive statistics of bottom-line measurement. Diagnostic analysis divides risk into more categories than market and nonmarket and identifies sources of various risks by security. It can be used to compare portfolio activity with a manager's stated investment style and forecasts for individual securities. It can also be used to measure and control a fund with several managers. Available diagnostic services differ in both concepts and techniques; there is not yet a generally accepted approach in this area. These systems are expected to gain wider use in the future as they incorporate an increasingly comprehensive approach linking analysis of specialized areas (such as earnings forecasts and trading operations), portfolio diagnostics, bottom-line measurement, and portfolio objectives.

INDEX

Standard & Poor Composite Index
(cont.)
  161, 162, 163, 167, 173, 174,
  175, 177, 186, 189, 192, 193,
  197, 198, 199, 205, 215, 237,
  240, 241, 242, 243, 244, 245,
  246, 247, 249, 253, 257, 265,
  271, 272, 273
Standard & Poor's Trade and Securities
  Statistics, 5
standard deviation, 4, 20, 36, 38, 42,
  45, 84, 85, 87, 96, 105, 153, 162,
  163, 164, 165, 167, 185, 192,
  237, 246, 270
Stanford University, 89
Statistical Bulletin, ii, 13, 112
stock and bond market indexes, 50, 85
stock/bond ratio(s), 84, 97, 101, 141
stock/bond mix(es), 88, 90, 93
stocks, bonds, and money market instruments, 3, 83, 98, 99, 100, 139,
  151, 181, 196
stock/bond/Treasury bill, 17
  combination(s), 18, 39, 45
  proportion(s), 17, 141
  ratio, 18, 20, 45, 98, 100
  returns, 45
stock/fixed income ratio, 142
stock price cycle(s), 140, 150
stock group research, 133
stock market indexes, 50
  Dow-Jones Averages, 50
  NYSE Corporate Index, 50
  Value Line Index, 50
  Standard and Poor's Composite In-
    dex, 50
stock price cycles, 54, 55
stock price movements, 54, 57, 58
stock price gyrations, 52
stock risk premium benchmarks, 50
structure of liabilities, 3
substitution swap(s), 112, 113, 114
Survey of Current Business, 12
systematic risk, 106

T

tax-free investors, 64
tax-paying investors, 64

technical analysis, 122
Telstat Systems, 256
*Theory and Practice of Bond Portfolio
  Management, The,* 111
time horizon(s), 33, 34, 37, 139
time-weighted rate of return, 221, 236,
  243, 244, 247, 250
time-weighted return(s), 233, 234, 235,
  250, 251, 256, 259
timing, 4, 5, 120, 121, 122, 124, 139,
  140, 145, 147, 150, 203, 214, 224
top-down approach, 146
transaction costs, 122
Treasury (U.S.), 72
Treasury bills (U.S.), 17, 36, 37, 44, 45,
  67, 70, 75, 83, 84, 88, 98, 99,
  132, 238, 240, 243
Treasury bonds (U.S.), 36
Treynor, J. L., P. J. Regan, and W. W.
  Priest, Jr., 30
trough-peak-trough analysis, 55

U

underpricing, 150, 171
  of common stocks, 150
underweighting, 102, 105, 150, 151,
  156, 159, 161, 168, 171, 204

V

valuation models, 75, 136, 137, 138
variability of returns from stock and
  bond markets, 50
variable income securities, 17
variable ratio, 141
variable value assets, 33
venture capital investments, 106
volatility, 3, 15, 16, 18, 31, 35, 37, 45,
  161

W

Watnik & Co., 265
weighting, 153, 155

Wells-Fargo Investment Advisors, 87,
    89, 90, 110
Wells Fargo model, 91
Wilshire Associates, 88, 89, 93, 258,
    270
Wilshire Associates model, 93, 94
Wilshire 5000, 197, 198, 253
Whitman, W. T., 140
World War II, 53, 62, 63

Y

Yale University Press, 170
yield to maturity, 70
yield pickup, 112

Z

Zarnowitz, V., 127